And Home Was Kariakoo

A Memoir of East Africa

Also by M. G. Vassanji

FICTION

The Magic of Saida

The Assassin's Song

The In-Between World of Vikram Lall

When She Was Queen

Amriika

The Book of Secrets

Uhuru Street

No New Land

The Gunny Sack

NON-FICTION

A Place Within: Rediscovering India

Mordecai Richler

And Home Was Kariakoo

A Memoir of East Africa

M. G. VASSANJI

DOUBLEDAY CANADA

Library and Archives Canada Cataloguing in Publication

Vassanji, M. G., author
And home was Kariakoo : a memoir of East Africa / M. G. Vassanji.

Issued in print and electronic formats.
ISBN 978-0-385-67143-9
eBook ISBN 978-0-385-67144-6

1. Vassanji, M. G.—Travel—Africa, East. 2. Vassanji, M. G.—Childhood and youth. 3. Authors, Canadian (English)—20th century—Biography. 4. Africa, East—Biography. 5. Africa, East—Description and travel. I. Title.

PS8593.A87Z462 2014 C813'.54 C2014-903139-4
C2014-903140-8

Cover image courtesy of the author
Printed and bound in the USA

Published in Canada by Doubleday Canada, a division of Random House of Canada Limited, a Penguin Random House Company

www.randomhouse.ca

10 9 8 7 6 5 4 3 2 1

For JKS Makokha

The Author's Travels

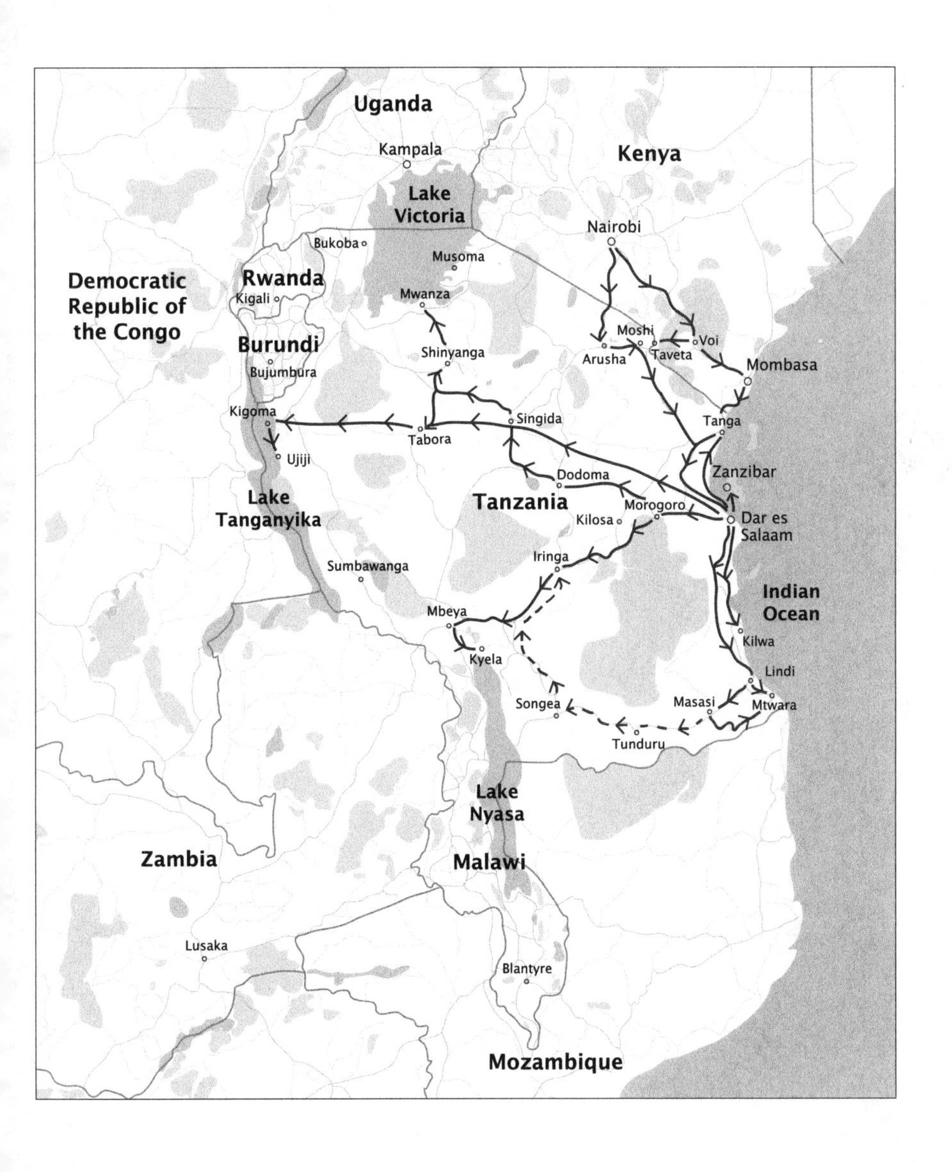

Partir. Mon coeur bruissait de générosités emphatiques. Partir . . . j'arriverais lisse et jeune dans ce pays mien et je dirais à ce pays dont le limon entre dans la composition de ma chair . . .

Je viendrais à ce pays mien et je lui dirais: "Embrassez-moi sans crainte . . . Et si je ne sais que parler, c'est pour vous que je parlerai."

To flee. My heart was full of generous hopes. To flee . . . I should arrive lithe and young in this country of mine and I should say to this land whose mud is flesh of my flesh . . .

I should come back to this land of mine and say to it: "Embrace me without fear . . . If all I can do is speak, at least I shall speak for you."

—Aimé Césaire, *Cahier d'un retour au pays natal*

Contents

Preface

From abroad, I often see Africa perceived merely as a place of war, disease, and hunger, a sick entity deserving pity and sustenance and all help possible. Schoolchildren gather to donate quarters to it. Men and women make professions pointing out its woes. Celebrities collect funds for it. People keep asking: Is there hope for Africa? Africa, it seems, is the world's perpetually poor relation.

Over the years I have often revisited East Africa, where I was born and raised, as were my parents and one grandfather. From the inside, the place is actually very different, and the world looking out also seems very different. It is as though a distorting lens separated these two realities. East Africa is an exciting place; to me it always was. During my revisits I saw problems, of course—some of them new, others merely larger—but there was much more. I walked through vast food and clothing markets, saw abundance as well as poverty; there was begging and sullen unemployment, but also there were games and festivals, there was joy. There was music and colour. Boys and girls in uniforms traipsing off to school early in the morning on city streets and country roads, people gathered for a wedding, men crowded under a tree after a funeral. Intellectuals ruing the lost days of idealism. I have witnessed poetry being made and discovered, in the language of the country; the youth in debate about their future, reminding me of the hopeful, exciting days of my own youth; early schoolers shyly come to a stage to announce their ambitions. Late one evening a man gave me a ride back from a literary reading at a bar and told me he had ambitions of building a supercomputer, and his own personal library. Every place is a universe in itself; I saw a vast diversity in a varied and teeming country. There was life, there were people. There was the geography.

Growing up in a country you absorb a sense of its multiple dimensions, carry images of its distant places, and hear the poetry of their name-sounds—and come away with a certainty or expectation that you'll see much of it during your lifetime. It's yours, after all. Circumstances took me away, and for a long time it seemed to me that I would never visit those lost dimensions, experience the land in its variety, appreciate the diversity of its people. I was wrong, all it required was a will to go and do just that.

One day I decided I would visit and experience that land as much as possible; travel to its different corners and write—not about the country per se but about myself in it; not as an outsider reporting to outsiders but as someone from there, who understood. If in the process I could provide a context, or indulge in history, which is a passion, or in memory, which is a form of history, all the better. There were moments when the thrill of travel and discovery was such that I wished I could go on and on, from place to place, and never stop. But I was not young anymore, and one lives with constraints; twice I had to be told *Enough*, and reluctantly, facing an inviting, unvisited landscape, I turned back. I had to stop.

— MGV

1.

Going Home

DOWN BELOW, OUT THE AIRPLANE PORTHOLE, lay the vast unconquered landscape of Africa—so different from the parcelled geometry of Europe which I had crossed over or the grey, highway-girded northeastern United States where I had made my home for the time being. The red earth and green scrubland, a few huts, a solitary figure wending its way on a trail to somewhere, perhaps carrying water, all under a cool morning sun that would in no time replenish its fires and begin to bake the earth. It must have been the arid north of Kenya, south of Somalia, down there below me, but it didn't matter, the familiarity was unquestionable and it filled me with a huge emotion. This was my country. This was East Africa and I was returning home.

I was twenty-one, it was only sixteen months since I had gone away, but that was a long time then. Mine was the overwhelming emotion of someone who had feared he might not see home again. The people, the places; the music, the language: everything that was suffused into my pores and my very being, now crowded out by new challenges and pushed back into memory. That feeling about my African home would never change over the years and decades that followed, during which I would go to many places, including Canada, which gave me a home, and my Indian ancestral homeland, which partially claimed me back.

Many from my generation left during those heady 1960s and '70s of the last century, soon after independence. Most went away to the United Kingdom, Canada, and the United States, and some have returned for visits, but few that I know with that intensity of emotional reclamation. Of mad belonging. Some of those who left never returned, having made good their escape, packing their bitterness with them—bitterness at the politics, the revenge racism, and the socialist policies and broken official promises that drove them out; others left simply to fulfill the colonial dream, finding their way to what had been the centre of their universe—London, now simply the West. Whence this sense of place in me, I have often wondered. To call it nostalgia is too easy; I recall harrowing moments from a deprived childhood, as well as happy ones. I don't long for the crowded bedroom of my childhood, the despair of a single mother on the brink of breakdown; they are gone. Dar es Salaam, where I grew up, has changed; Nairobi, my birthplace, has changed. I have seen both these cities which were my home metamorphose during numerous revisits—populations multiplied, violence increased, beauty and serenity reduced to squalor. Toronto, where I live and have made my home, has changed too; it has become friendly and cosmopolitan, its urban spaces look renewed, as they do in the American cities I have known: Boston, Philadelphia, New York. But, to use a metaphor, returning to the original home either one can opt to observe how everyone has aged and everything is no longer the same, and how ultimately, predictably disappointing it all is; or one sees the familiar and the dear in the older, broken faces. One has memory, and attachment and commitment, one is aware of change and history as it applies to everything.

Modern aesthetic—I mean the western one—prefers ironic detachment, a stony turning away from the emotion, a haughty look askance at anything that might give joy or sadness—seeing the inevitable winter behind the summer, the motive behind the charm, the spent passion, the bitter aftertaste. Does climate have anything to do with this? Those of us from the south—where fruits and vegetables actually rot and smell, and death is real, not irony—sometimes fear what the winters might be doing to us. I see my feelings about my place of birth to be mixed, obviously, growing older demands that, but disappointment does not poison the joy or the attachment.

Perhaps I judge unfairly this "western" aesthetic. It is novelists, of whatever country and culture, who in some sense never leave home, who keep returning to it—despite that old cliché. Why this need to return? My answer is this: there is simply too much of life unexplored that, at a distance and prompted by nostalgia, yes, and the clarity of observed youth, yields precious narrative and self-knowledge.

The question arises: Is the return of the Asian African different from that of an African African? The answer is yes, if only because for the former the ancestral South Asian homeland is a reality that looms closer today than it did on the streets of Dar es Salaam and Nairobi; the links to it are more realized. The returning African African at the same time comes with a global black consciousness. There is that unavoidable pulling away, then. And yet I've kept returning to this African homeland, and at each arrival there is that unmistakable tug at the insides, the same instinct to draw in deep from the air. The smoky coolness outside Nairobi airport at night, the salty humidity of Dar at the same time. The exclamations, the echoes of spoken Swahili.

2.

Gaam, Dar es Salaam: The India Town

FOR DECADES NOW BY DAR ES SALAAM'S LOVELY, open seashore its Asians have arrived in numbers to stare out at the ocean, carrying out a mysterious communion with the water that separates them from their ancestral homeland to the north and east. So it appears. In my childhood we came on foot, and during our frolicks we would go tumbling down from street level to water's edge. Two tugboats plied the harbour; a liner might depart at that hour, the passengers would wave, we waved back. Nowadays the Asians arrive in their cars or their oversize 4 × 4s, which they park in a long straight formation across the road from the water, and seated in their transport or standing beside it, they stare out at the blue beyond. Vendors, as they have always done, ply varieties of street food. Then as dusk falls, all depart.

The harbour is natural, a bay with a narrow inlet that is swimmable by the brave. The story goes that in 1862 Sultan Majid, the rather dashing Omani ruler of Zanzibar, whose domain included the long East African coastline, happened to arrive at this haven across the channel, and was so impressed by it that he called it Bandar es Salaam, the harbour of peace—hence the name Dar es

Salaam. He resolved to build a town here, with a palace—a private pad, a home away from the political clamour, family intrigues, and foreign machinations at work on his island metropolis. But he died in 1870, the dream unfulfilled. It was the Germans who completed it when they colonized the mainland a decade and a half later, making Dar es Salaam their capital and bypassing the nearby great market town of Bagamoyo, which had processed thousands of slaves over the years and perhaps deserved the snub.

The population of Dar es Salaam when I was a teenager reached 100,000. Consequently, at about the independence of Tanganyika in 1961, the town was declared a city—by what authority we were not quite sure but we were now in the big league. The world looked bright. Eminent visitors from all over the world dropped by in the sunshine of our new country, looking thrilled, announcing hope and promise. We had emerged from the backwater of an empire into a community of nations. A tower was erected to commemorate the "city status," at the centre of a traffic roundabout a block away from the harbour. It was a modest rectangular structure, painted a plain yellow and some twenty-five feet tall, with a clockface at the top; it proclaimed no ambition or lofty thought. The only other monument in the city was the bronze Askari statue, a mile away on the acacia-lined Independence Avenue, which honoured the African soldiers who gave up their lives during the First World War. How a European war was fought by Africans and determined the fate of this nation and city is one of the ironies of colonial rule.

The city-status tower stands intact now, surrounded by the same one- and two-storey buildings of yore and overlooking a decrepit parkette. Heavy traffic runs both ways past it, rendering the monument small and insignificant, almost invisible. Which is as well, for the population of Dar is now some four million.

—

A necklace of gleaming white buildings with a tall, grey-spired cathedral at one end graced the shoreline of the colonial harbour capital and met the traveller who arrived by sea. Unfortunately the white necklace is broken now, defaced by questionable or even haphazard modern construction. To the proposal, or protest, that historical buildings—German, Arab, Indian—should be preserved often comes the retort, Whose history? The answer requires some thought.

My forefathers left the small towns of western Gujarat—Jamnagar, Junagadh, Porbandar—with populations of 15,000 to 20,000 at the turn of the twentieth century, to settle on the East African coast. The old town of Dar es Salaam, the commercial section behind the elegant white shoreline, was their construction. It was the area of the first Indian settlement of Dar, and we called it Gaam, "Town"; in Swahili it was known as mjini, meaning the same thing; nowadays it is also referred to as Uhindini, the Indian (or Asian) area. A single long street, called Kichwele (later renamed Uhuru) Street, went down from Gaam past Mnazi Mmoja (then Arnautoglu) ground into the African area called Kariakoo; it was lined all the way with Indian stores and homes.

It was here, between Gaam and Kariakoo, that my mother opened her "fancy goods" store, when we moved fatherless from Nairobi to Dar. Running a small shop in a competitive market was hard work, and we all pitched in. It was here that the tailor Edward told me stories, where my cousin Shamim told me different stories, where my mother told me about her childhood. My strongest memory of her sees her seated on her high stool behind her shop counter, brooding, picking her chin. Awaiting customers. At night we would fight for the chance to press her aching feet.

Some time in the 1920s and '30s the Indians had replaced their old, slummy settlements with single-storey brick buildings; in the '50s and '60s came the double-storey and the rare three- and four-storey buildings, and the singular five-storey tallest building in town with its distinctive pyramidal front, overlooking Mnazi Mmoja ground. The owner of this pyramid was a man called Habib Punja, whom we kids knew as a somewhat short, round man who oscillated side to side as he walked—which he did rarely, since he was possibly the richest man in town and went about in a chauffeured Mercedes-Benz. But it was believed that he had made his wealth by starting out as a peanut vendor on the sidewalks, and he died of a heart attack when his many properties were nationalized during the heyday of socialism in 1971.

Dar es Salaam for all its smallness had six cinemas, a football stadium, and several cricket grounds. There were many schools, including three high schools, with their own sports grounds, and a few clubs. There were football teams, and two cricket leagues; only Indians and Europeans played cricket, coming out in all-whites on Sundays. There was an annual tennis tournament held at the Gymkhana Club and a national football competition for the Sunlight Cup, broadcast across the country and followed at the market and outside restaurants, over the radio, and a national school cricket trophy called the Isherwood Cup. There was the Little Theatre, where the elite might catch a local production of a Gilbert and Sullivan piece. The annual Youth Drama Competition for high schools was a literary feast lasting many days, staging the likes of *The Crucible* and *A Passage to India* (with Africans playing Englishmen, Indians playing themselves), and was reported avidly in the newspapers.

One day in 1971 the government announced the confiscation of all rental property, in keeping with its recent socialist doctrine proclaimed as the Arusha Declaration. This meant that for the Asians, who had arrived penniless to Africa, two generations or more of family savings invested in property disappeared at a stroke. Of course, most families, including mine, did not possess such savings. But the shock of this announcement, seen as the Great Betrayal by the businessmen, who could easily have kept their money in the banks or invested it abroad, led many to decide to emigrate. Since the mad dictator of Uganda, Idi Amin, following a divine revelation, had just expelled Asians in an ethnic cleansing (the term was not in use then), the decision to emigrate was relatively easy. Most went to Canada, some to the U.S. and U.K. The evacuation of Gaam, especially by the Khoja Ismailis, opened space for upcountry Indians to move into. Gaam changed its face and its ethos; the newcomers had the aggression and all the scruples of the pioneer; it is from among them that the wreckers of the old Dar have emerged. Meanwhile the business streets of these upcountry towns look haunted, as they wait to fill the vacuum left by their Asians.

As I negotiate the maze of dusty streets that is Gaam, which I know like the proverbial palm of my hand, as I turn into this one and onto that one at a whim, the provenance of this area is still evident in the names of the buildings, put up in Indian fashion on top of each—Salim Mansion, Durga Manzil, Jiwan Hirji Building. "Mansion" meant a two-storey building, not a grand home in its dictionary sense. In each "mansion" four or more families of five to eight people had their apartments, in three-room flats. Four to six kids could easily share a room; it was not unusual to share beds. It is almost bizarre to imagine that in many of these Dar families, living now in Toronto, Los Angeles, or someplace else in North America, the children have their own bathrooms, and sometimes even for a married couple to share one seems awkward. It's almost as if one were transported from the rowdy wooden front seats of the Empire Cinema onto Sunset Boulevard itself.

Some years ago I visited Jamnagar, Gujarat, and walking along a street I could have sworn that I was in Gaam: the yellow or white buildings with oil-painted window frames, the shop names, the variety stores for small needs, were identical to those you would see around Dar's Khoja khano (prayer house). My forebears had brought Gujarat with them.

My friend Walter Bgoya one day shed a new light for me on those cataclysmic property nationalizations that altered the demography of urban Tanzania. I met Walter first in the 1990s when I began returning to Dar and knew him as a publisher struggling in a hopeless book market. His books were in Swahili, small and simple in design, his market almost moribund. His office was a modest house on an unpaved street in Kariakoo, behind Msimbazi Street, where my grandmother had had her shop once. I had put up at a guest house called the Flamingo in Gaam, where for five dollars you could share a room and at night as you lay awake hear the tales told to each other by itinerant young Asian businessmen, in town from someplace like Mwanza or Arusha. My friends in Dar were always amused that I would stay here, but it was where the action was. You could run into someone from London or Toronto whom you'd not seen in a decade; you might gaze pityingly at an aged, sickly man whom you just barely recognized as the ghost of someone you'd last seen in childhood; you'd hear tantalizing stories of smuggling during the Uganda war and adultery in the community. Here were *characters.* And here one evening, the khano nearby blaring out a prayer on a loudspeaker, Walter picked me up in his jalopy.

He lived in a flat in a two-storey building nearby that was once owned by some Indian. As we went up the dark stairs, past the first floor to the second, he said, "Without the government takeover, I would never have lived in this area, next to an Indian family." Indians had lived in unofficially segregated community neighbourhoods, Africans lived next to Africans, in accordance with a town plan drawn up by the Germans during their rule and followed by the British who came after. Now Walter's son was close friends with the daughter of his Indian neighbour. Politics and economics aside, this revelation was an eye-opener for me.

Sadly, this Gaam, the India town to which I would come almost daily up Uhuru Street to go to the khano or the library, and lingered on the way back to play cricket at a friend's backyard; this Gaam which connected the bedroom suburbs of Upanga and the wealthy and expatriate areas of Oyster Bay and Msasani to humble Kariakoo and the airport; this city within a city was sealed off into an Asian ghetto soon after I left. Some expatriate city planners had apparently decided to construct a highway to bypass it so you had no need to go there unless you lived there or had some business; and for good measure they barricaded the area, putting up a pipe fence at the end of the key Jamhuri Street where it joined Uhuru Street. It takes an outsider to be so insensitive to a thriving, historical neighbourhood. I cannot help but wonder: Was this brutal closure prompted by that old animus towards the Asian in Africa, the tribe that always comes between white and black and so irked the Europeans? Or is this simply paranoia on my part, a residue of the old colonialism?

Cavafy says, of his own gaam, Alexandria,

You tell yourself I'll be gone
To some other land, some other sea,
To a city far lovelier than this . . .

There's no new land, my friend, no
New sea, for the city will follow you,
In the same streets you'll wander endlessly

And you ask me incredulously, How can you compare your measly backwater Dar es Salaam to Alexandria? Or, more obscenely, to Cairo and Bombay? To which I reply, Surely everyone inhabits his own space within a city, a space crowded by its characters and coloured by its stories. And Dar had enough for me—has enough for those who came after me—to fill the pages of a Decameron. Every Dar is a Cairo to its inhabitants; you only have to be able to see it.

—

My first return visit to East Africa, after a mere eighteen months in Boston, had been to Nairobi, the city of my birth, where my family—always nostalgic about it—had returned after the panic of the socialist takeovers in Tanzania. I first returned to Dar es Salaam after nineteen years, and a little nervously, for I had left under dubious circumstances, when travelling abroad was controlled by the socialist regime. How can you stay away from beloved Dar for two decades? Painfully; and by writing about it.

An aunt's brother had come to pick me up at the airport late at night, and took me to his home, a first-floor flat on Msimbazi Street, where he ran a shoe store. I went straight to bed. I had left Dar at a time when it was common to leave the windows open to the breeze at night, and a favourite childhood memory is of sitting at a window in the middle of the night looking down at the empty street below. My cousin's flat felt like a prison, barred to the outside and cooled by uncomfortable air conditioning. There were no children about, where formerly there would have been a clamour. There was a television, but only with one weak signal from, of all places, Zanzibar. Much had changed. Much had to change.

A block from where I lay awake was where my grandmother had lived with two of my uncles in one of those old-time iron-roofed mud-walled houses with a wide shopfront, a living quarter with one or two rooms behind it, and a yard with a large, sticky dining table covered with flies and a stinking hellhole of a pit latrine with crawling maggots and stifling smell into which I had a terror of falling. Next door was the pombe shop, an open-air communal bar the size of a football field, reeking of brew and throbbing with a deep and constant drumbeat, where shadowy figures moved amidst the smoky woodfires, some of whom emerged into the street chanting in mock, broken Gujarati or Kutchi to scare the young Indian kids in the shops. One drunk would come and stand before my grandmother's shop and sing: "Chapati Banyani nani kula?" Who eats the chapati of the Indian? And he would proceed to name the different communities who ate chapatis, who were mindless—he said—like cows. Dar es Salaam, for me at age four, was a comedown from the suburban Nairobi bungalow we had left behind, with its French windows and garden of roses. But later, Msimbazi was the place where my best friend lived, where I went to play cricket in his backyard with his two brothers. The family owned a pawnshop, with a noisy crowd always clamouring outside, waiting to cash in their tickets.

Early the morning after my arrival, after breakfast I came down and bid my relative so-long in his crowded shoe store and started walking the familiar streets. Down Msimbazi, eastwards up Uhuru Street, both lined with two-storey Asian buildings— all of which had been nationalized, many of their previous inhabitants now in Toronto. And on and on I walked, up the long street to Gaam, finally arriving at the thin line of the seafront, with its old Catholic and Lutheran churches, and the veranda-ed, white, one-storey office buildings, all from German times, which lasted from 1885 to 1916. Along the shore, northwards came the State House, the President's residence, also from German times, reconstructed after a British warship demolished it during the First World War; behind it were the dainty European bungalows; and on and on I walked past the golf course to the Upanga residential area, where my family had moved in the 1960s, to our old flat, outside which, to my amazement, the papaya tree still stood.

I was a being possessed, nothing could stop me that morning. From the Upanga flat I walked onwards to my old school, pronounced *Boyschool* those days, and noticed that the big brass bell

was missing from the garden where it had been mounted on a metal frame—every day one grinning fellow was picked for the privilege of leaving the class on the hour to toll the bell. Past the frame where it used to hang, I walked over to the science laboratories. The physics lab was on the first floor and I took the stairs with confidence. This was my school. I went in, walked through the aisles between the benches; to the back wall where the DC converter used to be; and to the office. There was no one in sight. On the way out I stopped in front of a wall. Hanging there was a solitary framed certificate. In fading typewritten letters, it bore my name on it, being the one that I had won at a Nairobi science fair, and that was perhaps instrumental in my admission to an American university—and consequently in my flight away, from which I was returning after all these years, heart full of emotion.

3.

Gaam Strikes Back: The Leaning Tower and Other Recent Developments

One afternoon not long ago after a meeting in New Haven I took a taxi for the intercity bus terminal, from where I would head off to the airport. The driver, a man in his thirties, was yammering away on his cell phone, had barely time to look up for instructions. My irritation, however, evaporated as soon as I realized that he was speaking in Swahili. I let him go on for a good twenty minutes or so, eavesdropping on a bit of trivial gossip, until finally he stopped the taxi and looked at me in his mirror. I asked him quietly, in Swahili, "Zitakua ngapi?" How much will that be? He gasped. We exchanged niceties, and went our ways.

There is something about Tanzania and its lingua franca, Swahili. There's a certain way to speak it that identifies you, and when there's a chance to speak it, you can't keep your mouth shut. You love to banter in it, it's your possession. Recently I arrived at Dar es Salaam airport with a friend, and found myself waiting while he obtained his visa. When he was finished I proceeded to an immigration wicket, where the officer asked me, a little agressively, in Swahili, "Why were you waiting?" I replied, "I was waiting for my companion." "Where did you learn your Swahili?" he countered.

There was a time when the border officials made you tremble; they could create a lot of trouble—confiscate your passport, for example. But I am older now, and the country has changed. And—time to come clean—I carry a Canadian passport.

"Uhuru Street," I replied to his question, naming the street where I grew up.

There was a pause. A smile. And I knew why. If I had named the street as I do in English, with the stress on the second syllable of "Uhuru," I would be a foreigner. But I had said "Uhuru Street," as I would in Swahili. There is no other way to respond in that language, which comes to the tongue as readily as the taste of a much-loved fruit: a mango, say, or a ripe jackfruit.

The man responded, "Hongera." Meaning, well done, congratulations. He stamped my passport. I was back.

The population of Dar is about that of Toronto, or any large western city. The country, once a small trust territory, has a population surpassing Canada's, and the East African countries, once again contemplating an economic community, have a combined population of 130 million or more. There are any number of natural resources. There is therefore all kinds of potential. The only question is whether corruption will eat up the wealth before it has a chance to improve the lives of people—bring textbooks and teachers to schools, for example, and illuminate the dark nights of the villagers. The city itself has expanded, swallowing up the outlying villages and neighbourhoods: in the evenings, blinding streams of headlights stretch for miles on end, almost as far as Chalinze, the junction from where the road branches north towards Kilimanjaro and Nairobi. Construction proceeds apace, and taller and fancier office buildings are in evidence everywhere in the newer business areas skirting the old Gaam. And yet the city only manages to look physically uglier. One has to admit, beloved Dar never had a sense of urban beauty and proportion, never saw much use for green spaces and trees. What there was of grace was due to its small size and colonial look; that has mostly gone.

But Dar to us is not what she looks like, it's what she is.

In Toronto there is a hangout called Safari where former denizens of Dar es Salaam gather in the evenings, where you might hear Swahili spoken, if not always full conversations then at least frequent expletives learned from the streets of Kariakoo and Gaam. It is a strange place, in a strip mall in an old European ethnic neighbourhood where an attempt to create an India Town around a cinema some years ago was snuffed out by the advent of VHS. The space is narrow, the lighting dim, and the patrons are all in their forties or over—bachelors, men who've taken leave from their families for a few hours, and couples, who can drink beer or whisky away from prying, sanctimonious eyes. The lingo is Dar. The owner and chef is also from Dar, a former rough-boy from Boyschool, now mellowed; a woman, perhaps with dyed hair, might stand at the front and sing sad Hindi film songs from yesteryear on karaoke, taking requests; a child might be waiting for her, at a table, with a book or laptop. You might wonder who exactly she is, why she has to do this. A depressing place, this, all in all, for its utter and unspoken nostalgia, its desperate and somewhat furtive ambience, and even the raucous laugh or argument sounds forced. You might come here before putting a bullet through your head. But it has other merits besides alcohol and familiar accents. It makes mishkaki, what the Kenyans call, crudely, nyama choma: grilled meat on skewers, East African style; it serves also fat, white mhogo (cassava) chips. But most important, what gives the Safari its imprimatur is that it serves meat kababs—round in shape, fried dark brown, and subtly spiced—that conform to the gold standard of Gaam's venerable KT Shop. With the kababs come coconut chutney. This is Gaam in exile.

KT Shop in Dar—abbreviated "KT"—is itself infinitely more cheerful, though a hole of a place. It's on a short road off Jamhuri Street that's not been resurfaced in half a century, a stone's throw from where years ago the Odeon used to bring regular fares of Bollywood. It is a narrow and shallow space, with six low tables set against one side wall, which faces a long and tall counter, behind which sits a bored manager. Behind him is an oversize Liverpool Football Club poster. On the back wall is another large poster, faded but framed, showing the great mosque of Mecca. The chai and kababs are legendary. For decades, Asian shopkeepers and salesmen stopped here for their mid-morning snack; nowadays customers from all backgrounds—bureaucrats, business people, housewives, truck drivers, tourists, the unemployed—come to share the small tables. It is a truly egalitarian place. A domineering, short waiter called Abdu in a dirty white apron sees to it, sternly, though not without a sense of humour, that when you finish your snack you vacate your seat promptly for a grateful someone else who's been waiting in the aisle, eyeing your progress. This is not the place to come to if you mind the small cockroach playing possum in a corner, or the hand that wipes your table with a towel from Abdu's shoulder also laying down your plate of kababs and chutney. But for the many who return to Dar, arriving late in the night when the overseas flights land, the first stop the next morning is for sure the KT. And they will swear, the tastes have not come down a notch from their perfection.

Outside on the broken pavement beggars stretch out their hands familiarly—with the taste of chai and kabab lingering in your mouth, you can afford to be generous; next door is a DVD store;

across the street two newspaper vendors sit with spreads of about a dozen papers. Behind them is a barbershop decades old, where four young barbers ply their trade, one of them an African. Such is the level of comfort now, between different peoples. Traditionally, Asians had their hair cut by Asian barbers, the nai or the hajaam, who came from the barber caste. When I go inside for a trim, the talk among customers is friendly and boisterous: kids' schools, football results, recent overseas visits, pilgrimage routes to Syria and Iraq.

This is quintessential Gaam. Its recent transformation, and there is that, seems drastic and yet is organic to its nature: haphazard, careless.

Some years ago, in response to a government dictat, the two-storey buildings in Gaam began growing more floors, sprouting into colourful six- to eight-storey structures, dwarfing their neighbours, but without a thought to zoning, safety, history, or aesthetics. The official ambition was to makeover Dar into New York. In the process, Dar's distinctive Indian and colonial architecture—the grilled wooden balconies, sloping roofs, arched verandas, and carved facades—slowly bites the dust. Every residue of the old Dar awaits helplessly the wrecking crew. But it is not the Asians who are objecting; few would care about architectural niceties. It is actually a few Asian developers in collaboration with corrupt bureaucrats and politicians who are responsible for erasing the former, gentler face of the city. There is some irony in that what property the government once took away in the name of socialism, with much gusto and racist applause, it is now selling back, to be defaced, deformed, or torn down and rebuilt in the name of the free market.

Gaam in its heyday, for seventy years, was the heart of Dar behind the seashore and the harbour; it reached out to the new suburb of Upanga and the expatriate strongholds of Oyster Bay and Msasani; it opened to the African areas of Kariakoo and beyond, and the industrial area of Pugu Road. Twice during the year, for three days, the Mnazi Mmoja ground would resound with the festive drumbeats of Eid. But during socialism, and especially after the Uganda war, Gaam had become a gloomy, flyblown place in the sun, bereft of its former joie de vivre. Those who had built it had departed, and business was in the dumps; landmark shops and restaurants had closed and there were food shortages. The streets were potholed and garbage was not picked up. To complete its demise, city planners had turned it into an Indian ghetto by closing off the two key arteries leading in and out of it.

But now Gaam is back. The new high-rises are attracting people and businesses; there are new hotels, mosques, and temples. And there is not only the KT to go and have your chai at, but also the AT and Qayyum's and Blue Room, within a block or two of each other, all sticking to the same formula: the same kababs, bhajias, samosas. No one's going to change the recipe and survive. Packets of biriyani and pilau are taken away by nonvegetarian residents during weekends. And Purnima, the vegetarian haven which sank into oblivion during the doldrums, is revived with crisp bhajias and the freshest chevdo. On Sunday mornings the new cake shop nearby fries jelebies on the sidewalk.

This is the capitalist revenge of Gaam. It is back and it does not need Oyster Bay. But the revival comes at a cost. Motor vehicles choke every street, SUVs being the preferred mode of transport. Every middle-class household boasts one or two or three vehicles, parked on the broken sidewalks, backsides poking out dangerously into the streets. In the evenings, when once people sat around to chat and children ran around playing, not only the sidewalks but also the streets are spread with parked cars—sleek, metallic ghosts in the dark, obstacles even to a simple solitary stroll.

Traffic jams, says a senior politician, are a sign of development. We are now like America. And he does not mean to sound ironic.

There are now essentially two Dars, connected by Selander Bridge. The other side is where only Europeans and a handful of the wealthiest Asians used to live. It was a beautiful dreamland to the rest of us. As children we went there only when a rich visiting relative took us for a drive past the grand houses. Oyster Bay, past the lighthouse, overlooking the Indian Ocean, was the place to go and sit in silence and feel a shiver while staring at the dark sea and the sky and hear the pounding waves; there would be the occasional European (that is, white) couple in their car, necking and doing whatnot, the car rocking as though possessed by a spirit, which in a sense it was. Oyster Bay today still has the beautiful houses; it has added the poshest hotels and restaurants in the city, and shopping malls and new developments for the foreigners and the wealthy. There are those who know only this Dar, who would not find their way around Gaam or Kariakoo. On the other hand, I who sometimes put up at Oyster Bay, don't feel I am in Dar unless I breathe the dust of Gaam. But the vicious bottleneck of the bridge can take two hours to cross at rush hour, and there is a growing tendency among people to move into the new residences of the old city. Yes, finally the revenge of Gaam.

Walter Bgoya, who benefitted from the confiscation of Asian buildings, is one of those who throws up his hands in despair at the blight that is the new, ugly reconstruction of the old city, its ruthless defacement. He's had a court order brought to prevent the wrecking of a historical building opposite the harbour. And his company has come out with an illustrated book showing Gaam's distinguished buildings: those already destroyed and those with the axe looming over their heads. Now they're preserved in print. But his is a rare sensibility. He has seen better fortunes recently, perhaps with a government or foreign benefactor, and having realized too the wisdom of publishing in English. The old idealist, publishing titles that would make a university press proud elsewhere, now owns a new, modern office in the industrial section of town and a storefront on Samora Avenue, hoping this part of the old town will revive and that people will flock to attend literary events and buy books. The avenue—called Unter den Akazien in German times, later Acacia Avenue, and later still Independence Avenue—was a promenade lined with acacia trees and fancy shops that displayed in their windows imported items such as shirts from England and tennis rackets and golf clubs and accordions and guitars; on Saturdays some of us would play truant from high school and come here to drink iced cappuccinos, recently in fashion, the Italians having arrived, and watch the girls. Now the shops sell anything from cheap ready-made clothes to cell phones, and in front of them, where once the flame trees were ablaze in their fiery red glory, the road is crowded with desperate-looking vendors selling anything from newspapers to worn-out books fifty years old, from peanuts to T-shirts with football logos from all the major teams of the world.

The shelves of Bgoya's bookstore have fattened recently, the titles are fascinating. I can recall the dusty wooden skeletons of only a few years ago. Where else would one see Soyinka's take on the new Africa, so abundantly displayed? Or a study of Ebrahim Hussein, the nation's iconic modern playwright, who suddenly went silent? Or the full set of the gritty urban novels of the Kenyan Meja Mwangi? A history of Dar es Salaam, a dictionary of Nyakyusa? Until recently only expatriates bought books; but now there is an elite, however thin the crust, and it has the money to buy books. But what are the James Hadley Chases doing here, 1960s-era pulp thrillers long out of date elsewhere, prominently on display? Walter Bgoya grins mischievously. The best sellers are the Bibles, he confesses. And then come the Chases. You have to draw the customers in before they go for Ebrahim Hussein, Issa Shivji, and Shaaban Robert. What about Qurans? No, the attendants are women and they don't know if they'll get into trouble handling the Muslim holy book.

One morning with a local friend I undertake a walk along my old streets. We depart from Mövenpick, where in its lobby café foreign-aid workers interview their local agents, who sit humbly before them like pupils before a principal, and where an espresso costs half the minimum daily wage, and head off to Jamhuri Street—Ringstrasse in German times, and later Ring Street. It used to have two cinema houses, the Odeon showing Bollywood and the Cameo showing Italian fare, a typical one of which had Hercules and Ulysses romping together bare-chested on the green hills where pretty young women in silk gowns played blindman's buff, and enemies and dragons lurked.

On the other side of Jamhuri Street, across the new highway that squeezes this venerable old ring road forever into the Indian quarter, is the Mnazi Mmoja ground. This open space was created by the colonial authorities as a cordon sanitaire separating the Asian Gaam from the African Kariakoo. But many Asians lived in Kariakoo, above or behind their small shops. Eid was celebrated with a frenzy on Mnazi Mmoja, to which people thronged in the hundreds. There were the local fast foods at every spot, the bands, the dancers and men on stilts, the merry-go-round, and gambling stalls. At night, oil lamps flickered in the dark, woodsmoke choked the air, shadows flitted about like jinns, and the sound of the ngoma drumbeats echoed far and wide into the suburbs. Sleepless in our beds only three blocks away, my brothers and I pined to be there "at the Eid." But tomorrow was school.

We walk along Uhuru Street, which begins near the customs house and goes down past the city-status tower and Mnazi Mmoja all the way into Msimbazi Street in Kariakoo. The street looks narrower than it did in my childhood, naturally. It is choked with traffic and fumes, and you push past crowds to walk on the sidewalk. Instead of the old green and beige Leyland city buses, the groan and grunt of its gears announcing the hour of dawn like a broken clock unable to chime but grinding away all the same, there are now the packed minibuses called dala-dala. They were introduced in the 1990s when government controls on businesses were completely relaxed; dala is "dollar," which had also arrived, it being forbidden to possess in the old days of socialism. A dollar or its equivalent was what the minibuses used to charge when they first came on the scene. A dollar was seven shillings when I first left; it's now sixteen hundred.

The corner of Uhuru and Sikukuu, where we lived two floors above, stands intact, awaiting the inevitable wreckers and cranes. It's uncanny. As I stand here in the noisy clamorous heat and dust taking photos, I think I could fill all the apartments around this crossroads with people and stories. No amount of photography could replace the memories of a life lived, of lives observed and known, of lives elaborated in the mind and on the page. Across from us a man nicknamed Toti had his shop; fat and sickly and miserly, always in singlet and loincloth, he had to be supported upstairs to his flat. He sold everything a modest African household would need day to day: grains, spices, matches, kerosene, cooking oil. I would be sent to Toti to buy bundles of used newspapers, which my mother used in her shop for wrapping. Where did Toti, sitting in his shop all day, get them from? They were all British papers, which I would pore over, reading news of child murders and football (Jimmy Greaves returning to Tottenham from Milan), and the comics (Andy Capp and Sooty). The Totis had the only telephone on the block, and the only car, a Ford Taunus stationwagon. With great reluctance my mother would pay 15 shillings a month, whenever she could spare them, to have me brought home from school with their son, a year older than I. Next door to us was a fair, chubby, and boisterous woman called Roshan Godoro, who sold mattresses and was rumoured to be having an affair with a police inspector who often came around. Across the street was a Goan family, whose older daughter was a seamstress and whose father drank a lot; when the British jet plane, the Comet 4, was introduced with much fanfare and arrived in Dar ("Good night, Dar! Good morning, London!"), the son took my sisters to the airport to have a look; they returned with the plane's plastic cutlery as mementos. And every once in a while the community town crier came limping along, stood at this crossroads, and announced a funeral or a special message from the Ismaili Imam. And once—the memory persists—here I was hit by a bicycle when returning with a loaf of bread from the bakery.

We walk into Congo Street, the open-air clothing market denser than ever and running for several blocks; my companion promised me a sight of Chinese vendors—still a novelty worth pointing out—in the area, but we don't find any. From here to Msimbazi, then back up to the vegetable market, which used to be open-air but is now—thanks to some foreign donor—all indoors. To the street it presents the grim permanence of a vast concrete bunker. Finally my companion and I go back up to Gaam.

We head towards Kumbhad wadi, the area of the potters. In the nineteenth century, I was told by a dhow owner in Gujarat, the Kumbhads (potters) would sometimes simply put their wares on a raft and let the trade winds carry them across to the African coast. In due time the reverse winds returned them home. The Kumbhad wadi used to be a very modest settlement, a village transposed from India. In the afternoons the Kumbhads would take to the streets, pulling their carts of clay pots and pans to sell, calling out, "Taawdi matli! Taawdi matli!" Now the area has three apartment buildings, and is still set off with a gate and a guard. Inside there is a temple and a playground.

Finally that afternoon, we stop to gaze at the site where one of those newfangled high-rises simply collapsed, leaving two people dead; not far from here is another tall building which, on its way to toppling sideways, has found support from a two-storey stalwart of yesteryear. The past upholding the present. This leaning tower of Dar es Salaam has people still living in it.

More recently, another building collapsed in the area while still under construction; this time more than forty people were killed and the incident made world news. The president and other politicians all came to have a look, and like Captain Renault in *Casablanca,* they all expressed their shock.

4.

The Road to Tanga

THE NAIROBI TO MOSHI BUS left early in the morning and made its lonely way south through the plains. I had been instructed by my hosts to decline in case a fellow passenger offered me a candy, because it was likely to be drugged, in which case I would be robbed and lose my luggage. It was the early 1990s and such was the fear for personal safety then. But my neighbour, a young Masai or Meru who was headed with goods for his father's shop in Arusha, seemed nice and I could hardly refuse the sweets he pressed upon me. Eating sweets seemed to be a common practice in the buses. It was an irritating and anxious journey initially, with frequent police checkpoints on the Kenya side. A grim-faced copper or two would step up and peer inside the silenced bus. If they felt like it these surly guardians of the law could search all the passengers, or even have the luggage brought down from the roof one piece at a time. At each checkpoint however they received their baksheesh. Once I heard the driver instruct the conductor, "Give him a pair of pants"; this was done, and we went speeding on our way. It was only when we had crossed the border into Tanzania, Kilimanjaro rising ahead of us in the distance, that the mood inside relaxed, the passengers became chatty. We arrived in Moshi in the middle of the afternoon.

The Khoja Asians used to have guest houses in many of the towns in East Africa; I had stayed in them in Dar and in Mombasa. They were clean and cheap, though often rooms had to be shared, but among familiars you didn't feel lonely in a strange town and there was plenty of free advice. I had been told there was a guest house in Moshi where I could spend the night, and also in Tanga, which was my destination. I got off at Moshi and took a taxi to the guest house, only to discover that due to the recent population depletions of Asians all over the country, it had been shut down. I had to look for another place to stay.

One of my fellow passengers was a young man called Pinto from Nairobi, a tour operator who had come from India only two years before. We found a hotel together and afterwards as we walked around were approached and befriended by a young Asian taxi driver called Dilip who took us to his home. The family was very modest, consisting of our friend, his young brother, and their parents. The father's leg had been amputated after a car accident, and the older boy was the bread-earner. I wondered why they took us in—perhaps they expected taxi fares from us, perhaps they were simply lonely. Driving a taxi was not an Indian trade. Only later I concluded that they must be from one of the so-called lower castes, who had recently left their traditional occupations. When the old man lost his "company" job following his accident, he had to give up the flat that went with it, and the family was forced to spend six months in the temple. After dinner and listening to incessant complaints from the old man about the state of the country—the general neglect (the refrigeration at the morgue was broken, for one thing, and there was a stench in the town), the rising cost of living, the shortages—Pinto and I went back to our hotel, which was above a noisy bar. It was the Hindu Navratri season, and during the night as the bar became quiet downstairs, I could hear strains of song from the temple.

Moshi, and its sister town Arusha, an hour away, always had an English-village feel to them, at least to those of us visiting from chaotic Dar. They were compact and neat, with tree-lined avenues and bungalows for houses; the weather was cool and the surrounding countryside lush and hilly. Moshi was the smaller town, with a set of streets named First Street, Second Street, and so on, giving it added distinction. But the wonderful thing about Moshi was Kilimanjaro, seen from the main street looming majestically over the town, the smooth, round, snowy peak clear in the pristine morning air, then gradually donning a veil of cloud as the day wore on. Elsewhere they talk incessantly about the weather, in Moshi they asked if there was a cloud cover yet on the mlima. This mighty mountain with its gentle contour remains the most awesome and yet heart-warming sight—even though I am not from the area—casting its benign gaze over the entire country. The story goes that originally—in the early days of colonization—it was part of British Kenya, but Queen Victoria presented it to her grandson Kaiser Wilhelm II of Germany (which had colonized Tanganyika) for his birthday, and the straight border between the two countries acquired its familiar bend in order to accommodate the change. At the nation's independence, Brigadier Sarakikya of the Tanganyika Rifles planted the national flag on its peak, a momentous occasion symbolizing freedom, hope, ambition—an event that was commemorated on the highest-denomination postage stamp.

Our friend from the previous day, Dilip, took us around. There appeared to be a subculture of drifters and expats in Moshi—consisting of hotel managers, tour operators, and others—that he took pleasure in showing off to us. The Asian section of town consisted of pleasant-looking, flat-roofed bungalows and townhouses built in the early 1960s. There was an older area that was eerily quiet, perhaps because there were no vendors or children in sight; the trees were ancient, and the bungalows staid, with high tiled or iron roofs. This would have been the old European area. Here we came upon a monument to "Hindu, Sikh, and Mohamedan" soldiers of the First World War. Close by, in a tidy compound enclosed by a white picket fence, was a rather extensive war cemetery where I walked around while the others waited with complete disinterest. The dead young men buried here wholesale in neat rows were all fully identified; many had been killed during the period March through May 1916. The cemetery was cared for by a British veterans' organization.

Few people I met knew or cared that a protracted campaign of the First World War—which changed so much of the world—had been fought in this region, that their town in Africa reposing at the foot of Kilimanjaro had a fascinating, dramatic modern history that was connected to the larger events of the world; that that European war had also dramatically changed the course of their African nation.

When war was declared by the great powers of Europe on August 4, 1914, the two colonies, British East Africa (Kenya) and Deutsch-Ostafrika (Tanganyika), became willy-nilly a part of it. Far away from Europe in every conceivable way, the East African campaign would seem pointless, frivolous, and bizarre, a waste of resources and lives that could have no possible impact on the outcome of the actual war, which in the real theatre in Europe would end up consuming millions of lives. But the British Empire stretched across the globe, protected by its navy, and therefore every corner of it was potentially vulnerable and strategic. The war in East Africa was fought using colonial proxies, Indians against Africans, and Africans against each other. There was a thriving Indian population in both the countries, but the Indian soldiers who fought on the British side were not local, they were shipped in from the Subcontinent.

Both colonies were recently acquired and settled. The dividing boundary had been drawn barely twenty years before. Kenya in 1914 had a mere 5,000 Europeans, of which 1,200 lived in Nairobi; the others, mostly farming families, were gathered in the lush highlands and the Rift Valley. There were 25,000 Indians. The Uganda Railway, completed in 1905, ran from the Indian Ocean to Lake Victoria—Mombasa to Nairobi and Kampala—following ancient caravan routes close to the border. Nairobi, founded as a way station and railway depot, had become the capital of Kenya, with a population of 20,000. In neighbouring Tanganyika there was a comparably small number of whites, concentrated in Dar es Salaam and Tanga on the coast, the highlands of the Kilimanjaro region in the north, and the Iringa region in the southern highlands. The Usambara Railway ran from Tanga up to Moshi, and like its Kenyan counterpart ran parallel and close to the border. Farther south, the much longer Central Line ran from Dar es Salaam to Kigoma on the other great lake, now called Lake Tanganyika. It was in this raw region, grabbed from its owners, and still unformed as colonies, that a two-year war took place.

Only days after the declaration of war, enthusiastic British settlers in Kenya, eager to fight for the motherland, had formed two ragtag volunteer corps, the East African Mounted Rifles and the East Africa Regiment. South of the border in Tanganyika, Paul von Lettow-Vorbeck, a professional soldier who would go on to become a legend even to the British, began to gather settlers and recruit African askaris in preparation for engagement. Like sparks presaging a forest fire, small units of armed men began darting across the border. These raids were indecisive, exploratory, and adventurous in nature, and more harassment than anything else. There were some notable engagements, however. On August 15 a German force of three hundred captured the strategic town of Taveta, twenty-five miles from Moshi, just inside the border in Kenya. This was a thorn in the British side, since from here the Germans could mount hit-and-run operations on the vital Uganda Railway. Farther east, on the coast, von Lettow-Vorbeck had his eyes on Mombasa. In late September, German askaris marched north along the coast and crossed the border but were beaten back.

Soon after, the British attempted two ambitious attacks on the German colony. In the first, in the Kilimanjaro area on November 3, 1914, an Anglo-Indian force of 1,500 men crossed the border and were soundly beaten by a German force half the size. In the second engagement, known forever as the infamous Battle of Tanga, a unit assembled as the Indian Expeditionary Force B, consisting of some 8,000 troops, arrived in a large convoy of ships to capture the port town of Tanga. They were humiliated by a much smaller but well-trained German-African force.

Finally in November 1915, worried by reports of these and other setbacks from the British colony, the Committee of Imperial Defence in London recommended that the conquest of German East Africa take place as soon as possible. This turned out to mean *immediately*, and the man picked to lead the invasion was Lieutenant-General Jan Smuts of South Africa, who arrived in Mombasa in February 1916. Smuts, a diminutive man, was of Afrikaaner background, therefore arguably an African. In the Boer War (1899–1902) he had commanded guerrilla raids against the British. He had tussled with Gandhi. He was as tough as von Lettow-Vorbeck.

Suddenly in early 1916 the quiet and arid border region between Kenya and Tanganyika, sparsely dotted with small villages, was overrun by thousands of soldiers speaking a dozen languages and from as many cultures: settlers wearing wide-rimmed sun hats, the British, South Africans, and Rhodesians in baggy khakis and helmets, Indians in a variety of turbans, smart African askaris in puttees and caps with a neck-flap. Armoured cars raced urgently on grass trails and new roads, vast tent villages sprang up, wildlife stayed away, and horses and pack animals raised the dust. Even today, this spectacle from the past makes you wonder. What would the natives in their rudimentary settlements—a few mud huts around a yard of packed red earth—someone at Mbuyuni, for instance, or Maktau—have made of this upheaval of their universe, this alien invasion that could as well have come from Mars? There are no accounts from their side, of course.

Smuts meant business. His plan was to attack the Kilimanjaro area from the west, throwing a full division at Namanga (where a present border post exists), and from the east along the Voi–Taveta axis, the two divisions later to join up. The British forces outnumbered Lettow-Vorbeck's Feldkompanies by 18,400 to 6,000. A railway line had been extended from Voi to Maktau, more than halfway to the border, to transport the British troops. By March 5, British forces, including several mounted, infantry, and field artillery units, had amassed at Mbuyuni, some twenty miles east of Taveta, and Serengeti, a village farther up. On the evening of March 7 the South Africans marched down in two columns, and the next day had displaced German positions on the Chala Crater overlooking Taveta. On March 10, the 2nd South African Horse unit expelled the Germans out of Taveta, which they had occupied the previous year. Meanwhile, Salaita Hill, just outside Taveta, where the Germans had twice rebuffed the

British, had been occupied unopposed by other units on March 9.

The Germans retreated towards Moshi, making British advance as difficult as possible. Early on March 14 the South Africans under Major van Deventer reached Moshi. At about the same time the 1st Division, arriving from the west, established contact. Von Lettow-Vorbeck's troops retreated east, along the railway. Smuts pursued. But, as the official history of the East Africa Operations states, "Although the Germans had fallen back, they had not been effectively brought to battle, much less suffered tactical defeat." Engage-and-retreat was in fact the tactic adopted by von Lettow-Vorbeck against the superior enemy forces, in a protracted guerrilla war across the country, north to south. There is some irony in the fact that the pursuing Smuts had himself used similar tactics against the British in the Boer War not long ago in South Africa.

Von Lettow-Vorbeck was never defeated and became a military hero and a man of legend.

The English poet and novelist Francis Brett Young was thirty-one when he accompanied Smuts's invasion as a member of the medical corps and gives a wonderfully impressionistic account of that experience in his book *Marching on Tanga*. In novelistic fashion he begins,

> When the troop train ran into the siding at Taveta the dawn was breaking. All through the night we had been moving by fits and starts over the new military line from Voi, moving through a dark and desolate land which, eighteen months before, had been penetrated by very few men indeed. In that night journey we could see little of the country. Not that we slept—our progress was too freakish, and the Indian railway trucks in which we were packed were too

crowded for that—but because the night seemed to lie upon it with a peculiar heaviness.

The title of the book is somewhat misleading: the troops did not go to Tanga but, always in pursuit of the retreating Germans, marched eastwards along the railway for some distance, and then turned south. Falling sick near Handeni, Brett Young appears to have been sent back to England after a period of recuperation near Nairobi, where he completed his book in 1916. The manuscript was censored, which is perhaps why it is at times vague and short on graphic detail. But it has passages of beauty, and the whole East African experience seems to have come upon him like a dream. He ends,

> But, though we do not always know it, the submerged memory of the dream lingers. And, in the same way, it seemed to me that though the forest tangles of the Pangani close above the tracks we made, and the blown sand fill our trenches and drift above the graves of those whom we left sleeping there, that ancient, brooding country can never be the same again, nor wholly desert, now that so many men have lived intensely for a little while in its recesses. Shall we not revisit the Pangani, I and many others, the country to which we have given a soul?

Since the "British" soldiers (including the South Africans and Rhodesians) were all accounted for, one assumes that it was the dead Indians and Africans who were buried on the road, the former to be remembered anonymously in that memorial in Moshi, the latter by the Askari Monument in the centre of Dar es Salaam. Brett Young went on to have a prolific career, publishing numerous books, some of which were best-sellers. His favourite novel, however, according to the Francis Brett Young Society, was *Jim Redlake,* now out of print, which uses some of the censored portions of *Marching on Tanga.*

To me the great war does not evoke Flanders or Vimy Ridge or Gallipoli, all vividly and multiply brought to life in novels and films, or the red poppies of November, in the same way it does the wind-blown thorny semidesert from Voi to Moshi under the mighty Kilimanjaro, the Usambara Railway, and the road to Tanga. And too, there is the overriding irony of it: the graves at Moshi, the anonymous monuments to the Africans and the Indians.

A week before my journey to Moshi from Nairobi, I had gone to visit Taveta from the Kenya side to look at the site of Smuts's great push eighty years earlier. On the way, however, there was a bit of family history to lay to rest.

Even before Kenya was colonized and its great railway was built, Indians had settled along that interior route to Uganda, running their little dukas (shops) that brought supplies to the local Africans. My great-grandfather, Nanji Lalji, was one of them, having arrived from the village of Girgadhada in the Kathiawar region of Gujarat to begin a business in the town of Kibwezi, not far from Voi. Here he was the local mukhi, or headman, of the Khojas and presided over the khano. This bit of family history I had learned only recently after a meeting with one of his daughters-in-law, my father's aunt, a shrunken old woman in a mattress shop in downtown Nairobi. Kibwezi turned out to be a typical nondescript town under the sun, with nothing of interest save the ruin of the old khano where my great-grandfather had presided. The Indians had all gone away. Several years later, I saw my ancestor's village in India. Here too the

Khojas had gone away, except for one family, and the khano was shut down, after the Gujarat violence of 2002. It was a strangely moving experience, to come to the place of my origins, but by this time I could also manage a sense of detachment.

The Uganda Railway was built in the early 1900s using indentured Punjabi and local African labour. Given various names, including the Lunatic Express and the Iron Snake, it was an engineering marvel of its time, traversing some six hundred miles, ascending to more than 6,000 feet before plunging down into the Rift Valley and rising up again to meet Lake Victoria. The construction was gruelling, and many workers died from malaria, dysentery, and sleeping sickness; and for a few terror-filled months some Punjabis fell victim to lions in the grassland who had become so emboldened by access to easy meat that they would creep inside a tent of sleeping men and drag one off. This grisly episode of the railways—the plight of the "coolies"—is captured vividly in the book *The Man-eaters of Tsavo* by Colonel Patterson, the man who hunted down the predators.

The Nairobi–Mombasa highway, going east, stays close to the railway. Arriving at Voi around noon, we turned into the Taveta road. It was rough and dusty, punishing for the car, and there was not another vehicle in sight, so that if the car broke down, as our driver worried, we would be stuck in the middle of nowhere under a burning sun. All around us the dry thorny shrub of the Taru Desert, a dull brown and green landscape relieved by the occasional baobab tree. Roads led into villages now obscure, which in that brief moment of the war had assumed such importance. There was no sign of the military railway from Voi, only a herd of cows and a few lanky Masai youth in red shukas with their herding sticks. Finally we entered a grassland, and soon thereafter the land was abundant and green with large shady trees and we were in Taveta. Straight ahead of us loomed Kilimanjaro, both peaks visible.

An eerie feeling. Could this be real? Is this where, under the eyes of this African god, the great war was fought?

Taveta was a sprawling village surrounded by hills and mountains. We found a decent hotel, from the terrace of which we could look upon a vista: the Pare Mountains before us on the left, Kilimanjaro directly in front, Chala Crater to the right. Behind us a stone church on a small hill, and behind that, Salaita Hill, whose occupation by a small party of Germans in 1915 had been the cause of so much British frustration. The hotel manager, a man in his forties wearing a Kaunda suit—a collared short-sleeved shirt of linen worn over matching pants—was a former schoolmaster and a history buff to whom I took instantly. He was delighted at my interest. Nobody knows about the war here, he rued; all that history, now lost. The church-on-a-hill behind us was relatively new, from the 1930s, but there was a cemetery, not very far, on the site of an old church destroyed in the war. There was a 1904 grave there, of a white woman.

He gave me a car with driver to go and have a look. The cemetery was a short distance away from the modern town, but I couldn't find the old grave. The place was lovely, however, shaded with mango trees and utterly quiet and peaceful. The graves seemed to have been reused, and even the gravestones. On our way back, a surprise awaited. Across the road from the church rose a site that made my heart race: old brick ruins crowning the top of a rise. We stopped so I could walk around. What remained of the original structure—a rectangular bunker—were the ruins of the outer walls, and in one corner an almost intact room with crenelated walls, a square opening in each of them, used presumably to fire down on the enemy. There was no roof, and the room was now used as a kitchen. The rest of the building had been patched up crudely with cement and brick and housed the church offices. Stones were scattered on the sides of the hill, debris that presumably had rolled away from the old structure. As we drove on, alerted, we noted occasional heaps of rubble that could very possibly—very hopefully—be signals from times past.

You have to go and see Lake Chala, the manager insisted, and the next morning we did just that.

The lake is inside a crater and invisible from the road, so that you have to walk up a hill to see it. And when you do so you come upon a sight of such pristine beauty it leaves you helpless. The sky blue, the leaves green, the dirt road an insignificant thin line. The lake below, crystal-clear blue, mysterious, deep; tiny ripples on the surface played by the wind like light fingers on a harp. You have no word to say; you walk away from the others. You think, This could be the site of Creation itself. And you want to hoard away this moment, so that years later you can say, I was at Lake Chala. When the tourists had not arrived and only a privileged few knew about it.

You can, if you try, climb down to the water. We meet two Masai youths who have done just that. We go halfway down, but the climb is steep, and without a stick (the Masai each have one) it does not seem wise to proceed farther. But at the top of the crater is a stone fortification, a wall, some nine feet high and twenty wide. This is where the South Africans had dislodged the Germans.

It takes some feat—amidst this spell-binding natural beauty that surrounds us—to imagine here tens of thousands of troops, animals, guns, motor vehicles. Dust, petrol fumes, animal odour in the air. They came, fought, and left, leaving only these stone clues behind, like men and beasts from another planet.

Lake Chala is fed by a stream from Kilimanjaro running underground. It runs, we are told, all the way to Lake Jipe, emerging once at the Njoro Springs. From the terrace of our hotel later we could see a green belt apparently following that path.

Now here I was in Moshi a week later perusing the names of the war dead: J. Watson of the Machine Gun Corps, and Private S.H.V. Palmer of the 12th Regiment of the South African Infantry, and D. Scott King of the 4th South African Horse, and W. Dawson of the Calcutta Volunteers Battery, and many other young men of Smuts's British army who died far away from home and were left buried here in Moshi.

5.

Tanga, Decline in the Sun

Late that afternoon in Moshi I took a bus bound for Tanga. When earlier in the day I bought my ticket, the company agent had confidently brandished a seating chart, and with the wisdom of a seasoned traveller I had put my name on an ideal place; to my chagrin the actual seat arrangement bore no resemblance to the one on the chart. Nothing to be done, a shrug of the shoulders by all concerned. That agent was nowhere to be found, and that too was par for the course. The bus terminal resounded with a football commentary: a Yanga–Simba derby was concluding, and a large crowd had gathered outside a stall to follow the match on radio. Yanga were the Young Africans and Simba were the former Sunderland, both Dar teams.

We departed at sunset, headed east, the mountain behind us, and night had fallen. Nothing else stirred on the highway, the bus the solitary creature grinding through the thick foggy darkness, its headlights sweeping across the hills and forests. There would be the occasional flicker of light, an only lamp at a distant habitation, drawing you in like a spell. Who lived there up on the hill, how would they spend the evening? Could one but peep into those lives and in some way share them. Did this habitual craving turn me into a novelist? What makes this primitiveness, this forbidding solitude of the jungle so wrenchingly attractive from a distance? There is in this stillness a certain spirituality, a welcome loneliness that I've often treasured in my travels, in which there seems to be only the universe and I, an endless moment devoid of fear or death. Perhaps it is death.

In the middle of the journey, in the pitch-darkness ahead a cluster of electric lights appeared in the distance, at which the bus arrived and abruptly stopped. It was a roadside restaurant. We were in Mombo, at a stop that was familiar to me from trips taken long ago in childhood; one always arrived here at night, it seemed. The place was still owned by an Asian, probably of the same family. The men's facility consisted of a dark windowless backroom with a stinging stench. You held your breath, did your job, and rushed out. I had a Coke and took my seat, and our journey proceeded

We reached Tanga at 2:15 a.m. instead of the scheduled 5 a.m.; some of us, who had no home in Tanga, opted to stay inside and snooze until morning broke. At 5:30 we were summarily cast out and the bus grumbled off to the depot. Outside, in the humid coastal coolness, I accepted a taxi with trepidation. It was an old car and had to be push-started. Barely a hundred yards on it turned off and came crawling to a stop, and started again after another push, then decisively sputtered out. "What now?" I asked, somewhat nervously. At this hour no one was about except the two of us. "No petrol," the driver said. "Isn't there a station nearby?" No. What to do, on this dark street, in a town in which I knew nobody? But I could see that the man had no evil purpose, he had only tried to eke out a fare in difficult times and his vehicle had betrayed him. I had not even seen his face clearly in the dark, though he was a small person and sounded as sleepy as I was.

"Don't worry," he said, "I'll take you there." We got out, he picked up my bag and put it on his shoulder, and we walked together to the Khoja prayer house, where I presumed I would be directed to the guest house. There was a mukhi there, the headman, chatting with two women after the morning's meditations and prayers; the guest house had been closed for some time, he said, and sent me with a worker to a local hotel where, however, there was no vacancy. I returned, had a wash in the shower in the ladies' room, and waited until seven, when two old men walked me to the house of the man whose address I had been given by a friend in Toronto. His name was Samji. He dismissed the idea of a hotel with "What's the need? Stay with us."

There were three of them in the house, Samji, his wife Roshan, and their son Karim, in his early twenties. After a rich breakfast of bread, butter and jam, and fried eggs, Karim said he would show me around town. This was typical community hospitality. It was the kind of welcome our grandfathers gave to new immigrants when they arrived penniless from India to start afresh in a foreign land. And I recall that during my National Service at a camp outside Bukoba, on a Sunday I only had to show up in the shop of a Khoja, introduce myself, and—in the home of complete strangers that seemed primitive by Dar standards—I would be treated to a hot bath, a longed-for Indian meal of pilau and curry, and after siesta be given a ride back to the camp. Here too, a complete stranger, I was given a home. (The mukhi, who had sent me to a hotel, was clearly an aberration.) But it was not easy to explain to my hosts my interest in their neglected coastal town. To them, writers were journalists who wrote in the papers and those who wrote books about life in Europe and America. What was there to write about Tanga? And what kind of writer could I be, a mere Asian from Dar?

No traveller or explorer of any eminence in the past has mentioned Tanga. An obscure Swahili port on the Indian Ocean coast, it was on nobody's itinerary, until the brief twenty-year period of German rule when its star began to shine. The Germans were fond of it. It was the entry point to the hilly Usambara and Kilimanjaro regions, where climate and agriculture were good. While farther south along the coast the fortunes of the old market ports and Swahili culture hubs of Kilwa, Bagamoyo, and Lindi fell, Tanga prospered and grew.

In the 1890s a certain Richard Hindorf ordered 1,000 plants of Mexican sisal to arrive in Tanga by way of Miami (direct export was forbidden from Mexico). Sixty-two plants survived the journey via Hamburg and were the beginnings of a sisal industry that would flourish over the decades to provide the country's pre-eminent export. Sisal estates, scored with row upon row of thick spiky leaves shooting up from the ground, soon characterized the landscape outside Tanga and became its welcome to the weary road traveller. As Tanga's economy grew, more settlers arrived. It became an important administrative centre, its port exporting twice as much as Dar es Salaam.

It would not have been unusual in Berlin to receive a postcard from Tanga, a pretty European town then, its gleaming white, veranda-ed houses tucked away nicely behind their green hedges. The town boasted three landmarks. The railway station, the bahnhof, was a two-storey building with sloping double roof, a wooden veranda, and a round stationmaster's clock prominent on the outside wall; a balcony on the first floor went around the building and was accessible by external stairs. The region's affairs were handled at the imposing, multi-gabled white boma, the German imperial flag prominent outside. And the Kaiserhof on Imperial (now

Independence) Road was the local hotel and the settlers' cultural centre. At the Kaiserhof you would go for your sundowners or the town Christmas party. Full room—guaranteed mosquito-free—and board cost five rupees.

The Usambara (or Northern) Line, went from Tanga to Moshi, roughly parallel to the Mombasa–Nairobi line across the border. In the 1960s a link was effected between the two lines, connecting the towns of Voi and Korogwe, providing the exciting prospect of a railway journey from Nairobi (or even farther-away Kampala) all the way to Dar es Salaam. I recall it as a miserable journey, spoilt by the agony of a long wait in the absolute dark at Korogwe in the middle of the night, under a massive onslaught of mosquitoes. In German times the entire Tanga–Moshi corridor was well populated by settlers. Once, when sixteen German peasants arrived from Jaffa in Palestine, the *Usambara-Post* gave the opinion that they would make excellent settlers, used as they were to "a hot climate and fevers." They would not have thought that a war back in Europe would drive them away so quickly from their new home.

Tanga has given its name to one of the most ignominious British defeats of the First World War, in an encounter that has become known as the Battle for Tanga. Soon after the declaration of hostilities, a unit called the Indian Expeditionary Force B was set up under Major General Aitken in India with instructions to "bring the whole of German East Africa under British Authority." Easier said than done. Said the confident Aitken, "The Indian Army will make short work of a lot of niggers"; and further, "I mean to thrash the Germans before Christmas." In Tanga he would meet his nemesis, the wily von Lettow-Vorbeck.

On October 16, 1914, a convoy of forty-five ships left Bombay Harbour, among which were fourteen transport ships carrying some 8,000 Indian troops. Aitken knew little of the conditions in East Africa. Moreover, his Indians were ill-equipped and ill-prepared, coming from different regions and castes, speaking different languages, and eating different foods, a requirement that was often not met. Many had been newly drafted. They were overcrowded and unhappy. According to one British officer, the two-week voyage to Mombasa was "a hell on crowded ships in tropical heat." To add to the Indians' misery, upon their arrival in Mombasa they were refused shore leave to recuperate. And finally, to top off the sheer incompetence of the operation and foolish confidence of its commander, there was the lack of secrecy; the Germans knew of an impending attack from any number of sources, besides what common sense had already informed von Lettow-Vorbeck.

The British troops landed at a headland called Ras Kasone, two miles from Tanga town. But it was fifty-four hours later when they began to advance, by which time von Lettow-Vorbeck had calmly reconnoitered the situation on his bicycle, having watched the transport ships from the land. His soldiers were in place and prepared. As the British—mainly the Indians—approached the town, through dense rubber and sisal plantations under a burning November sun, the Germans—mainly the askaris—fired. The Indians bolted in numbers. As the official history relates one instance, "The Madrasi troops, like the rest, were suffering much from the tropical heat and consequent thirst. In poor condition as a result of their miserable voyage, and short of sleep during the previous night, the companies of the 63rd began to disintegrate from the moment the German machine gun fire opened. . . . Nothing could prevent the Madrasi rank and file from pouring back and dispersing into the thick undergrowth of the rubber plantation." One group from the mainly Gurkha Kashmir Rifles, however, reached the Kaiserhof and tore down the German flag, before being forced to flee.

Von Lettow-Vorbeck writes of this battle, such as it was,

> no witness will forget the moment when the machine guns of the 13th Company opened a continuous fire. . . . The whole front jumped up and dashed forward with enthusiastic cheers. . . . In wild disorder the enemy fled in dense masses, and our machine guns, converging on their front and flanks, mowed down whole companies to the last man. Several askaris came in beaming with delight with several captured English rifles on their backs and an Indian prisoner in each hand.

And I would be told by a cultural officer in Tanga how his father recalled collecting chapatis from the bodies of dead Indian soldiers.

As it turned out, it was not only the askari bullets that created panic and mayhem among the Indians. The bees in their hives up in the trees, having been disturbed by gunfire, had also viciously attacked the soldiers. Bees and askaris, then, routed the poor Indians. And to give credit where it was due, the Battle for Tanga has also been called The Battle of the Bees.

The next morning, on November 5, Colonel Meinertzhagen from the British side went to meet the German command bearing the white flag of truce and medical supplies, and was warmly received at the Kaiserhof and given a breakfast. Meinertzhagen was a brilliant intelligence officer, a soldier, an ornithologist, and later a memoirist. The memoirs are valuable—few people have recorded the events of those times in East Africa—though he is generally regarded as an exaggerator. He was also a racist thug who took satisfaction in killing. In his accounts of the early colonial years in Kenya he seems to have enjoyed bayoneting Africans, including women. In Tanga, this is one account of his behaviour:

> As [Meinertzhagen] approached the British lines, still with his flag of truce, an Indian sentry, probably ignorant of the meaning of the white flag, fired at him, the bullet passing through his helmet and grazing his head. Meinertzhagen, enraged, jammed his flagstaff into the sepoy's stomach, wrenched his rifle from him, and stabbed him with his own bayonet.

The official history calls the Tanga expedition "one of the most notable failures in British military history"; it helped to prolong the war in East Africa and made a hero out of von Lettow-Vorbeck. The British casualties, wounded, dead, and missing, amounted to 817; the German, 147.

One day in Toronto I received a letter from someone called Ann Crichton-Harris; she wanted to talk to me about Tanga. A few days later in a coffee shop I met a cheerful, enthusiastic woman of middle age, and with her was a young friend who had recently escaped from Ethiopia via Djibouti and was keen to write about that experience. Ann's story was remarkable, though—as I've come to realize more and more—of a sort not unusual in Canada with its historical connection to the British Empire. Ann's grandfather, Dr. Edward Temple Harris—known as "Temple" to his family—was in the Indian Medical Service (IMS) in Bangalore when war was declared; soon after, he was recruited as a captain into the Indian Field Ambulance and accompanied the Expeditionary Force B to East Africa. He landed at Tanga with Aitken's doomed party. Dr. Harris wrote seventeen letters to his brother Tatham, which were hand-carried to India by IMS contacts and therefore not censored; they are chatty and candid, and sympathetic to the common soldier, and he describes his own fear in the face of fierce German machine-gun fire. After the Battle for Tanga, Temple was sent to Nairobi to recuperate from an attack of dysentery before being sent to Mombasa and then Voi. Here, like the other doctor, the novelist Francis Brett Young, he was a member of the medical corps of Smuts's army as it pushed into German East Africa. Following Edward Harris's letters, which came into her possession, and using her own research, Ann had written a book, titled *Seventeen Letters to Tatham*, describing vividly both the Battle for Tanga and the invasion at Taveta under Smuts. Her mission had taken her off to Tanga, a place she would never before have contemplated visiting. Here was someone whose chief interest had been her Cornish heritage now speaking as an expert about the landings at Ras Kasone, the fates of the various British regiments, and the layout of the Voi–Taveta plain. She had a photo of herself taken with an old German askari in Tanga.

I saw Tanga as a quaint town with remnants of the old architecture, but essentially in a state of decay. A typical house in the Asian section of the town had arched verandas on the ground floor, and second-floor balconies enclosed by latticed wooden barriers or wire mesh. Robbery was evidently a problem. The old European houses were more solid. The roofs were corrugated iron or tile. No longer was it the neat colonial town; the railway didn't run, the streets were potholed, the sisal market had been destroyed first by the arrival of synthetic fibres and then by the nationalizations of the estates during the two decades of socialism. But it seemed the Germans still loved Tanga. There was a German program in place to preserve buildings from their colonial days.

The Asian population in Tanga had declined considerably. Half the Khoja khano, a large two-storey white building within a

fenced compound, was in disuse for lack of people and partitioned off. It was a bleak sight. The khano and the Khoja development consisting of modern bungalows—portending the great optimism and cheer of the 1960s—were in the neighbourhood called Ngamiani—"where the camels are." Perhaps there was a camel station here a long time ago. But for the Asians who remained, business seemed to be fine. Samji's wife spent a good two hours every evening counting out the day's take. (To be fair, the counting took long partly because the currency had inflated so much.) They had four children outside the country. One of their friends, Ramji, had all his five children overseas. Both men were satisfied with their lives; they had cars, servants, remained busy. It was the wives who insisted on leaving. I couldn't help thinking of men of their age who had immigrated to Canada only to become useless and lonely, waiting to grow old and eventually die in a nursing home. For the women, emigration often was a matter of prestige and status. The Nanjis have gone, so should we the Ramjis; we are not nobodys. I held my peace.

The next evening Samji and his son put me on the bus to Dar.

The name of the bus, painted with a flourish on one side, was Scud. (The first Gulf War was a recent memory.) It was also decorated with pictures of Indian actors and the action-movie character Rambo. It left the station at 8:30 p.m. and at around midnight broke down. Groggy from sleep we got off one by one and came to stand around the right front tire, where the driver and conductor were inspecting a leak—oil or water, it wasn't clear. The mood was light, as though this were the order of the day, with joking, cussing, laughing. A bright moon lit up the pavement and the landscape. After some two hours, the driver gave up tinkering and caught a ride back to Tanga to fetch another bus. A young Bohra man borrowed a thousand shillings from me, frantic to get to Dar on time for something; when an overcrowded bus stopped, he got in and left. I never saw him again. The rest of us slept in a row at the side of the road, in front of the bus, using our bags as pillows.

In the morning it was surprisingly, intensely cold. It was after five, and I saw that we had stopped near a village and a roadworks; women were going off in a line to fetch water, barefoot and wearing khangas round the waist. A roadside stall had sprung up and we had sweet black tea and mandazi. The talk was fast and free and the government was openly criticized, with that casual sense of coastal humour. The freedom of the people was refreshing after the sombre, repressive mood that I had witnessed in Kenya. Someone mentioned that there could have been lions prowling about in the night. Yes, and they always dragged off a person sleeping somewhere in the middle of a row, not the end. A nervous tingle crawled down my spine. I thought I had been clever when I placed myself third or fourth from one end. I could imagine those man-eaters of Tsavo who had so terrorized the railway Punjabis, dragging them off even from their tents. On the Dar–Arusha route, the men around me said, a driver had abandoned a woman with two kids on the highway for not having tickets; one kid and the mother were eaten by a lion and the driver was in jail.

The relief bus arrived at seven, much to everyone's surprise.

A man complained, "Would the mzungus (white men) have made tools if you didn't need them?" Apparently our previous bus had lacked the appropriate tools. But the statement said much about the speaker's faith in the abilities of his own people.

Postscript

Twenty years later Tanga still looks as laid-back, as neglected, as forgotten.

I sit with a taxi driver called Taju on the large veranda of a seedy old hotel called the Sea View, waiting for the rain to let up; it's falling in sheets. The only other person around is the young Arab manager and a European guest consuming instant coffee. Inside the hotel, the paint is peeling, the furniture is shabby, the lighting is gloomy; a staircase goes up to the rooms, which have balconies. This is all that remains of the Kaiserhof. I ask the manager if there are any mementos in the hotel from olden times. He says no. And then, an afterthought: he points to a cello hanging high on the wall above reception. Perhaps in the past they heard Bach here on Saturday afternoons.

Across the road is a well-tended garden overlooking the sea; at one end of it is a modest clock tower marked with the year *1901*, only a few years after the Germans first arrived and took over the town. There appears to have been a coat of arms on it that has been removed. At the other end of the garden is the impressive-looking King George VI Memorial Library built in the 1950s, a long single-storey building with arched verandas, still in good shape. It was a gift to the town from the philanthropic Karimjee family. Here, on my previous visit, I had met a friendly librarian, who proudly showed me a small cabinet with a glass door containing rare editions of Stanley, Burton, and the like. Aware of their value, a predecessor had locked them up. I wonder now if the cabinet still stands there or has been "moved," as used to be said of theft, but that's impossble to ascertain on this Union Day holiday when everything is closed. The avenue and the streets behind contain a generous though rickety display of the old architecture—wooden buildings with latticed verandas and balconies, sloping roofs—of the kind that have been crushed and erased from the landscape of Dar. The wreckers won't be long getting here, though: a container harbour is planned and the Usambara Railway will be rebuilt, bringing new development. Soon will come the concrete high-rises—turning the town into what? A mock Boston to Dar's mock New York?

Taju's car is an ancient Toyota, to which the man himself, unshaved and unkempt, is a fitting match. My window doesn't close and rain pours liberally onto my lap. Pull the window up with your hands, he advises. I try, with partial success. We speak in Gujarati and there's a casualness to our relationship, a kind of familiarity. He says his father was from Punjab but died when Taju was three; he also says he was brought up by his grandmother who was from Tanga. I conclude that he is not sure, or is embarrassed by his origins, but since he affirms to being a Sunni Muslim he must be partly Bhadala or Baluchi. He has a heart condition and has recently had a consultation in Dar, but cannot afford to go to India for treatment. We pass Hindu and Sikh temples, stop at a chai shop. It is actually the front room of a house, with an ordinary door for entrance; inside, a man in his forties serves from behind an iron cage of the sort one might find housing a bank's vault. Chai is excellent but costs two and a half times what KT Shop charges in Dar. The man in the cage is chatty. He affirms that there have been robberies in the area. He's from Moshi originally; his mother died recently after a leg amputation from diabetic complications. She used to walk barefoot and one day punctured a foot. The chevda and the burfis look fresh and mouth-watering. The bhajias come straight from the pan in the backroom, where someone, presumably the wife, is cooking.

The European cemetery is in a densely overgrown area where the ground is so muddy and slippery it reminds me of going home from school in Dar. The old German graves, green with mould, occupy a dank corner. At another location, close by, the British war dead are commemorated with a rather comically small pyramid in the middle of a neat compound covered with loose gravel; it's fenced and gated. There is a wall of names inside, but they are too far from the fence to be read.

A walk away is the old Karimjee Secondary School, named after the well-known family that endowed it. It was renamed the Usagara Secondary School and looks as decrepit as any of the old endowed schools in the country that were taken over by the government.

In Dar, before leaving for Tanga, I met a former student of this once-famous school, a man of Asian origin called Colonel Kashmiri. He had volunteered into the King's African Rifles while still at school, trained at Sandhurst, England, then joined the Tanganyika Rifles. When the army mutinied on January 20, 1964, a sorry day in the history of the newly independent country, he was dispatched "to Bombay" by the rebels but actually went to England with a contingent of British officers. When the mutiny was quashed—in a day—he was called back and given the charge to place the leaders of the mutiny under arrest. He is not a large man but looks trim and fit; he says he plays squash three times a week. In the army he quickly saw the glass ceiling for an Asian—a man junior to him was made brigadier and went on to become rather glamorous. He wished to quit but agreed eventually to be transferred to head a state-owned enterprise after a lengthy entreaty from President Nyerere. It would not look good for the only Asian officer in the army to resign. And so the soldier became a businessman . . . or was he pushed to conform to the stereotype? Now he is a consultant, and a current project concerns inviting tenders for the construction of several harbours in the country, including Tanga. A project worth hundreds of millions of dollars. It is through one of his Tanga contacts that I have hired the services of Taju and his dubious Toyota.

It turns out that my hotel is on the northern coast of Ras Kasone, the peninsula on which the ill-fated Indian Expeditionary

Force landed in November 1914. Five troopships faced the coast on this side and landed their Indian men where I now sit watching the sunset. The map designates it as "Beach C," but there's no beach in sight. What a commotion then, how calm and peaceful now, how lovely the view. In the distance lies Toten Island, inhabited in the distant past, now barren. The yacht club is visible a few hundred yards away, a number of small boats bobbing on the water. The entire peninsula is lush and green, but there is no sisal anymore. A single road leads in from the town. On the way comes the Bombo Regional Hospital, the old stone building still standing and quite impressive; it was here that the armistice to end the Battle for Tanga was signed. It's fallen into disuse, and a new structure stands before it.

The next day Taju drives me around the coast to the tip of the peninsula, where the wealthy have their large houses and from where you look upon an infinite expanse of ocean.

6.

India and Africa: Of Entrepreneurs Old and New

ONCE WHILE TRAVELLING BY ROAD in western Gujarat, exploring my ancestral provenance, my companion and I stopped at a place called Droll. It was a typical Indian village of unpaved streets and make-do shops and homes. It could have been in Africa; there was, however, near the road a tall ancient gate bearing ornatery that suggested some history; it turned out that it was here that a Mughal governor on the run had stopped and killed himself in the fifteenth century. As we entered the village we asked around if there were Khojas living there, and were directed to a roadside paan-seller, who in a friendly gesture picked up two bright-green betel leaves, placed pinchfuls of various masala upon them, folded them into loose triangles, and handed us the finished paans. Only when we had the paans stuffed into our mouths did he give us the information we sought. The Khoja assistant headman, the kamadia, had his shop just across the road. He pointed it out.

We proceeded there, where a man sat on the floor at the doorway; after a brief chat, the mukhi, the headman himself, came by cheerfully and took us to his home. There, after tea in a cluttered yard that was the site of a cottage industry, he said he wanted us to meet someone special. Intrigued, we followed him to a rather dark room where we saw an intensely wrinkled and shrivelled old woman lying in her bed. She was "a hundred" years old. (The number, I discovered, was canonical in this part of India for very old people of indeterminate age.) Mongi Bai had been married to a trader from Dar es Salaam "during the war," and returned home when he died. Prompted by her family, in her feeble voice as thin as the rustle of a dry leaf, Mongi Bai spoke the Swahili greeting "Jambo" to me, and I replied appropriately. It was a trivial occurrence in its way, in a small dark room at a sickbed, yet for me a thrilling moment of connection.

The commercial nexus between the western coast of India and the eastern coast of Africa, part of the so-called Indian Ocean trade, is many centuries old. Portuguese sailors bound for India in the sixteenth century reported the presence of Indians and Indian ships in Kilwa, Mombasa, and Malindi. The ships hailed from the great port of Cambay (present-day Khambat in Gujarat) and took away gold, ivory, and wax in exchange for cotton, silk, and other products. Writes the Portuguese captain Duarte Barbosa, in his description of the East African and Malabar coasts circa 1500, "These ships of Cambay are so many and so large, and with so much merchandise, that it is terrible to think of so great an expenditure of cotton stuffs as they bring." The thirteenth-century sun temple at Konark in eastern India has among its wall carvings (many of them erotic) one of a giraffe that the guides delight in pointing out: intriguing indication of the connection between India and East Africa.

It was in the middle of the nineteenth century, when Sultan Seyyid Said of Oman moved the capital of his Indian Ocean dominion to Zanzibar, that Indian traders began arriving at the island and the mainland coast in larger numbers. By the middle of that century these Indians—who were from western Gujarat, specifically from the regions of Kutch and Kathiawad—had settled as traders in Zanzibar and ports along the coast from Lamu in the north to Kilwa and Lindi in the south. Most came as penniless young men from their drought-prone villages and remained modest, but a few grew in wealth and status to become merchant princes wielding spectacular influence, as chronicled by western visitors to the island. These men were, successively, Jairam Sewji, Ladha Damji, and Tharia Topan, all from the Bhatia caste of Kutch, to whose firms the sultans farmed out their customs collection and were often in debt.

The Gujaratis who travelled and settled abroad, then, were traders; they preceded the white man in East Africa and were instrumental in the western exploration of the region. In Zanzibar, British, European, and American travellers would stop at the larger Indian businesses for their supplies before heading off on expeditions to the mainland interior, and—nobody likes a creditor—sometimes wrote about them in the most unflattering, Shylockian terms. Richard Burton, however, having spent time in India before arriving in Zanzibar, had a softer spot for them and treated them as familiars. Here is how he describes meeting one of the more prominent Kutchis of Zanzibar at the start of his East African Expedition in 1857:

> We then took refuge against the sun at the shed called Place of Customs, where we were duly welcomed, whilst cloves were being weighed by the slaves. The Collector of government dues was a nephew of Ladha Damha [Damji] . . . the head of some ten Bhattias: they are readily distinguished by red conical fools' caps, and by their Indian Dhotis, or loin-cloths. . . . We determined him to be an exceptional man, but afterwards, on the coast, we received the same civilities

> from all Hindu and almost all the Hindi (Moslem) merchants . . . Pisu . . . seated us on cots, and served upon a wooden tray sliced mango and pineapple, rice, ghee. . . .

With the advent of British and German colonialism towards the end of the nineteenth century, Zanzibar's commercial power waned and businesses began to flourish on the mainland. Sewa Haji Paroo, also a Kutchi, dispatched his caravans from Bagamoyo and they went all the way to Taveta near Kilimanjaro. His apprentice, Alidina Visram, topped him to become "the uncrowned king of Mombasa," supplying the dukas (shops) that were springing up on the routes from Mombasa to Uganda, eastern Congo, and southern Sudan. In 1890, A.M. Jeevanjee, a Bohra from Karachi, arrived in Mombasa and, an astute and driven businessman of a new generation, soon made his presence felt. He began his fortune by supplying goods (and even workers) to the Uganda Railway, which had begun construction. Much of early Nairobi, a railway town of wood and iron, was built by his firm.

These great merchants remain largely unknown even in East Africa. They collaborated with the colonial governments because they needed them; they were also philanthropists and ardent supporters of their own communities. Tharia Topan and Sewa Haji donated hospitals in Zanzibar and Dar es Salaam; Alidina Visram founded a school in Mombasa, and has a statue there. A.M. Jeevanjee founded the *Standard,* forerunner of the *East African Standard,* still in existence, and he donated the Jeevanjee Gardens in downtown Nairobi.

By the early twentieth century, Indians could be seen everywhere in East Africa, in every town, large and small, where their distinctive business strips are still in evidence—often a short row of brick buildings, each with a wide storefront and a residence above.

In the even smaller village settlements outside the towns, often a single Indian family might subsist by providing essential supplies locally. But these "Jews" of Africa, as they were sometimes called, were rarely appreciated. To the poor Africans they were the ones raking in the cash. To the white colonials they were often an irksome, alien presence, the bone in the kabab—to use an Indian metaphor—spoiling their pure black-and-white picture of Africa—the whites the superior race out to convert and civilize the blacks; and later the benefactors bringing aid, the blacks the beneficiaries. In their writings and nostalgic musings about East Africa, the white settlers seem to have simply wished the brown man away. The "White mischief" television romances set in Kenya, for example, rarely figured the Asians.

One Sunday afternoon I read to an audience at Nairobi's museum, during the opening there of the Asian Heritage Exhibit, a remarkably detailed memorial to the history of the Asian presence in East Africa. When I finished, a man in his fifties came over to me in tears. Who tells our stories, he said, who tells about what we have been through? This exhibit was an attempt to do just that. But there was a telling irony to it in the fact that more than half of the Asians had already gone away by the time it opened, taking their untold stories with them.

It seems incredible today to imagine Africa as the land of milk and honey that it was for Indians. Some of our grandfathers would return to Gujarat to visit, often to marry wives, and often they came bearing "attitude," sporting western clothes (even hats) and looking conspicuously wealthy to the communities they had left behind. A small number of the returnees must have come to stay, however. The 1899 census of India reported some 100 Swahili-speakers. A Gujarali-Swahili dictionary was published in 1890.

During my visit to Droll in Gujarat, there was a woman present at the mukhi's house who was all set to go to a wedding in a related village. The groom, I was informed with a twinkle in the mukhi's eye, was a recent immigrant to Africa who had returned to marry. But he had gone to Angola. New frontiers had opened up in Africa, obviously, after the ravages of the long wars, and boys were setting off there to open shops and bring supplies, the way previous generations had done. Farther into Gujarat, when I visited a community office in the city of Junagadh to inquire about the village from which my great-grandfather had set off, I was told—over a cup of tea, naturally—stories of boys in recent times going away to Africa, and returning home arrogantly flaunting their new wealth. In other words, bearing "attitude." History repeating itself, and evidently the new prosperity of India had not reached these villages. But there was another side to these stories of glorious return. In Jamnagar, where my mother's family came from, I once sat in the shack of a poor family who were marrying off their sixteen-year-old daughter to a middle-aged man from Africa.

During my childhood one heard of exotic places upcountry where our people had settled—Mbarara, Mengo, Masaka, Nyeri, Isiolo, Voi, Nakuru, Mpwapwa, Singida, Mbeya, Lindi, Musoma, Sumbawanga, Moyale, and so on, dotted across the vast reaches of British East Africa—from the border with Mozambique to that with Rwanda, from the Indian Ocean to lakes Tanganyika and Victoria, between Zambia and Somalia, often with only one or two families to a village, doing the same old business—buying produce, selling essential supplies. These were names to stir the imagination, places one might visit one day. My cousins who stayed with us in Uhuru Street would set off during holidays for a village called Bariadi near Lake Victoria to visit their parents, and their stories of exciting train rides and dog-swallowing pythons and mysterious grandmothers made us goggle-eyed and envious. Kids from those interior regions—"bhurr" was the term for those places—would come to Dar for their high school education, and were treated as hicks; there was a naïveté to them, and yet, because they had stayed away from the watchful eyes of the larger, more fastidious religious community, they also seemed less inhibited. They would always carry the mark of their town; it identifies them often to this day—"Mehboob of Ifakara"—and some never completely blended into the rowdy familiarity that was Dar es Salaam.

Following the nationalizations of private properties in Tanzania in the 1970s heyday of socialism, and the expulsion of Asians from Uganda by Idi Amin soon after, and the Africanization policies in Kenya that we would now call racist, and the forced marriages of Asian girls in Zanzibar, the Asian population—frightened and uncertain—depleted, was welcomed to the cities of Canada. As a result there exist now entire ghost streets, shorn of their Asian populations, shops and homes not effectively occupied, in places like Tukuyu, Kilwa, Lindi, Kigoma. Coincidentally, in the village of my great-grandfather too, in Gujarat, following the widespread violence of 2002 the Khoja neighbourhood had been depleted, the prayer house padlocked. Thus the fate of minorities.

But in some, the indomitable mercantile spirit lives on; home is where the trade winds take you. The descendants of the merchants and pilots whom Vasco da Gama and Camõens and Duarte Barbosa met on the coast along the Indian Ocean will go to any corner of the world to do business, and still find East Africa a profitable place.

Property values are down, my friend Karim says, when we meet in Toronto for coffee. But don't believe what they tell you. He means media reports, I presume, soon after the 2008 recession. There is that perpetual smile on his soft, fair, baby face that makes you wonder sometimes if he's not pulling your leg with his fantastic tales about making money. The phone in his hand, at this patio outside a Toronto Starbucks, is of the cheapest sort—consistent with the manner of the typical Gujarati vania, the business caste: wealth is not for show, but to make. He's made and lost some millions in hotels and property in Canada, the United States, the Bahamas, and London. He's currently developing a resort in Zanzibar. And he's based in Dubai, where he and his partners have written off some twenty condominiums after the real-estate bubble there burst. Time was, he says, when you paid someone to stand in a queue to book a condo for you, and you turned a profit the next day. But now he's in neutral gear.

Karim and I went to school together, his family running a produce shop opposite the Dar es Salaam market, next to the post office. Ever since we finished school and went overseas to university, we've run into each other by sheer accident in the oddest circumstances, but rarely in Toronto. (This current meeting is an exception, and by arrangement.) The first time was in London, where I was stranded once, a student on my way to or from the United States. It was the 1970s. Soon after finishing his chemical engineering degree, Karim, having grown up amidst the fish smells of the teeming market near his father's Kariakoo shop, had the audacity to purchase a small supermarket in London. We had met at the Ismaili guest house on Gloucester Road where a bed could be had for five pounds and there was every likelihood of running into someone from back home, on a tourist visa but searching desperately for an accounting articleship, a secretary's job, or a place in a college. London, after all, had been the centre of our colonial universe, a magnet at a distance; it would take time to wean ourselves away from it. Come and visit me tomorrow, Karim said. I did so, taking the tube next day into Harrow and walking into a typical small English supermarket. That night he and another classmate, who had been a close buddy of his in Dar, took me to the Playboy Club. I was in a somewhat stunned state in that dark and glitzy hall, smiling white bunnies with bouncy breasts and long bare legs hovering around; none of us drank; all three of us were from simple families of the pious variety, and this was definitely not Karim's beginning on a path of debauchery—he still is the pious, prayerful sort. We soon escaped from the scene. Why had they brought me there? It's too late to ask, but I would guess it was to demonstrate their success in the world.

It seems to me that after he left Dar he's never had a home—a single, permanent dwelling. He's lived in many places, he's lived in two places at the same time. The last few times I've simply run into him in the streets of Dar. One morning while making my way from my guest house, the depressingly essential and affordable Flamingo, to Uhuru Street and Msimbazi, where Walter Bgoya had his publishing offices, a 4 × 4 stopped ahead of me and gave two sharp hoots. A voice called out my name from the window. You here? It was Karim. Get in, he commanded with a grin. I obeyed and he drove me first to an outlet on Samora Avenue where he took two bundles that could have contained sugar or rice or even books, but they contained instead Tanzanian currency, which had become so devalued it had to be carried in packages and baskets and changed into dollars as quickly as possible. Without asking me, he next whisked me off to KT Shop, where we had vitumbua, kababs, and sweet chai.

What was he doing here in Dar? Didn't he have property abroad? I've moved here, temporarily, he said. Business is good. In

Dar he owned oil mills and imported canned condensed milk; he had a partnership in a broadcasting company and a garbage collecting company; he brought in soap from Indonesia, packaging the same variety as detergent and body wash. He had had his life threatened by a competitor. Come, he said, and he drove me to the location of a new venture. To my utter amazement, it was on Uhuru Street right across from where my mother had had her shop. As I jumped out of the car, visions from the past assailed me; I gazed up fondly at Mehboob Mansion where I grew up; at Bhanji Daya Building, Salim Mansion. All two-storey buildings. The shop Karim took me to was in an old-style dwelling even in those days—a house with metal roof, a shop front, and living quarters at the back—where Baby Ndogo, famous as the fattest woman in town, had lived with her family. Karim's business was run by a local relative. It sold "mitumba," used clothing imported mainly from Canada. A large variety of fashions and sizes hung on racks, and bales marked "Babies," "Men Shoes," "Ladies Jeans," etcetera stood waiting to be slit open. The long rows of shops and the numerous tailors that had supplied the clothing needs of the city for a good three-quarters of a century had been run out of business by this incoming tide of stylish, ready-mades of the sort that once upon a time only the rich could afford. Now the lowliest menial could wear denim, sport Reeboks. Do you see anyone in rags now? Karim asked me with a grin, and answered after a pause, No. These are good clothes, better than what you and I wear. But we don't wear them, I said to myself.

Having shown me this latest enterprise, Karim drove me into an unpaved alley nearby, where at the back of a traditional and very modest African house, sitting on low wooden benches we ate bhajias made of ground pulse, a variety rare outside coastal East Africa, eaten with coconut chutney. He knew I would like them—who wouldn't, if only for old times' sake? In our schooldays, a young man used to go around on a bicycle selling bhajias like these; my mother would buy them while I was in school and save them for me.

Many years later, here at the Starbucks patio in Toronto, he asks rhetorically, would we let our twelve-year-olds go anywhere far? We wouldn't. When his father was twelve, his grandfather in India put the boy on a dhow and sent him off to Zanzibar, from where he went to Dar and opened a shop. The old man himself followed with another son and the three of them set up trading posts in three different coastal towns, importing cashews to Dar, exporting grain, copra, and oil. When Karim would return from school, his father would get him to sit in the shop and help. Never mind homework, first things first. And so in London when he went to the bank manager to ask for a loan to purchase the supermarket in Harrow, and the bank manager asked him why during a recession should he give him, a young nobody from the colonies, a loan, Karim replied: My father is a businessman; my brother runs a business in Congo; and I always helped out my father in his shop since I was yay high. I know business, it's in my blood. He got the loan. Soon afterwards he invested in his first piece of real estate, in Calgary.

I am convinced that it is not greed that drives him and his like; he's made and lost money, and made it again; real estate in Calgary crashed, but by that time he had property in New Mexico and London. He moved on, and kept moving. People like him don't really lose money. Business drives him as chess does a grandmaster. It's his passion. He thinks it, he talks of nothing else but. Opportunities lost, opportunities to gain; moves made; stories of success and tales of failure. He looks around and his mind calculates: rent, costs, profit.

Africa, he says, is full of opportunity. Believe me. There are millions to be made . . . though we are not young anymore.

Wary of my occupation and curiosity, still he cannot control himself. He looks at me earnestly, and his soft fair features light up with that smile which gives him the look of a simpleton. We've run into each other again in Dar, and we're sitting in the evening outside the old Odeon Cinema on the sidewalk, which every evening is cleared of vendors and cleaned up to convert it into an open-air restaurant; tables have been set up under tube lights and barbecued chicken comes off the fire and is served with soggy chips, the way they like them here. A few other tables are occupied. The atmosphere is hushed, and at this time it's mostly men who are about. On all sides of us, the normally noisy streets head off silently into residential darkness. And Karim talks.

He talks of the gold region of Tanzania, where a few years ago people might pick up gold pieces off the ground; if he were younger he would go south and clear acres of land, bought dirt cheap, and grow cashew. He runs off a quick budget for a cashew farm managed along western lines, efficiently. Millions to be made. He's currently surveying property in Zanzibar. His mitumba business has moved to Zambia—a country, he says, whose business potential was never realized by "us." Corruption is not as bad as reported. Don't believe what they say. But then he tells a hair-raising yarn about a road trip from Zambia to the Congo in the midst of the civil war. For me the very idea of the Congo is a nightmare; for him, sitting here like Conrad's Marlow turned into a businessman, that heart of darkness is just one more wrinkle in a life of commerce. There's no mineral the Congo doesn't possess, there's immense wealth in that country. And Kenya? Don't believe what they say, corruption's not so bad there either . . .

I gape. My life's taken an orthogonal turn to his, though I like to think that with my Gujarati heritage I understand business. I cannot but admire the sheer courage of men such as him, their spirit of adventure. Nothing fazes them, there's no trouble they cannot, Houdini-like, walk out of. This, my classmate, who would sometimes give me a ride home on his scooter. He did not come from the more pretentious segment of our small society, whose children came every summer from London and put on airs with their Beatle haircuts and fashionably bare feet, the girls wearing miniskirts; his were the old Gujarati bania type, who had more money but never flaunted it, living across from the market, quietly going about their business.

There are others like him. One of them, a former classmate and now a retired multimillionaire, would—I am told—take a drive through the streets of Kinshasa at night and throw bundles of currency at the despot Mobutu's soldiers posted at the street corners: insurance for times of trouble. There's the returnee from Toronto (a failure there) who manages a transport business in Dar. When I met him, he was on his way to Dubai to buy one hundred trucks. The rumour mill has it that the trucks are used for the stealthy transport of precious rare earths from Congo to a special location in Dar es Salaam harbour, and thence to America.

It seems to me that my friend Karim has seen so much and it's all unchronicled; he needs someone to tell his stories. He trusts and likes me, based on—I suppose—the ancient Indian respect for the harmless book person. I would like to raise a moral issue. Is it right to line the pockets of corrupt politicians and army men who feed on their own people? But the baby face dissuades me. It's I who am the child; these people take risks, after all, they move the goods and open up markets, they see the world. It takes more than one hand to drive corruption. What risks do I take, who simply watch and listen?

Recently, returning to Toronto from abroad I was with some impatience pushing my baggage cart in the customs queue when another cart nudged mine to vie for the space just ahead. I looked up to my side. Whom should I see but Karim, and we greeted each other warmly. He had flown in from Dubai. Are we always destined to meet like this?

7.

Kilwa, the Old City

THEY TELL US IN DAR that Kilwa—down the coast—is only four hours away, perhaps a little more, the road is all tarmac except for a small stretch; it's definitely the place to go, with unspoilt beaches and new resorts, and there is of course the ancient city on Kilwa Island; the French have an interest there; and so on. Even in my youth, flights of fancy would do in the absence of certain knowledge: it's what people want to believe. For people in Dar, Kilwa is a flight of fancy.

It takes us eleven hours to get there. The small patch of unpaved road so casually mentioned by the enthusiasts is actually sixty kilometres long and takes us roughly six hours to cover, a wet muddy stretch with craters large and small, and sometimes we're driving through three feet of water as though in some gruelling safari motor rally of times past. We stop at a truck station called Muhoro, where the only repast to be had is sweet black tea—"chai rangi"—from a tall thermos, over a table covered with a spread of torpid, overfed flies. A curtain of rain before us, through which we can see a wet and muddy square outside, with a few parked trucks. We finish our tea and depart.

The road, despite its ominous state, looks doable, until—one's worst fear—it comes abruptly to a stop in front of a deep ditch where a bridge has been washed away. A thin rain falls constantly, the day is still bright, the tree foliage glistens a variety of greens. The ground is red and drenched. A jolly crowd has gathered to watch a long queue of mud-splattered SUVs and trucks get their just desserts: revving their engines, bracing themselves when their turn comes, they confidently speed down the road to defeat the ditch—and almost inevitably get stuck in the swirling water. The onlookers, belying the proverbial kindness of the countryside, won't lift a finger to help. A tractor from a road-construction camp does service pulling out the stuck vehicles one by one, and sheepishly these safari-equipped SUVs crawl out and drive away. It's a slow process, taxing one's sense of humour. It's well past noon and muggy, and some of the vehicles will definitely spend the night here.

Our turn comes. Our elderly driver, Mzee Othman Bonde, the soul of respectability in his kofia and clean, pressed clothes, whom we have berated thus far as a timid slowcoach, has meanwhile silently taken the measure of the crossing, and picking a spot to enter he just manages to drive through the waterway on his own. There is applause. And Mzee Othman Bonde rises immensely in our esteem.

"You must have said a dua there," we say in admiration. A prayer. "I flogged out seven of the best," he replies with a grim smile, oblivious of the implied humour.

Behind us in the muddy ditch a truck full of cows is balanced precariously at an angle of forty-five degrees. It's too late to pause and watch their fate, and we race, or rather bump, along and away. There are light forests to either side; scattered mud villages that perhaps have not changed much in a hundred years. Periodically we see a figure, a woman or a child, standing still on the roadside, a bag of charcoal for sale.

It is about nine in the evening when we arrive at the intersection by a mango tree where an exit heads off towards Kilwa Kivinje. There is no other traffic on the main road, which continues on along the coast towards Lindi; the exit road is unpaved but dry, the headlights illuminating a forest. We arrive finally at what looks like a town, but it's covered in darkness, a few glows of light here and there. This must be Kilwa. When we ask some young men sitting about for a hotel in town, we are greeted with a silence and murmurs. We have posed a conundrum. The night is thick and salty in this backwater; and the thought occurs, what right do we have to create a ripple in this stillness, intruding upon this closed intimacy of a town? The website for the hotel we have in mind said clearly, "Kilwa Kivinje"; but there is no hotel here, there could not be one. We should go to Kilwa Masoko, up the main road, the young men tell us. We head back to the highway.

Some ten miles farther we enter another side road which takes us to Kilwa Masoko, "of the markets." There's a little more light and life here. Two modest beach hotels are made known to us, on a dirt road leading away from the main road, and we pick one due to its more imposing gate.

In Milton's epic poem, *Paradise Lost* (1674), when the angel Michael takes Adam to the Hill of Paradise to view the Hemisphere of Earth, which would henceforth be Adam and Eve's to inhabit after their Fall, curiously the angel points out more of the East African coast—"Mombaza, and Quiloa, and Melind, / And Sofala . . ."– than he does of India (only Lahore and Agra).

The name Kilwa (Quiloa), then, carries a certain mystique, for its connection to hoary times. When you've been brought up to skim over the contemporary surface of modern life, when history and the past were relegated to an unwritten irrelevant appendix of your existence to stay hidden or possibly receive a nod later, there is a certain thrill to discovering the verity and extent of these ancient connections; to *touching* them.

Seen from the vantage point of the nation's capital, Kilwa is this coastal region down south with a vague but distinguished history. But there are actually three towns called Kilwa, one sprung from the other. The oldest of these, known to the world in Milton's time and much before, capital of an ancient mercantile empire, is Kilwa Kisiwani, "on the Island"; after its somewhat mysterious demise arose Kilwa Kivinje, across the channel on the mainland, an entrepot of the nineteenth and early twentieth centuries; it was displaced in importance by a very typical colonial move, when the nondescript Kilwa Masoko, the market town, was founded and made the administrative centre at a place down the coast with its deeper harbour.

The hotel we have come to, Island View, is behind some scrubland but looks upon a pristine white beach. It has several cottages scattered about and a large hut-shaped structure that is the dining hall and bar, with a half-wall all around, so that you can look upon the ocean and the beach from inside, while a sea breeze passes through. The rooms are air-conditioned and clean, though dimly lit and filled with insecticide fumes; the bathrooms are modern. "Use the mosquito nets," we are instructed. Except for a couple of motorboats owned by the hotel to take you to Kisiwani to see the ancient ruins, there is nothing on the water. The boats lie unused. The Island itself is visible in the misty distance to the right. The other guests here are the occasional businessman and a hunting-tour operator, staying overnight, and two young Europeans surveying for a gas company with a crew of Filipino youth. The talk among afternoon arrivals is about the broken road into Kilwa.

Masoko consists of a few settlements, shops, and eating joints scattered carelessly about the main road, the only one paved, running the short stretch from the highway to the harbour. On the way comes the small airport, a bus terminal, called "Stendi," which has a couple of "bajaji" or Indian auto-rickshaws (manufactured by the Bajaj Auto company) servicing it, and a regional government centre. The colonial government moved its headquarters here, a few businesses set up to service it, people came to settle—and that's Masoko. The harbour, the raison d'être, now lies desolate.

This market town, because of the hotel, becomes the base for our daily excursions to the more interesting Kilwa Kivinje up the road.

Kilwa Kivinje has history, has structure, and this is immediately apparent as we sight the town once again, this time bathed in daylight; there is dignity—albeit a tired one—that comes from that history.

This town under the sun and by the beach, with its deliberately laid-out grid of streets, invites you to explore and imagine and reflect. It surprises you with discoveries and enigmas, it upsets you by its state of neglect. Much went on in Kilwa Kivinje in the last two hundred years. It grew in importance after the demise of Kilwa Kisiwani, the Island city, and therefore carried the prestige of that name that went back to the twelfth century. In its heyday it was a commercial, political, and religious hub. It was home to poets, Sufis, and slavers, to Indian, Arab, and Swahili merchants, and it was a colonial administrative centre. Standing at the head of the ancient caravan route that went southwest all the way to present-day Malawi (Nyasa), it took to the people of the interior goods such as cotton, metalware, beads, and guns, and received slaves and ivory in exchange. Besides these two commodities it exported gum copal, tobacco, rice, and grain to the markets of Zanzibar and beyond. It resisted German colonialism, for which it paid the price of a hanging site, and as proof of that resistance there are two monuments in the town. Not surprisingly it received many eminent, curious visitors.

On February 2, 1850, an avid German missionary, Johann Krapf, having already since 1837 travelled considerable portions of East Africa in the north, searching for souls to show the Bible to, agonizing over incorrigible Muslims, idolatrous "Banyans," and backward pagans, hired a Swahili sailing vessel in Mombasa to take him south along the coast to explore all the "havens and towns" as far as Cape Delgado in the Portuguese territory. Krapf was born on a humble farm near Tübingen, Germany, and has the distinction to be the first white man to see Mount Kenya and the second to lay eyes on snowy Kilimanjaro. He also went on to compile the first Swahili dictionary.

In the decades to come European governments would make their famous "scramble for Africa," but Christian missionaries envisioning a spiritual wasteland were already descending upon the continent in order to extend here the empire of their God. Says a fervent Krapf in his memoir, "May Heaven soon grant to the friends of missionary-teaching[,] opportunities of spreading the Gospel throughout the benighted region round Lake Niassa [Nyasa], and of establishing one missionary station after another! From that central region the Gospel might soon penetrate further . . ." He was a man with a mission, and the African landscape and the variety of its people seem to have inspired him not even a little.

On February 19, at four in the afternoon, past a spot called Fungu ya Baniani, the "Indian's Sandbank"—where once upon a time a passing dhow left an Indian to cook his own food and he met a mysterious death—Krapf's vessel reached the shallow harbour of Kilwa Kivinje—"the most important town between Zanzibar and Mozambique, with from twelve to fifteen thousand inhabitants." Unfortunately, this former farm boy of the cloth does not describe more. What he would have seen upon approach was a gentle nudge by the ocean into the side of the continent—an indentation marked by the scenic shoreline of a prosperous town, consisting of a row of white houses. On the left was the largest building, the boma, headquarters of the local governor and representative of the Zanzibar sultan. He would have sighted the sultan's bright red flag. The tide was in and the harbour was embraced on either side by a deep green forest of tall mangroves. Behind the town rose the green, majestic and intriguing interior of Africa.

The Indian Ocean coast, from beyond Mombasa in the north to Cape Delgado in the south, a thousand miles of a green fringe, with small Swahili towns and villages serviced by Indian dukas and small dhows, was directly under the rule of the Omani sultans of Zanzibar. A treaty of 1845 between Zanzibar and Great Britain limited the slave trade, but it continued at a brisk pace. Krapf was appalled by it and describes the scene amply as he saw it in and around Kilwa. Caravans set off in March for Lake Nyasa in the interior, he says, and returned with slaves in November; from here the slaves were dispatched in ships to Zanzibar and beyond. During the interim, the dhows would lie idle in Kilwa. The caravan journey itself took some fifteen to twenty days.

The slave trade was lucrative, with 25,000 humans shipped to Zanzibar annually, the government charging two dollars a head in duty. The Scottish missionary David Livingstone was touring the area to the west of the country, his dispatches home concerning the horrors of the slave trade making a large impact on British public opinion. In 1872 Britain sent a Special Mission to Zanzibar, "[bearing] a letter, as well as many valuable presents, from Her Majesty to His Highness" to negotiate a stronger ban on slavery. There was much resistance, but a treaty proscribing sea transport of slaves was agreed upon on June 8, 1873, and all slave markets were closed by decree. Even after this ban, it was estimated that 15,000 slaves continued to be smuggled annually by sea—at least for a period—into the nearby island of Pemba to service its new and fast-growing clove farms. Moreover, slave transportation by land continued. The sultan's authority on the mainland went only so far and was openly defied by the traders.

On December 11, 1873, a handsome, bewhiskered and somewhat dreamy-eyed young British official and member of the Special Commission, Captain James Frederic Elton, departed Zanzibar by dhow for the mainland coast to enforce the slave ban on Her Majesty's Indian subjects. He wrote,

> I have received orders to proceed to Kilwa to carry out the policy with regard to Indians holding slaves . . . and Lieutenant Pullen, RN, of HMS *Shearwater*, has arrived today in a dhow from Pangani, looking rather like a drowned rat, with leave from his Commander, Captain Wharton, to accompany me as a volunteer. I shall pass through the Copal Fields, and cross the Rufiji, I hope, above the Delta.

Elton was born in 1840, when Krapf was already three years into Africa. When the Englishman arrived, Indians—hailing from the areas of peninsular Kathiawad and Kutch, both now in modern Gujarat—had settled in small towns all along the coast, running their little shops, selling retail goods, and buying local produce—mainly gum copal—which was shipped to Zanzibar.

Elton marched from village to village southwards down the coast. The Indians he met belonged to the Gujarati Bhatia and Khoja communities, living separately. He describes a Khoja shop thus: "It is noticeable in the Khoja houses that they are built with an upper loft and rough ladder for the storage of goods." Presumably this storage was a safeguard against native thieves. Of a Bhatia home he says, ". . . they have built an enclosure and planted a garden round a covered and raised terrace, on which they meet for meals, which, with inner sheds, forms at once a fort and pleasant lounge; and here we slept for the night."

In those early days of settlement the Indians were mostly single men, and their slaves would have been their concubines and house servants. But our forefathers cooperated readily with the Queen's agent and their slaves were duly freed, in some cases opting to stay with the household. Elton describes in pithy detail his meetings head-on with the slave caravans bound north from Kilwa, whose leaders were well armed and often hostile. Elton's brief did not include interfering with these traders. On December 22 he estimates that he must have passed seven hundred slaves. And he notes that the villages he visited were often used as caravan stops:

> the inhabitants do a large stroke of business in buying half-dying children, fattening them up, and reselling them at a profit, so that the place [Kisuju] is full of walking skeletons.

The leaders of the slave caravans and the traders were described as "Arabs"—though even the upper-class Swahili could be described as Arabs. The most prominent slave trader of the period, Tipoo Tip, renowned from Zanzibar to the eastern Congo, who went on to write a memoir, was a Swahili. The slave trade was a multicultural enterprise, involving Arabs (whatever that description meant precisely), Indians (financiers at one end, and keepers of concubines and servants at the other), and Africans of various tribes. As Krapf remarks, "Many a Wahiao [Yao] and Waniassa [Nyasa], returning to Kilwa from his own country, is caught at night in a snare, laid in the way by the Wamueras . . . when the captive has a forked-like piece of wood placed round his neck, and his hands bound, and so the poor wretch is taken to Kiloa."

Elton arrived in Kilwa around December 24 and had a miserable time there. He was sick with fever and from his writing it appears that he had lost his earlier zest for his mission.

> [In Kilwa] bad waters and severe fevers fall to everyone's lot; and the town itself, with its scattered stone houses, winding streets and thickly peopled native huts looks dry and feverish in the hot glare of a January sun; the green hills

> in the distance, and the broad, rippling sea, are the redeeming features of the scene. "Places of Skulls" mark the various roads on which the slave traffic is carried on; skeletons are strewn on the beach.

Perhaps with its terrible history as a slave depot, Kilwa Kivinje's current neglect is poetic justice; but politics and inept government are undoubtedly the actual cause.

James Elton died before he was forty, in 1877 or '78, of sickness while on a march from Lake Nyasa back to the coast.

Just eight years later happened the so-called "scramble for Africa." The area called Tanganyika was annexed by Germany to be administered by the German East Africa Company.

A short, preliminary excursion to Kilwa Kivinje the morning after our arrival. We park at the end of the main road that comes in from the highway, and stroll about. The side streets are unpaved, most houses are mud and wattle. It seems reasonable to ask for the boma, where once upon a time all government business was conducted. It should be the most prominent sight, a focal point. We see it on the promenade facing the shallow harbour, a large building of three floors, all beaten and broken. Gaping holes where the windows used to be. The sight of it takes the breath away. How to interpret this ruin that is history; that is metaphor and reality? We ask for the German cemetery—there must be one—and are directed. At the end of a long crossroad, at the edge of town, past the shops first, then a residential stretch, we arrive at a small shady area giving shelter to a couple of dozen graves. Some are large, most are piles of tumbled grey brick. We manage to read a couple of headstones. "Hier Ruhet Carl Staeck," says one. Born May 31, 1872, in Waren; died May 9, 1897, in Kilwa; age 25. What hopes dashed, for this young man from Waren who set off for distant lands to help found an empire?

Where is the Muslim graveyard? we ask some women we find chatting outside on the porch of a Swahili home. A foolish question, obviously, but we are groping for some hold: how do we go about exploring this town? A group of boys walk us on a long sandy trail through a field of grass and out of town, staying close to the shore. Past a saltworks we arrive at a graveyard with two prominent graves, said to belong to sharriffus, holy men, the headstones unevenly etched in Arabic script. Smaller graves are scattered about on either side of the trail, flat headstones stuck edgewise in the ground, marked and unmarked. As we inspect the graves a couple of men, one on a bicycle, pass silently by without even a curious look at us. The boys are a cheerful, chatty lot, wearing singlets or bare-chested with elastic-waisted shorts, and all are barefoot; one of them sings to himself. The oldest of them answers me that he will go to an Islamic school after primary school. Secondary school, of course, costs money. We find a kiosk and have sodas with the boys; several others come and join us.

It appears that women here no longer wear the buibui, the black, full-length, translucent drape they used to put on over their dresses, but instead cover their heads informally with a loose khanga or, more formally, cover the head and shoulders tightly with a white or coloured chador in the now international style of hijab.

The pounding heat of the January sun that Elton wrote about 140 years ago we can attest to now, for it's the same month. It's the kind of heat that has a wasting effect—the body sags, the clothes cling, the face flushes and drips as you hopelessly breathe in the hot air. It was in such heat, though, that as schoolboys in Dar we walked two or three miles back and forth to school; we are now older, and softer. But we've taken a measure of the town, walked its length and breadth, stood at the harbour, caught glimpses of buried history. We've been observed and raised curious eyes.

Tired and still jet-lagged, my cold acting up, we repair back to Masoko.

In the afternoon I sit on the hotel patio in front of the beach, writing my notes, drink at hand, watching the sea recede. Boats floating, sea shimmering, Kilwa Kisiwani, the Island, looming to my right—a low, hazy hump in the sea. It all looks idyllic, postcard-perfect; the journey in, long and nightmarish, hot and muggy, a thing of the past. We remain wary of the return. Our elderly driver, Mzee Bonde, fits in with the pace here; he was so timid coming in—we remind ourselves—that he would stop for an oncoming vehicle half a mile away. But he was grand at that ditch. We suspect his night vision is bad. His sore throat I blame for my terrible cold. I suffered from it last night and it's not gone away. But the sight of Kilwa Kivinje, its calm sense of itself, of its past, and speaking with the men and women in town, and with the kids, has left a nice feeling of anticipation. This afternoon is just to rest and bide our time. The waitress who served us is young and pretty, called Mwana Hamisi; she is from Lindi and married, with a three-year-old. "Ubwabwa" is cooked rice; I hadn't heard that word in ages. Kilwa Kivinje, said a waiter, had many Asians once. There are Shadiliya and Qadiriyya Sufi centres in all the three Kilwas. There is so much to explore, so little time.

The next morning I am awake at four, and the omens look good. My cold is gone, and the infection I brought with me, due to which I had almost called off the entire trip, is miraculously gone too. The sea laps quietly at the shore, before full tide, and the sunrise when it arrives is breathtaking. Growing up on the coast, I recall, watching it had been a casual, at times a daily, affair at dawn.

After breakfast we drive to Kilwa Kivinje once more.

On the main road going in, just outside the town itself, is the hospital; next to it is the site of the famous hangman's mango tree, called Mwembe Kinyonga, from where the Germans used to hang their rebels. It died only recently and was cut down. We park inside the town, farther up close to the main crossroad, which is also the country bus terminal; conductors wearing vests or shirts with the sleeves cut off, their arm muscles gleaming like polished ebony, hang about cheerfully calling out impending departures to Lindi, Dar, points between. A moderately busy chai shop does service nearby.

Across from the chai shop is a site which must have been a small plaza once but is now a garbage dump and parking space; in the midst of it, partly visible, stands out something strange and white. We cross the road and find it to be a memorial to two German men—Gustav Krieger and Heinrich Hessel of the German East Africa Company—who died in 1888. I surmise they must be the two men who—according to sources—were beheaded by local people resisting the German occupation. They were the first Germans (after Krapf) to set foot in Kilwa. Reports say that they arrived to take over the town on the day of the Eid festival, and they entered a mosque with their boots on. The white cenotaph stands like an alien object fallen from space, neat, geometrical, and upright, its inscription executed precisely on a marble plaque. It is a certainty that no one in this town today would have an inkling of who these men were.

Farther along, where the main road ends, is the three-storey ruin of the boma, and facing it to the left is the shallow harbour. There is no beach, the harbour consists of an inlet between tall mangrove stands, but the oceanfront is a wide space, with shady trees, stone benches—a plaza or promenade of sorts. One easily imagines here, once upon a time, vendors of corn, cassava, oranges, mangoes; children running about; men sitting down for a game of bao or cards in the late afternoon as a brisk wind blows; Indians out for a stroll in the evening, men in ones and twos, the women in groups. Today we see two eyesores of recent vintage: a utilitarian customs shed and a bar.

Behind the plaza run two parallel, wide streets, with an abandoned look to them, also reminders of another era. One—in ghost-town fashion—contains the brooding remains of large stone houses of two and even three floors, with balconies, grilled windows, Arab doors. These broken dwellings are now only partly and haphazardly occupied. The neighbourhood bespeaks a period when Indian life thrived here. The former Khoja khano is a large broad building next to a chowk, or square. It's been abandoned. The mind drifts to conjure up families sitting outside their houses at night, the men playing cards and chatting, the women gathered separately, the children running in and out, playing hide-and-seek and "thuppo!" Life before television or video. I recall people who lived here once, part of the community: a chronically down-and-out uncle; my friend Karim's mother.

Behind the ghostly Indian residential neighbourhood runs the old Indian bazaar. It currently has a pharmacy, an outlet selling Islamic inspirational videos from abroad, a restaurant with a large veranda that's a mockery of its former self. It would have served samosas and kababs and bhajias, there is an elaborate entree menu fading upon a wall; but today there is only mandazi and black chai. Across from us, where we sit on the restaurant veranda surveying the scene, there is the small but well-constructed town market, empty but for three women sitting before meagre heaps of mangoes.

Where are the meats, grains, vegetables? Mango trees proliferate in the area—who would go to the market to buy mangoes?

Both streets head off towards the old German and Muslim cemeteries we visited yesterday. Behind the streets, as well as farther up along them, are the original native quarters of mud and wattle and thatch. We head back to the plaza. Looking out at the harbour, to the left, the water enters into a creek; a paved walkway runs alongside, facing a deep green wall of mangroves across the channel. The telltale smell of rotting garbage accompanies the walker. To the right of the harbour is possibly the fish market, next to a smaller harbour.

In January and February 1959, the English writer Evelyn Waugh, at the age of fifty-five wishing to winter at a place not wasted by tourism or politics (and without a prohibition on alcohol, like parts of India), came to eastern Africa on the *Rhodesia Castle* and landed in Mombasa. He then travelled south, mostly by road, visiting many towns and taking full advantage of his privileged status to receive hospitality (and information) from local British officials. On February 24 he flew from Dar to Kilwa Masoko and the next day was driven to Kilwa Kivinje. His travels were quick and what he saw was fragmentary, but still the observations were often quite apt:

> Drove to Kilwa Kivinje—well laid out, well planted, picturesque, decaying. There are no European inhabitants. . . . In the ramshackle little German hospital Indian doctors rather ironically displayed their meagre equipment. A few youths squatted on their doorsteps playing the endless and unintelligible game [bao] of dropping nuts very swiftly and earnestly on a board hollowed out for them as for marbles in solitaire. No crafts survive in the town except, among the women, very simple grass matting. . . . There are a few Indian grocers and a pleasant little market of fish and vegetables. Meat is almost unprocurable. . . . It was a regrettable and much regretted decision to move the boma [government offices] to Masoko. Anyone having business at headquarters has a walk of nearly forty miles.

Visiting Kilwa Kivinje every morning to look around, we are a curiosity in a town where very little happens. It is assumed that we are looking around to buy property. What else would Asians want here? The plaza, facing the harbour, pulls us like a magnet every time. Once, when the tide is out, we walk on the squelchy wet sand out to the dhows, watch the repairs in progress, listen to the tock-tock-tock of small hammer on wood, as pull-carts arrive carrying sacks of salt to be loaded.

One afternoon we stop on the main road at the site of the

mwembe kinyonga, the hangman's mango tree. I first read about this tree in Dar's daily paper, the *Tanganyika Standard,* as a schoolboy, at about the time of the country's independence. Julius Nyerere, the prime minister designate, the report said, had visited Kilwa and was taken by the town's elders to the site where their fathers were hanged for resisting the Germans. A casual bit of news, but it intrigued me sufficiently that this became a place I wished to see someday. But now as we walk over to this almost mythical site, as significant surely as any war memorial elsewhere, it turns out to be a disappointment that signifies to me many things at once. The dead tree—and the hanged men—are memorialized by a rather forlorn white monument standing at the roadside by itself, close to two huts and a vegetable patch; there is no ornamentation or boundary, any relief to give it stature and draw attention. The inscription is crudely painted by hand in black, its uneven lines ending abruptly with broken words. The information presented is inaccurate. This careless memorial is the contribution of the independent African government; and—one thinks in despair—it was probably constructed with foreign aid, anyway. It is further irony that the century-old memorial down the road to two Germans martyred to colonialism is more impressive, the inscriptions precise.

Behind the adjacent hospital is a cemetery that could have been used to bury the hanged.

German colonialism was resisted all along the coast and in parts of the interior, from 1885 to almost 1910. The leaders of these insurgencies showed courage and resilience and fought to the bitter end; sometimes they used Islam as a rallying cry, and only the Germans' well-equipped and greater numbers, with the aid of sea power, defeated them; when captured, the leaders were hanged from a locally designated tree. One of those hanged in Kilwa, at its famous tree on the site where I stand, was Hassan Omari Makunganya, a chief of the Yao tribe.

One morning when the German forces based in Kilwa were away in the interior to quell Chief Mkwawa's now legendary resistance, Hassan Omari attacked the boma with a large force. He almost took it. But the boma proved a good fortress, the askaris with their superior weapons were adequate, and Makunganya was forced to retreat. He continued a guerrilla war in the area, until von Wissmann, the soldier governor in Dar es Salaam (and Bismarck's personal friend), became utterly exasperated and sent reinforcements to capture the chief. Makunganya fought to the end and was captured but not killed. Von Wissmann himself came to Kilwa to give him a trial, bringing the rope with him to hang Makunganya and three of his companions.

Makunganya was a charismatic figure, and his capture and public hanging from the mango tree by von Wissmann, who himself was already feared and held in much awe in the country, must have been a momentous occasion for Kilwa. It is described in some detail in a Swahili long poem, called "The War Against Hassan bin Omari" by Mwalimu Mbaraka bin Shomari.

There are in fact a number of historical poems describing resistance to the German occupation of mainland Tanzania. Swahili poetry is traditionally a public form. The poems are sung to an audience, always to the same tune, in a low droning intonation. I can recall, while walking in my Kariakoo neighbourhood, hearing poetry recited on the radio somewhere. It is a haunting, unforgettable sound. Even today, Swahili newspapers will devote a column or two to poetry sent in by the public.

Among Makunganya's collaborators there were four Indian

shopkeepers of Kilwa. According to the poet Mzee bin Ali bin Kidigo bin il-Qadiri, who narrates the proceedings of the trial in his "The Poem of Makunganya," upon the Indians' denial of the charges against them, the German officer Hans Zache stormed to their houses and found the incriminating evidence in a book in the house of Kasum Pira. This was presumably a log of the revolution to come, when all the Germans, including Wissmann would be dispatched to Berlin.

By official German accounts the death sentences of the four Indians were commuted to imprisonment and heavy fines. The poet narrates:

Wahindi wakatiwa nyororoni, wakawekwa karakoni
sitima wakangojea, ilipokuja wakapakiwa
wote kujisafiria, wakafika Bender-Essalama
. . .
wakashukwa kama watumwa, kette ilivowangia.
Leo mnajuta nini baa la kujitakia?

The Indians were chained and put into prison
waiting for the steamer. When it arrived they were put into it.
They all travelled, reached Dar es Salaam.
. . .
They were brought out like slaves, chains cutting them.
Today why regret the trouble you yourselves invited?

From Dar es Salaam, the poet says, they were sent to Tanga to work on the railway, but this is disputed by scholars.

The poet was from Zanzibar and his name implies that he may have been from the Qadiriyya Sufi sect. (I have altered the translation a little.) His tone is sycophantic towards the Germans and mocking towards Makunganya. Wissmann "has a pure soul," "is glorious . . . has no fear," "is a good man."

(Such poetry, with "Uncle Tom" attitudes, have been found extremely embarrassing, especially by the intellectuals of the 1960s, who would rather have wished them away. Perhaps there's greater tolerance—and wisdom—now, enough to separate poetry and history from sycophancy, and even to understand the sycophancy. And with so much dependence on Europe today—even the volume from which I quote the poetry comes from Germany—who dares cast a stone with a clear conscience? We should not forget either that Makunganya himself was a businessman and traded in slaves.)

Mwalimu Shomari, another poet who deals with the subject, leaves no doubt about local feelings following the hanging of Makunganya:

nawahubiri wenzangu
hii ezi ya Wazungu
shikeni maneno yangu
wepukane na hatari

babu zetu madiwani
kwanza ni masultani
sasa atajua nani
kwa mato kutubusiri

I tell you, my friends
it's the time of the European
hold on to my words
and avoid trouble

Our grandfathers were diwans
they were sultans
now who knows us
who notices us?

Il-Qadiri's poem was translated and published by Hans Zache (known locally as Bwana Saha); Mwalimu Shomari's poem is from an edition by Carl Velten. Both Germans were present at Makunganya's trial and hanging, as was Mwalimu Shomari, who, according to Velten, helped him translate the letters incriminating the plotters.

There is a Makunganya Street in Dar, next to Indira Gandhi Street. But there is no mention of him on the memorial to the mango tree where he was hanged; it mentions Kinjikitile, the prophet of the great Maji Maji War of 1905–08, as having been hanged there, but according to historical sources, Kinjikitile was captured and executed elsewhere.

We are sitting at the restaurant on the main crossroads one morning, over a breakfast of mandazi and chai. Outside in the glaring sunshine, on the road, as cheerful as ever are the buffed-bodied bus touts. All that coiled-up energy, you feel, bears some menacing potential—perhaps it needs only a spark to set it off? And you wouldn't want to be in the way. Barely visible across the road is the white German monument. Down from it is the opposition party office, looking lively—it's hardly surprising for the opposition to have a following in this long-neglected town. We've noticed that the breakfast of choice here is "supu"—a beef soup with one big bone in it—and chapati. The only people who can afford it are the bus touts and a few others who we look like businessmen.

One such businessman, a slight, well-dressed man in shirt and pressed trousers, upon overhearing our inquiries, volunteers the information that he belongs to the Qadiriyya Sufi tarika (order) and agrees to show us his mosque, which is close by. It turns out to be a fairly new, tall white structure. Outside it stands the sheikh, a handsome, tall, black-bearded African in immaculate white kanzu and cap. Yes, they do the dhikri, the sheikh answers with twinkling eyes, a silent meditation every day, and yes, once in a while they do have the chant—and in a beautiful voice he sings it, "*La illaha ilallah, Muhammadur rasoolullah, Abdul Qadir Jilani . . .*" The second name upon whom God's blessing is invoked is that of the twelfth-century Sufi mystic from Iran, founder of the order, whose branches can be found all over the world. It is an enchanting experience.

Later that morning we have tea with the businessman, and he tells us he is an exporter of timber to Zanzibar and beyond. He has a mill in the forest.

We return at night from Kilwa Kivinje, the landscape pitch-black except for the occasional solitary lamp outside a dwelling: a family cooking, or sitting down to eat, or simply chatting for a while before turning in. And it hits me, something that is so obvious and that I always knew: so much of the country lies in total darkness at night.

But the African night is unforgettable; it sits forever on your heart.

8.

Quiloa, the Island

MILTON'S "QUILOA" WAS KILWA KISIWANI, THE ISLAND. A view of the Island is what our beach hotel promises its few visitors, and provides, in the hazy distance towards the southeast; but tourists come to Tanzania for its animals, not its history. Tanzania's history is of little interest to the world, or even apparently to itself. The Island is a UNESCO World Heritage Site, but that means practically nothing so far.

We decide to visit the Island.

Masoko harbour, a short distance from the hotel, is quiet. Under a large tree some hundred yards from the water a group of men and women stand and sit waiting patiently for something to happen. The two European prospectors from our hotel have flown to Mombasa; their ship, heavy with equipment, is set to depart soon with its Filipino crew to join them. One of the young men waves at us. We hoped to visit the Island by dhow, but the wind is wrong—it will take us three hours to cross the channel by dhow, the motor boat operator tells us, but he can take us in fifteen minutes. We have no choice and negotiate a price. We board the boat, and this being their signal, the waiting men and women come down at a trot to take their seats around us, without charge—they're going our way anyway. The sea is choppy, and the full boat cuts diagonally across the channel towards the other shore. When we arrive we remove our shoes and wade to the beach. By this time a man with a cell phone has attached himself to us as guide. He seems quite unnecessary; at the ruins he tells us what's already on the plaques, which tell us exactly what's written in our slim volume on ancient Kilwa. The published literature on the ruins is sparse and out of print. Here, at the site, there is no resident office, no literature; no one who knows anything more than us.

No other town or city on the East African coast, no other place in southern Africa has a written premodern history all its own. Kilwa does. The story of Kilwa has been told in the Kilwa Chronicle, or *The Book of the Consolation of the History of Kilwa*, a history set to paper around 1550 in Arabic, at the instigation of the ruling sultan, who feared that the story of Kilwa would soon be forgotten. Says the writer of the Chronicle, whose name is not known (because the page bearing it is missing),

> Historians have said, amongst their assertions, that the first man to come to Kilwa came in the following way. There arrived a ship in which there were people who claimed to have come from Shiraz in the land of the Persians. It is said there were seven ships: the first stopped at Mandakha; the second at Shaugu; the third at a town called Yanbu; the fourth at Mombasa; the fifth at the Green Island [Pemba]; the sixth at Kilwa; and the seventh at Hanzuan [in the Comores]. They say that the masters of these first six ships were brothers, and that the one who went to the town of Hanzuan was their father. God alone knows all truth.

This is the founding myth. Besides the oral tradition there is ample evidence in the form of coin finds, pottery, and inscriptions (for example, at the mosque in Kizimkazi, Zanzibar, dated 1107) of ancient Persian connection to the Swahili coast. Iran is known to have had a strong maritime presence in the Indian Ocean from pre-Islamic times, and there were Persian settlements in many ports. In East Africa, many coastal people consider themselves Shirazi, after the city in Iran. (The ruling party in Zanzibar, soon after its independence, was called the Afro-Shirazi Party [ASP].) The first sultan of Kilwa, and a Persian according to the Chronicle, was Ali bin al Hasan; copper and silver coins found at the site and nearby bearing his name attest to his existence, and place his rule at around 1070. He was known as Nguo Nyingi ("Much Cloth"), says the Chronicle, for having bought Kilwa Island for a lot of coloured cloth.

According to archaeologists interpreting Kilwa's desolate, grey stone ruins, by the late eleventh century Kilwa already boasted a stone mosque. It had a flat roof of coral laid over mangrove rafters supported by nine wooden pillars. What remains of that structure today are portions of the boundary wall with arched entranceways, the roof having collapsed. During the economic boom of the fourteenth century in Kilwa this mosque received a large extension, with fifteen domes, most of which still exist, and octagonal pillars of composite stone, also now very much in evidence. This larger combined mosque is called the Great Mosque. It marks a period of extensive and grand construction on the Island, the most impressive of which would have been the Great House, or Husuni Kubwa, only the foundations of which remain.

Kilwa Island was the southern extremity of the Islamic world and its rise as a commercial empire corresponded with the rise of the Abbasid Empire centred at Baghdad and the growing market for gold, copper, ivory, timber, and many other items. Gold and copper were mined in Zimbabwe down south, brought to the port of Sofala—on the Mozambique coast—and dispersed through Kilwa to the commercial centres abroad.

Sometime probably in March, in 1329, that remarkable Moroccan globetrotter Ibn Battuta arrived in Kilwa, having sailed from Aden, gone round the horn of Africa, and touched port at Mogadishu and Mombasa. This was before his more famous voyages to India and China. Ibn Battuta says, of his visit to East Africa,

> After one night in Mombasa, we sailed on to Kilwa, a large city on the coast whose inhabitants are black. A merchant told me that a fortnight's sail beyond Kilwa lies Sofala, where gold is brought from a place a month's journey inland. . . .
>
> The city of Kilwa is among the finest and most substantially built in the world. Its sultan at the time of my visit was Abu'l Mazaffar Hassan, surnamed Abu al Mawahib [the Father of Gifts], renowned for his humility, generosity, and hospitality. I saw at his court many sharifs from Iraq and the region of Mecca.

The Kilwa Chronicle nicely corroborates this, and a copper coin minted in Kilwa has been found in Zimbabwe, bearing al-Mawahib's name.

Such was the reach of Kilwa on the Isle. It had wrested the southern African gold monopoly from Mogadishu, and its merchants were among the wealthiest in the region. They lived in multistoreyed houses of stone and marble with sunken courtyards and indoor plumbing, they wore silk and cotton, gold and silver, they ate off porcelain dishes. The Island's reputation had reached legendary status abroad, though few had seen it. Milton would equate it (or Sofala) with the biblical Ophir, from where King Solomon received gold and silver. Other accounts described it along the lines of a walled, European city surrounded by luxurious vegetation, forgetting that it was an island off the coast of Africa.

While in the mind of Europe Kilwa belonged to the realm of fantasy and myth, the city had a more mundane and an older relationship with India and China. Leopard skins, ivory, and rhino horns had a market in the Far East. Correspondingly, Chinese porcelain has been found in many coastal towns where it was used to decorate mosques and the better homes. Cotton from India was a valued commodity, as was silk from China. In the fifteenth century giraffes were shipped to China, one particular giraffe making a stopover in Bengal, whose ruler then presented it to the Emperor of China.

Europe's contact with Kilwa (and the East African coast) began with the search for the sea route to India.

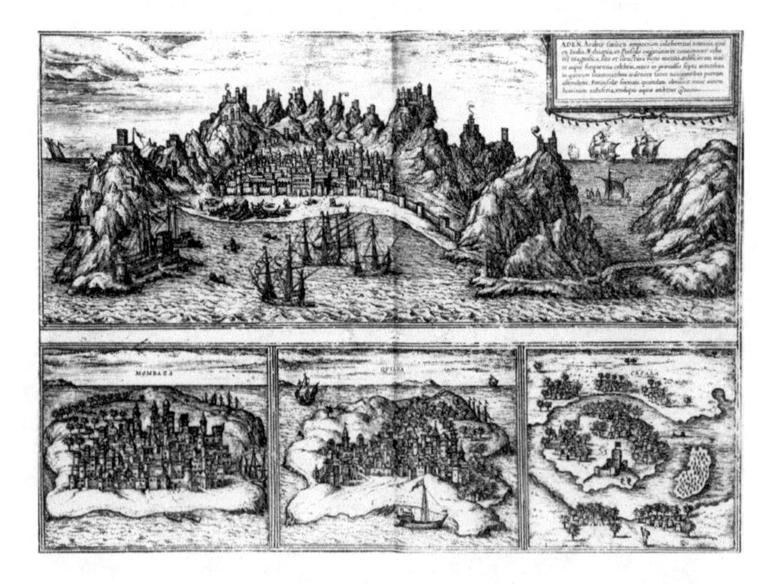

In 1497–98 Vasco da Gama rounded the Cape of Good Hope at the tip of Africa with three Portuguese ships, looking for India. This was just six years after Columbus had set off in the western direction from Europe, with the same objective. The voyage was hazardous, and the attitude of the Portuguese towards all whom they met was belligerent and mercenary. They came with superior weapons—crossbows, canons, and muskets—and body armour, and among the crew were select hardened criminals who had already been condemned to death in Lisbon. With that voyage a new era began on the Indian Ocean, that of European commercial and naval dominance.

In March 1498—according to the account by Gaspar Correa (d. 1583)—the ships arrived in Mozambique (the island, in the northern part of the present country of that name), having captured a "Moor" on the way. This Moor did not speak Arabic, and did not drink wine, and was from the great Indian port city of Cambay (Khambat today, shorn of all its former glory); therefore we can only presume that he was a Gujarati, perhaps a Muslim. That he was described as a dalal, or broker, only makes one smile. He agreed to assist them, likely under duress—he was captured only because, unlike the others who were with him, he could not swim. His name was Davane. The Portuguese in their accounts use the term "Moor" somewhat loosely, because they did not know the people they were dealing with—a Moor could be an Arab, a Swahili, an Indian from Gujarat or from Malabar, a Christian, a Muslim, or a Hindu; and "fair," "dark," or "swarthy." How Davane of Cambay was able to carry on lengthy conversations with them is unclear. According to Correa's account, this stretch of coastal East Africa had a governor representing the sultan of Kilwa. Besides gold, silver, ivory, and wax, he says, pepper and "drugs"—it's unclear what this term refers to—were also shipped out to Cambay.

What followed in Mozambique, this trading colony of Kilwa, when the Lusitanian ships arrived is a tale of intrigue and treachery that includes a skirmish with the natives. The Mozambican port is described thus, as Davane the Moor comes ashore on behalf of the Portuguese:

> The Moor went ashore, and Nicolas Coelho carried him in his boat, and then returned to the ship. The Moor was surrounded by many people, and so he went to the house of the sheikh, who is the captain of the country on behalf of the King of Quiloa, and who was in this town as agent collecting the duties from the merchant ships, which are many in number, and some from many countries, with much goods of various kinds . . . ; and with these goods they go along the coast, and up many rivers, which they find, in which they effect much barter of silver and gold, ivory and wax. . . .

The Africans were naturally nervous about these white men in armed ships who spoke of the great wealth and power of their king. Informed by Davane of Cambay about a treachery planned by the "sheikh," or governor, of Mozambique, da Gama pretended not to be aware of this and left, restraining himself from firing on the sheikh's ships—he had a long way to go still and didn't want news of his aggression to precede him. He left behind one convicted murderer, Joan Machado. Joan was joined by a fellow convict who swam ashore from a ship to join him and the two lived happily with the sheikh.

As in all such chronicles, the local facilitator remains a cypher. Who was Davane (whatever the actual name was) and why would he attach himself to a foreign ship whose success was not guaranteed?

Da Gama was informed by his pilots that Kilwa was a great city where ships came from all parts of the world, including India and Mecca—presumably Arabia—and that there were even some Armenian Christian traders dwelling there. But, according to the faithful Davane, treachery was afoot. This is how the Portuguese poet Camõens describes it in his epic, *The Lusiads*, which he wrote to extol da Gama's exploits and Portugal's glories:

Then, subtly as when Sinon to the Trojans
Sang the praises of the Wooden Horse,
He let slip that close by, on an island,
Lived an ancient race of Christians . . .

There he saw his plot maturing
With strength and numbers far
Greater than Mozambique's, the island's fame
There being widespread. Kilwa is its name.

Fortunately for da Gama and his crew, "the Lord sent them a contrary wind" and they missed Kilwa, going to Mombasa and Malindi instead, before heading off to the port city of Calicut in India.

In 1502 Vasco da Gama undertook a second voyage to India, this time taking ten large ships and five warships. He arrived in Kilwa on July 12. Says Correa,

> The streets of the city are narrow, and the houses are very high, of three and four stories, and one can run along the tops of them upon terraces, as the houses are very close together: and in the port there were many ships.

Da Gama fired a series of salvos to frighten the people. Then he had the nervous sultan visit him in a boat with a few of his men, and demanded of the ruler that he become vassal to the king of Portugal and pay an annual tribute, with the threat that he had the capacity to "put the city to fire and sword." In return, da Gama would give him a written guarantee of protection from the king of Portugal. The sultan acquiesced. The Portuguese standard was raised upon a spear and brought to the shore where it was received with trumpets and carried around the city. Thus began the demise of Kilwa, and indeed of the city-states of the coast. In time Mombasa and Mozambique became important, in the former of which the Portuguese constructed Fort Jesus. The Portuguese eventually left Kilwa, which was ruled by local sultans, before the Omani Arabs of Zanzibar took over.

Much of East Africa would eventually end up in British hands; the Portuguese clung to Mozambique until 1975, fighting a bitter guerrilla war to keep it. The liberation of Mozambique, Angola (also Portuguese), Zimbabwe, and South Africa was a cause we grew up with in the 1960s in newly independent Tanzania, which had become a champion of African freedom. In National Service, where we were sent after high school, we sang about all these causes, wishing death to the enemies of Africa during our morning jogs, and on long route marches over the countryside, dressed in khakis and boots, our G3 rifles in our hands. The headquarters of the Mozambique freedom movement, FRELIMO, was in Dar es Salaam, on Nkrumah Street, where the leader, Eduardo Mondlane, was killed by a letter bomb presumably sent by the Portuguese. The head of the Angolan freedom movement, Samora Machel, was later killed in a plane crash believed to be arranged by the South Africans. Dar's Acacia Avenue, its name already changed once to Independence Avenue, is now Samora Avenue.

Yes, says our guide, there are ghosts on the Island; and there are also people who are descended from those early Arabs. He shows us a boy of about eight with an almost translucent brown skin and a round head. They are called Shombe, says the guide. We see another man, black, but with a greenish glint to his eye; he claims that descent too, on his mother's side. Many of the Shombe have gone to Dar, the guide adds. I recall that "Shombe" in my childhood was a derogatory term for a half-caste.

We walk farther inland through a field and come to an immense baobab tree, its girth some ten feet across. Looking up into the gnarly, leafless branches coloured a grim shade of grey, one can well believe them to harbour a ghost; an important spirit of the air, a captain among djinns. This would be an eerie place at night. Past the baobab we walk along a path and come to a settlement, all mud and wattle, and no electricity. In fact the Island is not electrified at all; from our hotel it appears totally dark at night save for some pinpricks of light. We come to a table where a few men sit idly and, just to bring business, we join them and ask for tea, which is brought for us. There are no jobs, the men say. Yes, there are the ruins, but the government has brought no development; what do we eat, the stones? Our guide takes us to a large, square structure closer to the shore. It is a madrassa. We walk inside and meet the principal. They teach Islamic doctrine, he says, up to Standard 6, and also English and Math. But the teaching is in Arabic, no Swahili is used. The boys come from different parts of the country on scholarship. After Standard 6, some of them get further scholarships to go to Egypt, Libya, and other places. This appears to be a madrassa of the Shadhiliyya Sufi group.

The guide uses his cell phone to beckon the motorboat, which is ready for us when we arrive.

The sight of the ruins and the present state of this Isle has left many a visitor in a contemplative or depressive mood. "Such is the state of a settlement which in 1500 the Portuguese found prosperous in the highest degree," wrote Richard Burton, who visited it in 1859. "Every grace save that of beauty has now passed from it and . . . we see the wild 'smokes' of the tropical coast, and we hear the scream of the seamew harshly invading the silence and solitude of a city in ruins."

According to Krapf, who visited not long after, the Island should be turned into a place like Sierra Leone, a haven for freed slaves.

9.

The Mystics Down the Road: Discovering the Sufis

By the time the prayer starts in the mosque this blazing Friday afternoon on Sikukuu Street, Dar es Salaam, the sidewalk is close-packed with worshippers, and more are arriving, converging from the neighbourhood, some wearing their kofias and kanzus, some bringing their own mats to pray on. Not to be taken as unbelievers, as we more or less are, we go down on protesting knees on a proffered mat on the hard pavement and follow the motions of those around us. No one spares a look at us. As the prayer proceeds, in a rich, throaty voice heard clearly over a loudspeaker, the people on the street, as though charmed by a mesmer, stop in their tracks, go down on their knees, and begin to perform the familiar motions of the Islamic prayer. Traffic has stopped.

We have come to see the Shadhiliyya Sufis at prayer. Is this a purely voyeuristic desire? Perhaps, but can you distinguish that from an intense curiosity about those amongst whom we lived, a desire to make amends for the sin of ignorance? I carry a tiny flame of resentment inside me at the fact that most of us, Africans and Asians, had grown up in such insular communities that we did not know how people down the street from us lived or worshipped. I had heard of the mystical and unorthodox Sufi Muslims, but believed that they resided elsewhere, in the countries of the Middle East and South Asia. That they existed in East Africa, and moreover were important in the spread of Islam in these lands, I discovered only recently—much to my embarrassment—in the accounts of some western scholars. Soon after my arrival in Dar, therefore, I stood outside the city's main Jama Mosque and as the men emerged from their prayers I inquired about these Sufis: where could I find them, the Shadhiliyyas and the Qadiriyyas? No one seemed to know of them. This was not too surprising, for the orthodox do not view the Sufis very positively; and one group of worshippers is not going to send you to the doors of another. (I discovered this also when inquiring about Hindu temples in Dar.) In Kilwa Kivinje, however, I had been shown a Qadiriyya mosque and its sheikh had sung to me. And on Kilwa Island, in the madrassa next to the stone ruins, I was informed that indeed the Shadhiliyya had their centre in Dar, on Sikukuu Street. And here it is, in the midst of the noon prayer, hardly a mile away from where I had made my fruitless inquiries; and hardly a mile away from where I grew up.

Sufis are intriguing for their oddball nonconformism. Their mysticism is manifest in expressions of devotion to God, either at the abstract level of meditation on the Absolute, or at a personal, devotional level. Sufi sects or orders have formed around hierarchies of spiritual teachers or masters. Devotion to God is often expressed through the dhikr (Swahili: dhikri), consisting of meditation or chanting, and sometimes singing and even dancing. The whirling dervishes of the Mevlevi order who sometimes tour North American cities express their devotion by their dance. For such unorthodoxy, and their close fraternity, they have often been despised. The medieval Iranian Sufi, Mansur al Hallaj, for repeatedly uttering, I am the Truth, implying We are all God, was—according to legend—hanged and decapitated, then burned and his ashes thrown in the Tigris; even then, it is said, they formed the words I am the Truth.

Sufis exist everywhere, often in small numbers, practising innocuously. In the old city of Jerusalem I once came across a Sufi; he ran a tiny general store and when I made my inquiry agreed to take me to the local centre, which was on the first-floor terrace of a building nearby. It was Thursday, sacred to Sufis, and that evening the group was to meet and performed the dhikr, but much to my regret I had to be elsewhere and therefore missed it. For the moment, I could only peep through the grille door into the long, dark, silent hall laid with carpet. And in Toronto, on a winter morning, the ground covered in snow, my friend Munir took me to a Sufi meeting in a modest suburban home. This group was defined by its devotion to a master of Sri Lankan origin, now dead, who has a shrine in Philadelphia. This day the group, seated on the carpeted floor of the modest living room, spoke with veneration about their master—his demeanour, his simplicity, his wisdom. A visitor from Philadelphia was present. Towards the end of the meeting the devotees sat in silent meditation, after which a discussion took place, and then a simple meal was served. A far cry from the whirling dervishes, but these were also Sufis.

Why my own interest in Sufis? The act of human devotion to the sacred intrigues me and draws me as an observer; perhaps there lies here a nostalgia for the simplicity and humility of devotion that I knew and saw around me in our prayer house as a child. I was brought up in the syncretistic Khoja tradition, containing the elements of both esoteric Ismailism and the Indian Upanishads, as well as devotional mysticism of the kind demonstrated in the songs of Kabir and Mira. I could add that the quest of fundamental physics, which became my specialty for a while, is also a quest for absolute truth.

The African variety of Sufism—more often known as the tarika, or "path"—is little known, and most books on Sufism completely ignore it. Unlike in Iran or South Asia, there are no major Sufi shrines in East Africa, where people from all backgrounds and faiths can go and pay respects and ask for blessings.

The Shadhiliyya path is North African in origin and named after Abul Hassan Ali ash-Shadhili (d. 1258), a Moroccan mystic. In the nineteenth century the Shadhiliyya movement had found a footing in the Indian Ocean islands of the Comores through a connection to Palestine. From the Comores the movement spread to the old settlement of Kilwa in Tanganyika, which became a local centre.

What is in my mind as I go through the motions of Islamic prayer, up and down, both hands to the ears and back to the sides, mimicking my neighbours to the right and left and the man in front, is memory—fleeting visions of this street, Sikukuu Street, as it once was. It ran all the way down to Uhuru Street, where I lived at the intersection, and for several years it was the first leg of my long trek to school. The houses were of mud and wattle. As I passed, early in the morning at seven, elderly men in kanzus and kofias might be sitting outside playing bao; on the ground at some of the doorways there would be bottles of togwa, a light porridgelike drink, for sale. Across from where I now perform this ritual like a nervous robot was a rudimentary store of the poorest sort belonging to a friend's family; sometimes I would stop and pick him up—he was always late—and we would then hurry off as I was regaled to a catalogue of dirty stories. The street was unpaved, and often we removed our shoes, not to pray but to wade through rainwater and mud. If there was a mosque at this location, a simple one, I didn't know. Now the street is paved, there are one- and two-storey brick buildings, many motor vehicles. At the end of the street, a block away on this side, is the Fire Station, which had in those days a wall clock in a front room. Viewed from a distance through the window the clock was my timekeeper: How many minutes to bell? Should I run or keep walking? The vice-principal, Mr. Duarte, delighted in greeting latecomers with a swinging cane.

And on the way back from school down this street in the hot afternoon I would stop at some shop and beg for water. At one of the shops the owners were especially generous, and some Thursdays, which were holy days, they would even hand out sweets to passing schoolchildren. A few days ago, while I was walking outside the Khoja khano, an Asian woman came to beg me for money. It was an unusual and embarrassing experience; Asians never begged in public. Only when I had walked away did I realize, recalling the name she had given me, that she was from the shop on Sikukuu Street that had so generously given me water to drink and even some sweet on special Thursdays. Perhaps she had been sitting in the shop watching as I stood outside dripping with sweat and gulping down water.

The prayers over, the men on the sidewalk get up and, without ceremony, except pausing to shake hands with familiars, disperse up and down the street to where they came from. They do this every Friday, of course, if not every day. The mosque begins to empty as a tide of men emerges from the two entrances. But now something strange happens: a number of men are conspicuous, easily discernible in crisp, extra-white kanzus and kofias, and against the emerging tide they are going *up* the steps and inside. Something is going on there. I inquire of a man beside me, and he replies, "They're doing dhikri inside."

I walk up the steps, remove my laced shoes outside the door, and enter the cool shade of the interior. I go and stand against the back wall. Elderly men come to shake my hand, put their right hand to their breast in the Islamic greeting, very happy to see a stranger among them.

At the front end of the hall a small tight circle of men forms, and then expands as they take a few steps back. And they begin swaying back and forth, back and forth, chanting, "Allahoo, Allahoo." The name of God. Such is the absorption, such is the collective murmur, a humming and a buzzing, that it holds me spellbound. Against the front wall before them stands an ancient-looking, frail man with two companions. He is, I guess, the khalifah, the master of the order here. Occasionally someone comes and kisses his hand. The chanting gets louder, the swaying energetic. It becomes apparent in time that one of the men is leading the dhikri, and soon he enters the circle and is joined by another, and the two conduct the chanting and swaying, gliding in long strides from one end of the circle to the other. A group of young boys, perhaps eight years old, have meanwhile formed a smaller circle of their own.

These are the Shadhiliyya, then.

I lived in this city, at the end of this street, yet never saw or dreamt anything like it, was never aware that prayers of this sort went on in our midst. Now after many years I have returned, and connect this ritual prayer to a larger history, to the world, see it as a part of a global mystical fraternity.

Politics have not been far from the life of these tarikas or Sufi orders, which is not surprising, because they are both populist and nonconforming and reach out to the simple and less privileged. In India and Africa, many believe, it is the Sufis and mystics who have been largely responsible for the spread of Islam among the masses. The following is cultish and centres around the spiritual master, in much the same way that among many Indians worship often centres around a guru like Sai Baba. The language used is the vernacular and accessible, and joint worship and song are the expressions of devotion to God. It is the opposing, judgemental orthodox faith, Arabic- and scripture-based, that has the ear of the sultan—or whatever ruler is in place. If everyone were to declare, like the Iranian mystic Mansur, "I am the Truth," where would government be? Where would orthodoxy be?

In 1905 in Tanganyika, a massive insurrection against German rule erupted and spread out in a good swath of the country, involving many ethnic groups. The war was inspired by a medicine man called Kinjikitile, whose village, Ngarambe, was close to Kilwa. Kinjikitile introduced blessed water to his followers, instructing them that if they took it (drank it or sprinkled themselves with it, the ritual is not quite clearly described in the texts) and followed certain rules of abstention, then any German bullets shot at them would turn to water and be rendered harmless. Thus began the Maji Maji War. The blessed water (maji) spread, taking the war with it. It has been conjectured that members of Sufi orders were among those who initiated the warriors with the water ceremony. There is no hard evidence for this, but it would not be surprising. People of many beliefs resented the Germans, and the Muslims had special grievance against the European domination of the Muslim areas of the world. The Germans in turn were wary of the Muslims, wavering between policies of tolerance and hostility. They even considered encouraging natives to raise pigs, in the hope that a liking for pork would discourage them from adopting Islam.

Following the Maji Maji War, the Germans remained nervous about the Sufis. In 1908 a pamphlet called the Mecca Letter began circulating in many parts of the country and caused much excitement; written in Arabic, it was read in the mosques and discussed by the sheikhs. Millenarian in content, it warned Muslims against deviation from the true faith. And furthermore, those who did not pass the letter on would face dire consequences. Implicitly anti-European, it put the scare into the government that it could instigate another uprising, along the lines of Maji Maji. A number of people were arrested, and in 1909 the colonial government banned the practice of dhikri, the collective Sufi chanting. It was allowed again two years later.

Not much is known about the origins of the mysterious Letter. According to the historian August H. Nimtz, "there is at least circumstantial evidence that the Qadiriyya [Sufi sect] was involved in [its] dissemination"—a few prominent members of the sect have been named as disseminators. But Muslims also learned to work with the government, which had a "Good Muslim" list. The Ottoman–German alliance during the First World War was played upon, with the raising of both flags, German and Ottoman, at public places. "In locations where brotherhood [that is, Sufi] leaders had friendly relations with the Germans . . . it is likely that they helped by spreading word of the holy war as well as by resisting the British efforts."

In 1914, the leader of the Qadiriyya movement in Mpwapwa was a detective, presumably a spy.

10.

Burton and Speke, and the East African Expedition of 1857

The Romance of Exploration

ON A BRIGHT SUNNY DAY AT NOONTIME ON JUNE 16, 1857, the English explorer Richard Burton departed Zanzibar for the Tanzanian mainland on Sultan Majid's corvette, the *Artemise*, which fired off a gun salute as it sailed off. "We quit Zanzibar Island in dignified style," wrote Burton, and thus began the so-called East African Expedition sponsored by Great Britain's Royal Geographical Society. Sub-Saharan Africa was still Europe's "dark continent"; little was known about it, besides ancient speculation and fantasy, and more recent accounts by a few missionaries relentlessly afoot on the bush trails with their Bibles. A mid-century map of Africa shows an empty space in the east, in a region between the Indian Ocean and a vast slug-shaped lake in the centre, which by its odd shape betrays the ignorance of the cartographer. The coastal towns—Malindi, Mombasa, Kilwa—and Zanzibar were of course known, but more as belonging to the Indian Ocean trading zone. The purpose of the expedition was to explore the limits of that inland lake, which Burton called the Sea of Ujiji or Unyamwezi Lake and later the Tanganyika Lake. With Burton were his English companion, John Speke, two "half-caste" Goan "boys," two African gun carriers, and eight Baluchi armed guard, courtesy of the sultan.

Burton's description of the Zanzibar coastline as it receded behind him that June day is quite marvellous: with a few deft strokes he paints a picture of the island as it appears from the sea, a picture that has not changed much in a century and a half.

> [The *Artemise*] slowly gliding out of Zanzibar harbour, afforded us a farewell glance at the whitewashed mosques and houses of the Arabs, the cadjan-huts, the cocoa-grown coasts, and the ruddy hills striped with long lines of clove. Onwards she stole before a freshening breeze . . .
>
> the land faded from emerald to brown, and from brown to hazy purple, the tufts of the trees seemed first to stand out of, then to swim upon, the wave, and as evening, the serenest of tropical evenings, closed in over sky, earth, and sea, a cloud-like ridge, dimly discernible from our quarter, was all that remained of Zanzibar.

The Zanzibar coastline has evoked the romantic impulse in many a traveller, and Burton was no exception, especially when recalling it some years after the voyage took place. The *Artemise* carried all the supplies the expedition would need, and across the channel on the mainland Burton had already arranged to hire a large number of porters to carry them on the journey ahead.

At the height of empire in the nineteenth century, accounts of explorers in East Africa made gripping reading in the western world, providing details of an alien, unknown, and dangerous landscape, at the same time describing the heroism of the men who undertook these journeys, which lasted many months. The books were cleverly marketed, keeping in mind their exotic subject and readers' sensibilities, the illustrations in them selected and redrawn from the explorers' own sketches. (It should not surprise us, then, to see in them grotesque racial caricatures.) Thus, within a year of its publication by John Murray in 1857, David Livingstone's *Missionary Travels* had sold 25,000 copies in England, thrilling its readers with stories of a heroic and good Christian man in a savage and cruel land. Livingstone had set off for South Africa—by then long settled by the Dutch—in 1840 as a missionary, and ended up travelling vast tracts of the African interior with only Africans as his companions and guides. *Missionary Travels* was published after his first return to England, sixteen years after he left, when he was arguably perceived as more heroic explorer than missionary.

The lives and personalities of the explorers had become the stuff of marketable legend. As Louise Henderson writes:

> . . . a host of Victorian mythmakers made it their business to profit from turning individual explorers into heroes or villains, ensuring that reputations would often be well-established before these adventurers had even returned from the field.

Speculations about David Livingstone's unknown whereabouts for long periods after his return to Africa fed the public imagination, as did his death there, and Henry Morton Stanley has been immortalized for his "I Presume" moment, when he found Livingstone.

It was in this climate of celebrity exploration and best-seller travel-writing that the Burton–Speke saga took place. Burton, who led the East African Expedition, was already famous as a traveller to exotic places; Speke, the junior member, was relatively unknown. The two men's accounts of their journey, which lasted a little over two years, provide fascinating descriptions of the country, Tanganyika, the mainland of Tanzania, that they travelled through—the landscapes, the peoples, the cultures in all their diverseness, even when we allow for their narrators' biases and misunderstandings, and their personality quirks. They are even more fascinating when you come from the place itself and see a piece of its history revealed through this objective yet infuriatingly faulty lens. Little else has been written about the country in that period. To an East African it would be of interest that the Nyamwezi people of the Tabora region were famous as porters and seasoned, knowledgeable travellers (and their donkeys as especially good for the arduous journeys on diverse terrain); unlike their later caricature as beggars, the Gogo (properly called the Wagogo, or singular Mgogo, and their land Ugogo), inhabiting the vital centre of the country, were feared, and held the key to any access to the interior; the Zanzibar sultan's reach extended in various degrees into the hinterland right up to eastern Congo. We learn about the habitations of the different peoples, how they covered and adorned themselves, what their politics were.

But Burton's and Speke's accounts also reveal a very human drama, and it was this, not the country itself, that grabbed the western imagination in the decades that followed. The story of that expedition has now become one mainly of the conflictual and ultimately tragic relationship between the two men, so opposed in their personalities, that developed during the return leg of the journey and continued to its tragic end after their arrival back home. That story is linked to the obsession with the discovery—at least from the European point of view—of the source of the River Nile. It has been retold many times.

The East Africa Expedition and Its Tragedy

The two men left the East African coast at a point called Kaole near present-day Dar es Salaam and headed west into the country with a large entourage of porters, soldiers, and other assistants, and a quantity of supplies to last them two years. They marched single file, led by a "half-caste" guide called Ahmed bin Salim, and a man from the coast called Mwinyi Wazira, whom Burton describes as a "huge, broad-shouldered Sawahil with a coal-black skin"; in the vanguard were also the Baluchi soldiers carrying the sultan's red flag and armed to the teeth with matchlocks, sabres, and "khanjars" (daggers); in the middle were the porters and various assorted men; the rear was brought up by one of the Englishmen. Someone in the front carried the Union Jack—Burton doesn't tell us who.

They set off on the old trade route that began at Bagamoyo—the major slave and ivory depot at the Indian Ocean—and terminated at Ujiji, a similar depot at Lake Tanganyika, where slaves and ivory were brought from Congo, across that long lake that forms a natural continental boundary. The route initially followed the valley of the Ruvu (then called Kingani) River southwest from the coast until the tributary Mgeta branched off, from where they then turned northwest. The landscape was wet and at times marshy, the river shrouded in bush. At the lower end this trek is well inside what is now the Mikumi game reserve, therefore not surprisingly an abundance of wildlife was seen. Crossing the Uluguru (then called Usagara) range, which reaches heights of over 6,000 feet, they arrived at the semidesert terrain of Ugogo. Here the land is flat and dry, covered with thorn bushes and low trees for miles on end, interrupted by isolated outcroppings of granite.

The country traversed, east to west, from the Indian Ocean to Lake Tanganyika, was observed and described in terms of five geographical sections: Ruvu (Kingani) valley, Uluguru (Usagara) highlands, Ugogo semi-desert, Unyamwezi, and Lake Tanganyika. On this busy highway or "trunk road," caravans numbering a thousand or more regularly passed each other, pausing to exchange messages (the Europeans sent reports and requests to sponsors in Zanzibar), inquire about road conditions, and barter for essentials which had run out. At the important way stations, such as Zungomero, at the Kingani–Mgeta junction, and Ugogi, at the beginning of the desert, the caravans took long rests, replenished manpower and food. Armies of touts descended to offer services, as at any road station today. At Zungomero, "a hotbed of pestilence," the expedition waited fourteen days for the arrival of promised porters. Neither Zungomero nor Ugogi now exist on the maps.

Each porter carried a load of seventy pounds (two "frasilahs," in the measure used in the shops even up to the 1960s). The loads consisted of shells, copper wire, and cloth; provisions for cooking; arms and ammunition; camp furniture; surveying and other instruments, tools, and stationery. The first three items were the "currency," for buying stuff and paying off chiefs for permission to travel through their land. Shells came in numerous varieties; wire was used for ornamentation such as armlets. Cloth came in three major varieties: marikani, a coarse white cotton from Salem, Massachusetts; kaniki, a light black-dyed cloth from India; and coloured checkered cloth from India. (Marikani and kaniki were disused after independence in 1961, perhaps because they were seen as demeaning to the African.) Among the "miscellaneous" items were needle and thread, a little coffee and a lot of tea, brandy and cigars, "curry stuff," and a Union Jack.

On the way the travellers suffered extreme discomfort and encountered malaria, sleeping sickness, and small pox. As early as the Kingani valley, dubbed by one of his men as the "Valley of Death," Burton became delirious with a malarial fever that lasted twenty days, accompanied by nightmares and the sensation of a "divided identity"; his companion seemed to fare worse. "Unhappy Zungomero," where he describes his hut thus, "the roof was a sieve, the walls were systems of chinks, and the floor was a sheet of mud," he also calls the "Slough of Despond." They were frustrated by tribespeople, hyenas feasted on their donkeys, bees swarmed them, and the men quarrelled, became mutinous, molested women, or absconded.

After the desert of Ugogo, the next important terminus was Kazeh, site of the modern town of Tabora in Unyamwezi, where they were given hospitality by a Khoja Indian called Musa Mzuri. Departing from Kazeh they arrived on the shores of Lake Tanganyika in February 1858—eight months after they had departed from Zanzibar.

The two men turned back from Ujiji, arrived at Kazeh, where Burton was sick. Speke, feeling better, took the northbound trail towards a lake he had heard the local Arab traders speak about. At a town called Mwanza he came to the shore of the lake, which was vast, and he named it Lake Victoria, convinced that it must be the source of the Nile. It was a moment of inspiration. The fact that one man named a lake using local custom, while the other named it after the reigning English queen surely reflects a difference in their personalities. Speke returned to Kazeh, but Burton did not believe his theory about the Nile. As Burton would write, Speke had no scientific reason for his conclusion except "a woman's reason": I think so because I think so. They quarrelled. On the way back to England from Zanzibar, they arrived at Aden, where Burton stayed and Speke went ahead. According to Burton, who was the leader of the expedition and upon whose recommendation Speke had been taken on, they had agreed that Speke would not reveal the results of their expedition until Burton arrived. He returned to England on May 21, 1859, twelve days after Speke, to find that not only had Speke revealed his "discovery" of the Nile's source, but also he was being feted in London, and moreover had been asked by the Royal Georgraphical Society to undertake another expedition to confirm the discovery. The following year, in 1860, Speke left with James Grant to prove his conjecture and the two returned almost three years later to great acclaim, having announced previously by telegram from Khartoum that "The Nile is settled."

The immensely egotistical and accomplished Richard Burton, long used to the limelight, was sidelined. He still did not believe that the Nile question had been settled, and a meeting was set up in Bath on September 16, 1864, where the two men were to present their points of view. But on the afternoon before the meeting, Speke shot himself in an apparent accident while hunting. Speke was an expert hunter, familiar with the gun he had used; and so the speculation arose, was his death a suicide or an accident?

The Protagonists: Two Victorian Englishmen

So different were Burton and Speke from each other that it almost becomes incumbent upon us to take sides, and biographers of either one of them and storytellers of the Nile have not failed to do so.

Richard Burton is the most intriguing and enigmatic of all the Victorian travellers, a man entirely self-educated, familiar with many cultures and languages, a self-admitted depressive, moody but with a sly sense of humour. With his dark, sombre features he has been called a "Victorian Heathcliff," and an "explorer, scholar, poet, supreme linguist, student of pederasty and nymphomania, popular hero, prolific author, mystic." A romantic, and attractive from a distance. Livingstone disliked him. So did Stanley and many others. As a disguised British secret agent Burton had intrigued with warring peoples in Afghanistan in the machinations of European empires in the East that came to be known as the Great Game. He gained fame by entering the city of Mecca, forbidden to non-Muslims, in the garb of an Afghan Pathan that he donned while still in London. In the words of his wife, "He did not go disguised; he simply *became* a Moslem, identifying with every aspect of Moslem life and faith. Arabic became his native tongue." According to one source, he even had himself circumcised for the purpose. And unlike other travellers to Africa, he did not brandish a Bible; in fact in his writings he does not display a religious sensibility at all.

He was of course a racist of his time, and apparently more so with respect to Africans. (But we should not forget that the Africans and Indians had their own disparaging observations of the white man among them. As Burton and Speke arrived in one village, the women gathered to laugh at their looks; at another place a rumour had spread that they were cannibals.) He makes vast and quick generalizations—a tendency in travel writing that's surely still not gone away. Of the people of the mrima (the coastal territory between Mombasa and Kilwa), who were a mixture of African and Arab descent, he says, "The Wamrima are an ill-conditioned race; they spend life in eating, drinking and smoking, drinking and dancing, visits, intrigue, and low debauchery. They might grow cotton and coffee . . . but whilst a pound of grain remains in bin, no man will handle a hoe." And of the Baluchi soldiers who accompanied him, and whom he finds gallant elsewhere, he says also: "Abject slaves to the Great Gaster, they collect in swarms round a slaughtered goat, and they will feast their eyes for hours on the sight of a rice-bag." He has intense dislike of "half-castes"—as did other Europeans, perhaps because they seemed not to know their place—but approves of the Nyamwezi porters. He is not consistent, and it appears that he displays in his observations the frustrations of a traveller, especially a westerner, being openly ripped off, and one imagines the locals chuckling away at their small triumphs over the strange white men—who wrote in their books, worked with strange instruments, were influential in Zanzibar, and dangerous with their weapons, but who could also be easily duped and evidently afford to be robbed. But Burton is never aloof or patronizing; he learns and speaks the people's lingo, bargains and argues with them, moves amongst them, and in his pages he recreates them vividly as characters. Before his departure he goes around listening to bazaar "gup"—using an Indian colloquial term for gossip; he visits a coastal medicine man to ensure good luck for the expedition; he listens in as two Bhatias discuss in Kutchi the improbability of the white man's impending journey's success, later telling one of them that he had understood him. His prose makes use of Swahili words with ease, and in one footnote he gives a quick primer on Swahili word-formation. He quotes in Arabic, Greek, Latin, French, Kutchi, Hindustani.

Who but Burton among the explorers, or any of his compatriots, would relate a pudding at an Arab house to the Indian firnee (khir); or slyly hint that the name of the coastal town Mbwamaji puns with a Swahili slang for penis; or discuss forms of pilau; or scold his compatriots for not learning how to cook rice properly?

Burton's companion John Speke, tall, slim and blond, with what one modern admirer calls a willowy figure, could not have been more different. His writing style is sober, efficient, and formal, and he appears to be a good organizer. Rarely does he show emotion or frustration, evoke a person or a place beyond naming them or their function. But he is not beyond racist generalizations. The African is the "curly-headed, flab-nosed, pouch-mouthed negro," the unfortunate, the cursed progeny of Ham, therefore a "strikingly existing proof of the Holy Scriptures," and he is by nature devious and lazy. And though Speke admits once that the African can be taught and is a good learner, at other places he presents him as incorrigible. "Laziness is inherent in these men." The African "works his wife, sells his children, enslaves all he can lay his hands upon, and, unless when fighting for the property of others, contents himself with drinking, singing, and dancing like a baboon, to drive dull care away." Having lived in India, he apparently uses Hindustani to communicate with some of the men, but Speke is not a linguist, nor a show-off, and unlike Burton does not quote in any other language. The narrative is almost entirely in English. The speech he quotes is stilted and sounds artificial. Many observations are provided about "African" ways, but we wonder how precise they are. When he describes a child sacrifice, for example—before telling us that such events are rare—we wonder if he actually witnessed such an event. According to him the African lives only on instinct, he does not possess thought or culture. It appears that Speke, prone to being a victim of cheating, mischief, and misunderstanding as a foreign traveller, uses these instances in his portraits of the "African" character. He quotes a bizarre theory that the ancient Indians knew the source of the Nile, and equally bizarre etymologies for some place names: Uzaramo (the country of the Wazaramo people), according to Speke, is the land of "Ramo," whoever he is.

Those Unknown Others

The story of that expedition, as the background to a tragic relationship between two extraordinary English explorers, polar opposites of each other in their personalities, has been retold many times and from various perspectives. Their public argument, which ended in

Speke's death by gunshot wound just prior to his scheduled debate with Burton in the city of Bath, belongs to the lore of nineteenth-century European explorations of Africa. It is a colourful narrative linked to the mystery of the Nile source and has benefitted much from the rich publishing culture of Great Britain. Having paid that due, one cannot help but wonder today, long after the end of the colonialism that began in the wake of those explorations, about all those *other* characters, the Africans, and Indians, and Arabs, who were also part of the adventure. Who were they, and what went on in their lives? How did *they* perceive the goals and the day-to-day events of the long journey? We might have heard from them *different* romances, tragedies, or travails. The maligned Baluchis and the even more despised Goans might have given us their own observations of the two wazungus, or goras (white men). But what we know about the rest of the caravan is almost entirely from the writings of the two Englishmen. There is enough for us just to wonder, and to regret that there is not more.

A mischievous, enigmatic character like a self-effacing jinn slips in and out of the nineteenth-century explorers' accounts: it is that of the Zanzibar-based Indian trader who facilitated the journeys. Ladha Damji was an Indian from the Bhatia caste of Kutch—in present-day Gujarat—and therefore a speaker of Kutchi, as are many Tanzanian Asians to this day. He was a vania, the quintessential Indian trader. We may well question how successful the Burton–Speke expedition would have been without his assistance: his firm offered a vast quantity of supplies, ranging from sewing needles to camp chairs, tea to gunpowder, everything two Englishmen might need to survive in the jungle for two years, plus the porters and asses to carry them.

Imagine: Burton arrives at the mainland port of Kaole on the

Artemise and finds that most of the porters he had arranged to have hired for him—having been informed of the arduous journey that awaited them with the white men—have absconded with their advance pay. How will he find more porters, what can he afford to take with him under the circumstances, what to leave behind? Arrives this Indian wearing his national dhoti and red conical fool's cap, on a "native vessel," and says, Not to worry, and reorganizes the journey, substituting donkeys for lost men, giving comfort and assurance, negotiating and cajoling all around, promising to send remaining supplies to follow. Nothing looks impossible—or so it is made to seem, such is the nature of the pliable vania (who of course takes his cut), and the journey can proceed.

Waiting in Kaole as the details of the journey are being worked out, Burton builds up a relationship with his facilitator Ladha. Before the expedition departs, he happens to overhear a conversation in Kutchi between Ladha and a relation, Ramji, questioning the wisdom of his impending journey. The two men give him reasonable chances to reach Ugogo in the centre of the country, but no farther. Burton later tells the man, to his embarrassment, that he understood the conversation all along. And when Ladha objects to the shooting of a wild hippo, which has just caused the deaths of three men, Burton asks him, why should he, who bought tusks and therefore "encouraged the destruction of herds of elephants" and had no compunction about destroying a rival in business, "object to the death of a 'creek bull'?" Says Burton, "Ladha received these futile objections contemptuously. . . ." But "When Ladha left," he confesses, "my spirits went with him."

According to H.M. Stanley, arriving much later in Zanzibar in 1870 to begin his search for Livingstone, who had not been heard of for months, Ladha was still around, "a venerable-looking old man, with a shrewd intelligent face . . ." and he calls him "the great Ludha Damji."

But who was Ladha really? Was he tall or short, thin or fat? Did he have a family? We don't know. He died in 1871.

The Bhatias originate in Sindh and Rajasthan. Muhammad Ali Jinnah, the founder of Pakistan, was from this caste, though a Khoja. (The difference was the practice of faith.) The Khojas and the Hindu Bhatias were the two largest groups of Asians on the East African coast. Tharia Topan, another great Zanzibari trader, who interacted with Stanley but had not yet reached his eminence in Burton's time, was from the same caste and a Khoja as well.

Says Stanley, "[The Indians] can produce scores of unconscionable rascals where they can show but one honest merchant. One of the honestest among men, white or black, red or yellow, is a Mohammedan Hindi called Tarya Topan . . . a proverb for honesty, and strict business integrity. He is enormously wealthy, owns several ships and dhows and is a prominent man in the councils of [Sultan] Barghash. Tarya has many children. . . ."

Legend has it that Tharia came as a twelve-year-old runaway on a dhow from Kutch to Zanzibar and worked his way up. He always maintained good relations with the British consul. After Barghash's unsuccessful attempt to snatch the throne away from his brother Majid following their father Seyyid Said's death, he was advised by the British consul to leave the island. He went to Bombay accompanied by Tharia, who also later accompanied him to London, where he was described as a stout, fair-skinned man with a red-dyed beard, wearing a blue, embroidered robe. He was a philanthropist and Khoja mukhi (headman) for a while, and definitely more flamboyant and travelled than Ladha Damji, who had employed him as a young man. He was knighted by Queen Victoria in 1875 in London, apparently for helping the British government's efforts to end the slave trade; his business dealings with the slave and ivory trader Tippu Tip, however, raise a question.

Perhaps the most remarkable man associated with the European expeditions was Sidi Mubarak Bombay, the so-called African factotum, a former slave who was hired as a gun-bearer but became an indispensable man for all purposes, a guide, a translator and interpreter, a negotiator. Burton describes him thus:

> The gem of the party, however, is one Sidi Mubarak, who has taken to himself the agnomen "Bombay." His sooty skin, and teeth sharp-pointed like those of the reptilia, denote his origin from the Ohiao [Uyao] . . . Bombay, sold at Kilwa in early youth, a process of which he talks with many broad grins, was carried to Cutch [Kutch] by some Banyan, and there became a libertinus: he looks fondly back upon the hour of his adoption, and he sighs for the day when a few dollars will enable him to return. His head is a triumph to phrenology; a high narrow cranium, denoting by arched and narrow crown, fuyant brow and broad base with full development of the moral region, deficiency of the reflectives, fine perceptives, and abundant animality. His hair is of the woolliest: his twinkling little eyes are set close together. . . . He attends us everywhere, manages all our purchases, carries all our messages, and when not employed by us, he is at everyman's beck and call.

Thirteen years after the Burton–Speke expedition set off, H.M. Stanley arrived in Zanzibar. Stanley was an American journalist; the

United States had only recently emerged from the civil war and seen the emancipation of its slaves. His attitude to Africans was different—he says. Walking around Zanzibar gave him a certain realization about the African: "From here he [the white visitor] begins to learn that negroes are men, like himself, though of a different colour . . ."

To begin his voyage, in Zanzibar he had gathered Speke's "Faithfuls," those who had travelled with Speke and Grant before, and some with the earlier expedition under Burton. One of them was Sidi Mubarak, who was called back from the isle of Pemba, where he had retired. Of Mubarak, Stanley says he was

> . . . a slender short man of fifty or thereabouts, with a grizzled head, an uncommonly high, narrow forehead, with a very large mouth, showing teeth very irregular and wide apart . . . [his] face was rugged, his mouth large, his eyes small, and his nose flat.

Sidi Mubarak accompanied four expeditions: the one with Burton on a tour of the coast in 1857 when he was hired as a gun carrier; the Burton–Speke Expedition (1857–59), when he was Speke's personal servant and interpreter; the Speke–Grant Expedition (1860) all the way to Uganda and the source of the Nile, when he was a captain; and finally the one under Stanley (1871), when Livingstone was discovered in Ujiji. He was an indispensable man, yet one whose relations with Stanley and Speke, at least, were fraught. Reading Stanley about him one is aware of an independent-minded, opinionated, and passionate man. Stanley didn't like Mubarak, despite his first impression upon seeing him. There were confrontations between the two, but of course the white man held the power, including that to punish and humiliate. "Bombay gets a thrashing," is one subheading of Stanley's account, *How I Found Livingstone.* Sidi Mubarak Bombay stands as an example of the contradictions in the wild and racist generalizations made by these explorers about the Africans.

When Burton and Speke reached Kazeh, they were welcomed by the trader Musa Mzuri. Burton calls him "the Indian doyen of the merchants settled at Unyamwezi. . . ," translating his name as "Handsome Moses," though "Good Moses" is perhaps more accurate. Musa, says Burton, was one of those people who developed Kazeh into the eminent market it now had become. So well respected was Musa that Burton devotes a good few pages to him:

> Musa Mzuri is now a man of the uncertain "certain age" of between forty-five and fifty, thin-bearded, tall, gaunt, with delicate extremeties, and with the regular and handsome features of a high-caste Indian Moslem. Like most of his compatriots he is a man of sad and staid demeanour, and he is apparently faded by opium, which so tyrannizes over him that he carries pills in every pocket, and stores them, lest the hoard should run short, in each corner and cranny of his house.

He had come to Kazeh with his brother Sayyan from Surat, India, and had made his wealth starting from twenty loads of cloth and beads. Sayyan had since died. Musa dressed smartly, wearing a "snowy skull-cap," and perfumed himself with jasmine and sandalwood. His abode was almost a village, with lofty gates, crowded with buyers and sellers.

James Grant, who accompanied Speke in 1860, was also impressed by Musa, who along with others came out a mile to welcome the party. "Guns were fired, jambos and salaams with shaking of hands followed, and we were lodged once more under a hospitable roof."

> Moossah [Musa], an Indian in whose house we resided, was a fine benevolent old man, with an establishment of 300 native men and women round him. His abode had, three years ago, taken two months to build, and it was surrounded by a circular wall which enclosed his houses, fruit and vegetable trees, and a stock of cattle. The lady who presided over the whole was of most portly dimensions, and her word was law.

He also never missed his opium pill in the afternoon, had several wives, and chatted all the while the Quran was being recited to him by a sheikh from Madagascar. He had slaves, like all men of any wealth, and, what is truly remarkable, he told Grant that "The Egyptian river flowed from the Lake Nyanza [Victoria]." So much for the Nile controversy.

Grant and Speke stayed with Musa for fifty-one days, at the end of which Speke presented the Indian with five hundred dollars and a gold watch.

I've learned much about Speke and Burton, and about Livingstone and Stanley, since elementary school, when the "I Presume" moment was firmly etched in my mind. Perhaps the first place I went to see, as a wide-eyed colonial abroad, of London's many historic sites, was Westminster Abbey and specifically the exact place where Livingstone lies buried. It was a moving moment for a variety of reasons. And then the question persisted, Where was *I* in all this history?

We can hardly blame the others for celebrating their own heroes, writing their own stories; the question is, why did "we" not produce our own stories? (If I may be forgiven the temporary distinction between "them" and "us" to make my point.) I was brought up with only the vaguest sense of my own history as an Asian African, much of it mythological or even recently concocted. As Asians growing up in East Africa we didn't know how our forefathers had arrived, how they lived, or even what they looked like. It was later, while living abroad, that this information seemed vital for my sense of who I was. The stories of Ladha Damji and Musa Mzuri and Sidi Mubarak and Tharia Topan, the descriptions by James Elton of the Bhatias and the Khojas, lonely in their shops in the coastal towns of Tanzania—bare glimpses of these men (no women or children were mentioned)—were my stories; they were part of my projected completion as a person. To find them in the pages of the explorers' accounts, therefore, regardless of ignorance and jaundiced perceptions, was a thrilling experience, and I was thankful to these men who wrote.

Who were these men *as people*? As fathers, husbands, community men? To some commentators, Musa was a drug addict and a greedy businessman. An easy enough caricature. I see him as an Indian who arrived penniless and went native in East Africa way back in the mid-1800s, whose mixed children spoke no Indian language, who welcomed the white strangers to his home, and who knew quite casually that the Nile began at Lake Victoria. And then he disappears from our view. Did he write home? What were his relations to India? There is even scanter information about Ladha Damji; I imagine him in his shop worrying about his mother as Indian men are wont to do. Tharia Topan's descendants are known. Once I had tea with a grandson in London, and he had some stories about the old man. A descendant was superintendent of a hostel in Mombasa.

A Question of Language, Understanding, and Truth

One obvious question that arises regarding the journeys is, how good was the communication among the various parties involved?—those who helped to organize the caravans, those who went with them, those in whose lands these strangers arrived. Burton, Speke, and Grant, having spent time in British India, all spoke Hindustani—the older and more vernacular form of Hindi and Urdu—and reportedly could communicate with Sidi Mubarak in that language. Yet none of these four men was its native speaker. Sidi had spent time with Kutchis and would have spoken Kutchi better, though hardly like a native. One can only imagine the confusion and misunderstanding that arose, the more so when whatever Hindustani was spoken was translated into Swahili or English, or even some of the other languages. One imagines a mixture of Swahili, Hindustani, and English used to communicate, along with hand gestures. Sidi Mubarak was a man of the coast and would have been fluent in Swahili. But until quite recently many peoples in the interior did not speak or spoke only a little Swahili. It is far from obvious that Sidi could make himself completely understood to a Mgogo or a Mha. And yet the problems of communication were entirely glossed over, by either the travellers themselves or their numerous commentators and admirers.

Burton writes the first name (actually a word describing Africans in India) of Sidi Bombay as "Seedy," and in an article in *Blackwood's* as "Sudy"; in *Zanzibar*, he writes it as "Sidi." Grant calls him "Seedee." This seems a minor point but it surely reflects the levels of misunderstanding possible, simply on the basis of pronunciation. Burton's Kutchi quotation in *Lakes* sounds marvellous, and one can only admire his linguistic skills, yet it is not entirely correct. Imagine Speke's message in English and broken Hindi, conveyed to Sidi Mubarak, fluent in neither, and reaching a Mgogo via a Swahili in which *he* is not fluent.

And then, how good was the understanding *outside* of language; whose word do we, as modern readers, take? If Burton and Speke do not always tell the same story, and Stanley takes time repudiating Burton (concerning the features of Sidi Mubarak, for example), how much can we trust their accounts of the Africans, Asians, and Arabs? Burton was often contradictory; he was moody and depressive. Sickness made these men delirious. As Burton describes one instance, "I had during the fever-fit, and often for hours afterwards, a queer conviction of divided identity, never ceasing to be two persons that generally thwarted and opposed each other; the sleepless nights brought with them horrid visions, animals of grisliest form, hag-like women and men with heads protruding from their breasts." At the same time Speke had a fainting fit "which seemed to permanently affect his brain." And further, how much of what they report is what they saw and how much was overheard? How much was tall tale? How much was received or written down under the influence of alcohol or rage or fever; how much was reported to them out of fear, spite, a need to please? Did they always know when a native was pulling their leg, in the Swahili manner of "kutania"?

There was a clear power relationship during these long, arduous journeys: the white man was the boss, the black man the servant; obedience was exacted with punishment that could be cruel and humiliating. As Stanley says of Sidi Mubarak, when he hires him in Zanzibar,

> An ugly rent in the front row of Bombay's teeth was made with the clenched fist of Capt Speke in Uganda, when his master's patience was worn out, and prompt punishment became necessary . . . months afterwards, I was called upon to administer punishment to him myself. . . .

Speke of course makes no mention of this incident. And although Stanley says he has black friends in America, he himself had Sidi Mubarak flogged on at least two occasions and even put in chains. We should not forget that Sidi, in Stanley's time, was a captain of the caravan, an elderly man—a "mzee." Stanley's attitude, perhaps under stress, reminds one of a slave owner, patronizing yet harsh, the slave's dignity at the hands of the master.

Animal comparisons demean even the most courageous and helpful of the Africans, reflecting perhaps Victorian anthropology; painting Africa in strictly black and white terms catered to the voracious appetites of a public for these accounts of heroic adventures. Twenty-seven years after the East African Expedition, H. Rider Haggard would begin to publish his wildly popular adventure novels set in Africa. At about the same time began the "Scramble for Africa," when much of the continent was portioned off.

11.

The Old Westbound Caravan Route

FRANTIC UBUNGO STATION, early in a Dar es Salaam morning, hums with the growls of a dozen buses arrayed in rows, impatient like hounds to fan out across the country. It's a vast terminus, outside the city; simply to arrive here is an ordeal. But the sheer volume of transport necessitates its location. Vendors weave in and out with their small goods, touts shout their destinations.

"Mwalimu, where are you?" I ask over the cell. "I'm here, Daktari," Joseph informs me, "I've just arrived." I tell him I'm waiting beside our bus and where to find it. Soon I see him approach, pushing through the crowds, a bag on his shoulder, and go to meet him. It's been four years since we last met, in Nairobi, though we've corresponded in the meantime. "Let's have tea," I suggest, "there's still time." We sit down at a tea stall, renew familiarity, and then get on our bus and are soon on our way.

A thrilling feeling, a wonderful excitement, takes hold of us—the sun bright and the air cool, the familiar coastal vegetation rushing by, villages and farms in the midst of their morning rituals, and the wheels rolling on the earth beneath our feet. We're headed west, our cares are behind us, and we chat like schoolboys. The entire country, the entire continent stretches out ahead.

The highway follows the Central Line, the railway built in the years 1905 to 1914 by the Germans. For some reason of convenience the railway headed out straight westwards from Dar, along a sparsely populated plain, instead of following the populous bend of the Ruvu (Kingani) valley, which route the caravans and the European explorers had taken in the past. Burton's "Slough of Despond," the busy station of Zungumero on the caravan route, was therefore bypassed. Instead there grew Morogoro, which if it had existed before was too insignificant to be mentioned by the travellers. Zungumero I cannot find on any map now.

I first travelled on this road in a rattling old green-and-beige Albion with my mother and brother, on our way to Nairobi. I was ten, he twelve. The month was December and schools were out. I had been promised a sea voyage to Mombasa, thence a train to Nairobi, but this road trip was all that proved possible. On the way to Morogoro the bus got mired in a muddy stretch, from which it had to be pushed out with much heave-ho, and we reached the town in the evening, twelve hours after starting out. We had travelled 120 miles. My mother had a cousin in town, so we washed and had dinner at her place before proceeding. On the northern branch road to Kenya the bus got stuck again, but there was another cousin somewhere who fed us. It was a memorable journey, my first one out of Dar; there were giraffes, zebras, deer, and elephants on the way, and I recall being restrained from sticking my head and shoulders out to watch the passing scenery. My brother never knew until the last day that he would be left behind at a "Boarding" in Mombasa on the way back. That changed us all.

Almost all the roads are paved now—thanks to the Chinese—reaching every corner of the country, and the bus terminals are as busy as airports are elsewhere. With efficiency, good roads, and comfortable buses comes another modern development—we don't have to enter the towns we pass. Time is saved, but something surely is lost. We say adieu to Morogoro without entering it, picking up passengers at the terminal outside the town. The Uluguru hills rise in the blue mists in the distance; the earth is red, the sky a trembling translucence in the heat. Past Morogoro we enter the land of the Gogo people; the terrain is flat, the vegetation sparse, thorny and nondescript. This is an arid region, prone to droughts, which is why not very long ago the Gogo would come to Dar in such large numbers to beg at the shops. The Gogo are a tall, lanky people who keep herds by custom. They were a feared people in the nineteenth century; caravans dreaded the prospect of crossing their land, for which they would be subject to heavy hongo, or tax, in the form of cloth, beads, and wire. In 1857, we recall, the Indian businessman Ladha Damji of Zanzibar did not put much stock in Richard Burton's party advancing through this region. Burton says that while neighbouring peoples wrapped themselves in grass or skin, the Gogo proudly wore cloth; many wore leather sandals. They were doing well.

The urban centre of the region is Dodoma. It was made into the nation's capital in 1996. In my childhood the town was known for two things: the nation's best pedas—the Indian sweets—came from Dodoma, made by one or two Indian families; and all the "crazies" went to Dodoma, to the only mental hospital in the country. Dodoma was thus a euphemism for madness. But later, laughable Dodoma became for me a place of very special and vivid memories. I did the military part of my National Service in this area, at a camp just off the highway. Asian youths hated the idea of being forced to go into the jungle immediately after high school, to eat the most rudimentary food and march about aimlessly in the sun—but the experience turned out to be profoundly, positively transforming. It gave us the opportunity to travel into the country and live with young people from different places and backgrounds.

Every National Service camp had its own peculiarities; Ruvu had lions lurking just outside. In Dodoma, a daily horror—until we hardened ourselves to it—was the sight of starving Gogo villagers waiting anxiously for us to finish our meals so they could get the leftovers. Sitting outdoors on the ground, we ate from aluminum mess tins. The moment you stood up, finished with your meal, a bunch of desperate Gogo spectators would come racing towards you, men, women, and children, grandmas, grandpas, and toddlers, arms stretched out, begging for the leftovers. You had to select from the staring faces whom to give your leftovers to. If you lacked the steel to face such a crowd and opted simply to go and throw the remains away in the grass, a crowd of the beggars would make a rush for it: maize meal and beans, boring but healthy food in generous government helpings for city-bred young men and women training to build and defend the nation. Our pathetic audience were skin and bones, barefoot and covered in rags and blankets, their faces unwashed and eyes often diseased. How more memorably awakening could our experience of the nation have been? How more humbling?

There were fun moments too, daring escapes we still talk about, into the town to get away from the camp's rigorous monotony. A few times I asked permission to go to the government hospital and, after the consultation there, would have lunch with a friend at the posh Dodoma Hotel, which I could not really afford. We would arrive here in our military uniforms. There were white tablecloths, the service was formal, and we ate English fare with forks and knives. I had never been to such a place before, but my friend seemed undaunted. She had a tooth problem and a couple of times I feigned that malady to accompany her, and allowed myself to suffer a gratuitous drilling from a rather confused dentist.

We reach Dodoma at 4 p.m. and head for—where else but—the Dodoma Hotel. It is situated at the end of a quiet, shady street away from the town and behind the station, just as I remember it, but evidently has been remodelled since my visits. The rooms, sprayed with insecticide, are good but not luxurious, constructed around a square courtyard at the back. Meals are served mostly in the courtyard, but there is a dining hall towards the front in which I discern the place where I would come for that English lunch.

After a journey of eight and a half hours, having showered, we happily sit down to a few beers and a lavish Indian dinner in the courtyard. There are only a few other guests. The night is cool, the sky above us dark and clear; it is eerily quiet. What we have to beware of are the mosquitoes.

We've hit it off completely, Joseph and I. He's chatty and knowledgeable, with a sense of humour. To come with me he's had to delegate his extensive teaching duties and bear the wrath of his first and the critiques of his second wife. He married the first one when he was only twenty, has two children by her, a boy and a girl. She's kept the boy, "of course," and given him the girl, who is twelve and very close to him; knowing he's away in Dar, probably having fun, the first wife has demanded more money. The second wife is recent and they have a little boy. She too demands more money. "You wonder if it's worth getting married." He has a doctorate in literature from Berlin. When he arrived there first, he says, there was no one to receive him at the airport, everyone he turned to would say words equivalent to "No English" and turn away. He waited for taxis, but all that arrived were Mercedes-Benzes, which he imagined would charge him more. No Toyotas or Nissans! Finally he took a Benz and arrived at the train station. No one to help him get a ticket to Leipzig, where he had to spend the first few months to learn German, until at long last he found a Moroccan worker who helped him. He arrived in Leipzig station in the middle of the night to see a bunch of skinheads busy making a ruckus. He waited nervously at a McDonald's, and when morning came took a taxi to his university department. In four and a half years he was never invited to a colleague's house; he frequented an African bar where he heard all kinds of "narratives," the stories of lonely Africans in Europe. There was a Camerounian who went to Nigeria, crossed the Sahara to Libya, waited until a boat took him to Italy, worked at an orange farm in Spain, walked to Austria, and finally arrived in Munich, where he was immediately arrested and deported. Now he was back.

I have with me a fine storyteller.

It's rained all night and I worry about our journey onwards. The plan is to go to Tabora tomorrow, and then onward to Kigoma and Lake Tanganyika, following the old caravan route. We step out into a quiet, shady street. The morning is cool and dry, pleasant to walk. We are at 3,600 feet above sea level and the sun sets later here than in Dar.

If there was hope that moving the nation's capital to impoverished Dodoma would charm it into a burgeoning city and change its fortunes, this has not happened. Like other purely political capitals, there is the sense of a quiet, tidy dullness, of seasonal activity, which explains why our hotel is almost empty. Parliament is not in session. Dodoma did not exist before colonial times; like Nairobi it is what the railway left behind. But Nairobi prospered.

First thing, we walk up to the bus station. On the way we pass an opulent two-storey white building with a dome, a structure dominating a major intersection. It's the "jamatini," the Khoja prayer house, or khano. One of the cross streets is named Jamatini, so is the dala-dala (bus) stop. A man inside the gates tells me there are about 150 Khoja Ismailis in town. At one time there would have been a thousand. We walk onward, passing a row of young Masai "doctors" from the north, men in traditional red or brown togalike body covers sitting under the trees on the sidewalk, selling local medicines for potency, good luck, and the like—you are shown a printed list of ailments they can cure that is as long as the menu of a Chinese restaurant. Business appears to be not bad.

At the station, we face a dilemma. Kigoma via Tabora, following the caravan route, is a tempting destination. Tabora is the Kazeh of former times. Kigoma is close to Ujiji at Lake Tanganyika, the actual caravan stop and slave market. Opinion is universal among the touts, however, that the road all the way to Kigoma is unpassable due to the rains. We decide to get tickets for Nzega, a three-way junction, and there to decide which direction to turn: north will take us to Mwanza and Lake Victoria; south will take us to Tabora and perhaps, with only the slightest chance, on to Kigoma.

We come back to Jamatini, choose to turn left and head towards the mental hospital. It's a long walk away and finally we arrive at the gate, from which a road leads inside. The hospital grounds are quiet and look well tended; two men guard the gate. A vehicle goes in, a small bus comes out. We have no desire to go inside, and return to Jamatini by taxi.

On the other side of the prayer house is the town's business section. It could not have changed much from when I knew it—a few intersecting streets and moderately busy. There must be a chai place here, I tell Joseph, and he looks surprised. How do I know? Obviously we have enough to learn from each other. Where there are a few Asians, there is a chai place, I explain to him. He's all for it. We ask around and are finally escorted by a young man to a rather small, narrow joint, run by an Asian woman, serving the usual fare: kababs, samosas, bhajias, and chai. We sit down and are served. This food is a revelation to my friend, he's not had it before; soon he'll become addicted to it. But instead of chai he prefers soda.

On our way to Dodoma, at the road stops, boy vendors would come by to the windows offering fried termites for sale. Termites, says Joseph, are a delicacy, raw or fried; in the latter case they taste like chicken. His folk spice them with chilies. He is from the Bukusu, a Bantu people. They live in northwest Kenya by Lake Victoria. Some years ago, he says, a Meru district officer (DO) was sent to their area and created havoc, imposing his alien ways upon them. Driving around in his Land Rover with two bodyguards, he came upon some elders outside the village gorging themselves upon a termite mound, and assumed they were drunk. He arrested them for "loitering with intent"—a grin comes over Joseph's face at the ludicrousness of it, but it's a crime in the books introduced in colonial times, presumably to restrict the Africans to their neighbourhoods. Another time this same Meru DO came upon a gathering of villagers drinking the local brew. The custom is for the youngest wife to sit in front of her husband, between his legs, while he drinks his beer. She's his favourite. The DO was furious, convened a kangaroo court right there, and had an elder whipped. "First you drink illicit alcohol, then on top of that you rascals rape your young women!" There was an uprising and the DO was withdrawn.

We talk about various East African groups, or tribes—the latter a somewhat controversial term because it's associated touchily with colonialism. Scholars consider the Meru to belong to the Bantu group of peoples, but many Meru themselves believe their origins lie in the north, as far as Egypt perhaps or the Near East. Even a Jewish origin has been claimed. They could easily pass off as Somalis or Ethiopians. Their ancient occupation was metalworking, i.e., they are not like the other Bantu, natural tillers of the soil. On linguistic evidence the Bantu appear to have originated in western Africa and dispersed. Secondary dispersals took place more recently, and some tribes in Africa show evidence of this—the Luhya in northeast Kenya are related to the Hehe in central Tanzania, and people even farther south.

I suggest—uncertainly—that the Boers came to South Africa before many of the African peoples did. He agrees emphatically; even before his own people came to Kenya, he says. He's had Afrikaans literature introduced into his university African Literature curriculum. I suppose that coming from a smaller tribe makes him more accepting of differences. His concept of modern Africa is very interesting.

The bunge, the new parliament building, is in a quiet area set off not far from the town centre; designed by a Kenyan firm, it is an impressive structure modelled on the traditional African round hut. The pity is that it's hidden away in a section of a small town where few Tanzanians will happen by to see it. We return to the hotel by a shortcut across the railway tracks.

The new Dodoma University, apparently the previous president's legacy, where we arrive in the afternoon also looks impressive—it's stunning, actually, consisting of a number of white buildings gleaming under the open skies, scattered across a vast plain. Each is a separate department. You can imagine the parking lots of the future, playing fields, commuter buses. The student body has already expanded to 20,000, but Natasha, our host, tells us there are not enough lecturers or books, and there is no easy access to the Internet as yet. Students have to rely on photocopies of texts. Lunch has just been served in the cafeteria of the department where she teaches—History—and the sweet vapours of ubwabwa—steaming local rice—greet us warmly as we enter. We have tea. My lecture has been advertised as "Burton and Speke and the Kutchi Bhatia (and others): The Importance of Telling Stories." The subject of my talk came to mind when I saw a small but lively controversy about the two explorers in the pages of a well-known literary journal, following the publication of a book on John Speke, and I began to wonder about the African angle to the story. In my lecture I make the point that while we have been told so much about the European explorers who passed here, we know little about the local Indians and Africans who made their journeys possible; we have so little recorded history, so few personal accounts from those times. I expand on that: we read over and over about the great men of Europe and America—there must be hundreds of books on Lincoln, not to mention films—yet we know little about our own. We should be telling our own stories. One lecturer reminds me that Tippu Tip, the nineteenth-century slave and ivory trader, did write a biography; another reminds me of the Kilwa Chronicle from the sixteenth century. These exceptions only serve to prove the point. The Chronicle is only a fragment in Arabic, its author unknown; Tippu Tip's is the only Life from these parts and from his time. I produce UN statistics comparing the number of books published in the U.S., U.K., and Tanzania: 206,000, 172,000, and 179. Even though the number for Tanzania is for 1990, whereas the other two are from the mid-2000s, the disparity and its implications are staggering.

When I finish and look around the room, I get the sinking feeling that the students, some fifty in number, have all the time been staring blankly at me. They don't know what I've been talking about. The problem is partly language. They come to university, especially here in rural Dodoma, with only a rudimentary knowledge of English, from places which have not seen libraries—and here I was, speaking of literary journals and the latest books published in England and

America. They are here for a degree with a minimum of fuss, in order to get jobs afterwards. They would rather hear of accounting, computers, business. Abstract issues such as history and culture are not as relevant to them as they were for an older—my—generation, better educated and bred on the rhetoric of idealism—which, these young people would argue, was what held the country back in the first place and why they don't have sufficient English. But surely it should matter to them what the world reads, and especially what it reads about Africa and how it sees Africa on its screens?

Natasha my host is different. Hers is the only Asian face in the hall besides mine, but that's not what makes her seem alien. From Dar es Salaam, the daughter of a university professor and one of the country's leading intellectuals, she went to high school in Botswana and university in Canada. She's small and strikingly delicate-featured, but a sophisticate, earnest and serious, though perhaps with a tendency to trip into jargon. She's young yet. I imagine her scaling her chosen mountain: teaching with passion, poring over books she's ordered with her own money, copying chapters for her students to give them the latest and best in political and historical theory, organizing seminars. She lives by herself in a university-supplied apartment. She was on the same bus as us coming in from Dar, her father having come to drop her off. It was a touching sight. She could have taken a plane. While she teaches she's waiting to join a doctoral program somewhere, her proposed subject the traditional modes of conflict resolution in Somalia. All this enthusiasm in a world in turmoil makes one want to be young again, until I recall the silent phalanx of students I had just spoken to.

After the lecture we have tea at her place, where she serves us the traditional Indian fare sent to her by her parents. She talks of rethinking the state, and I wonder what that means practically. Joseph is smitten.

We leave early the next morning for Nzega.

His life—"sansar," an Indian might call it—pursues him over the phone, each of his wives demanding more money. He has yet to find a way to send a course outline for his students in Nairobi, he's not found an Internet service that works. He promised too rashly, I think, to accompany me, though I'm sure he finds it rewarding. I feel a bit guilty, though. My own phone's suddenly quit on me.

We speak in a mixture of Swahili and English; he speaks with passion and humour, doesn't judge, just states. He's a joy to be with.

He tells me of his experience as a teacher in Somalia, where he worked two years for a Norwegian NGO, which took him there. There was skimming at the top—he signed for more money than he received, and he describes his amazement at seeing the ultra-posh residences of his superiors in Nairobi. The flight back and forth from Nairobi to Djeberra was on an old Russian plane, the seats coming loose, the co-pilot tipsy as he wandered up and down the aisle in singlet, the Somalis shouting at each other at the tops of their voices, from one end to the other. It's a scene easy to picture and laugh at. The senior members of the NGO used a better airline, he adds.

He describes a scene:

In a class, outdoors, while he's speaking on a point of grammar, a student raises his left hand (the right hand is used to ask for permission to go to the toilet) and stands up, and asks, "Sir, do you know what to do when you are walking and a plane is dropping bombs?" A nonplussed Joseph says, "No—what?" "You stand up still and don't move—and they will think you are a tree."

There were many instances of battle-shocked young men; places where there were only boys and old men, the young men having gone away abroad to send remittances or having been killed. When the Americans put the squeeze on the hawala system of remittance, a large number of people were left without money. British and Italian companies dropped tons of toxic waste near the Somali coast, poisoning the fish, Natasha says as we discuss Somali piracy.

The world from here looks different. CNN is far away.

The ride from Dodoma to Nzega is so smooth and speedy that we feel exhilarated; surely nothing can impede us on this trip. The landscape is vast and flat, a sparse bush country, except for a short, very hilly stretch, and a scattering of tors—heaps of grey boulders. These are the granite protuberances that both Speke and Burton mention. We see maharage (bean) patches here and there, which supply the food staple, taking advantage of the recent rain. It surprises Joseph that there is so much empty land in the country. In Kenya, he says, where land is scarce, all of this would have been distributed and planted; the stone boulders of the tors would have been cut up and carted away for building. That's why, I remind him, the Tanzanians are nervous about a free market with Kenya. Kenyans are aggressive and greedy.

The huts in this Gogo country are rectangular and flat-topped with thatch. Soon we see them with V-shaped roofs, and presumably we have left Gogo country; the people are darker. It is ironic, I observe, that the Gogo, who seemed to fill the European explorers with trepidation (Stanley called them "a powerful race" and "ferocious"), are now seen begging. What a twist of fate, Joseph replies. The Masai, he adds—and here do I trace a shade of schadenfreude?—once feared from central Kenya down to the Serengeti, and perhaps the reason why the slave routes did not pass through Kenya, have been reduced to working as watchmen and taking up hair-braiding, which they are good at; you can see them at bus stations practising this trade. As he says this we are observing, in a town bus station, a Masai walking about with a stick and a red blanket over his shoulder, and a Gogo standing erect, leaning on a stick, wearing a black blanket. Both men lean and angular, handsome. The town is Singida, fairly busy and well known; several of my Asian high-school classmates came from here.

We left Dodoma at six and arrive at Nzega at eleven feeling happy and positive. But it's now that our troubles begin.

Nzega is a busy way station, a T-junction with no other character to speak of, with one road leading off north to Mwanza, another south to Tabora. One paved, the other bovu—rotten—as they say; on one side the Sukuma people, on the other the Nyamwezi, both major tribes. Which direction to pick? Our bus takes its place alongside others, waiting before a row of stalls and chai shops, all under a red metal roof painted with large white Coca-Cola signs. Vendors sell fruit and soft drinks from their carts, and an exuberance of coloured small cottons, plastic travellers' bags, and knickknacks, all made in China. There is the ubiquitous cell-phone kiosk, bright and adrift at the edge of the station, a link to the world. We pick a place to have our snack. And after that begins a frantic search for a suitable bus.

Touts and agents abound. The choice is still between the uncertainty of the Tabora road and the safety of the Mwanza one. We decide to risk it and buy tickets for a Tabora-bound at 1:30 p.m.; but when we push through a crowd to claim our seats, we find that they've been double-booked. After a heated argument with the present occupants, we get off, defeated, and demand a refund. We wander around. A number of buses have now left and suddenly the choices have diminished. One bus, undergoing much repair, has painted on its back an angry, oversize José Mourinho, the charismatic coach of the Real Madrid soccer club, berating someone. We resign ourselves to missing Tabora and pick a bus bound for Mwanza. It would be nice now just to sit down and arrive somewhere. It's hot and dusty and we're tired. But at the last minute the Mwanza driver decides to mend a puncture. Meanwhile the two agents who first sold us Tabora, feeling guilty, have found us another Tabora bus, ready to depart. We take credit for the Mwanza ticket and follow them to a waiting bus, where we find excellent seats behind the driver. It's too good to be true, and surely enough all are asked to get down, the bus has to go for servicing. Another hour passes while we wait outside the tea stalls. We've become a fixture, Joseph and I, earning pitying looks and sympathetic commentary from onlookers. Most of the buses have gone, but Mourinho has not budged, we wonder what ails him. Finally our bus returns, we sit down, and it begins to fill, and fill. Packed, it drives out slowly from the station, and our hearts leap with joy, we grin at each other. But rounding a corner, it stops again. The driver jumps out. More people squeeze in, the aisle is packed right up to where sits the new driver, a calm elderly man in a kofia. We depart finally at 4:30 p.m.

The old driver seems to know his potholes and drives expertly and carefully. The countryside is denser than before, scattered abundantly with mango trees of a short variety with spherical crowns. Houses are intermittently strewn about next to the road. Men sitting around doing nothing, waiting for the sun to go down. It's a strange sign of muted life: no market, no children, no cattle, no electricity. Inexplicably, after two hours the driver stops in the middle of nowhere, "kuchimba dawa," dig for medicine—a pit stop. No one asked for it. Some fifty people clamber out, get back inside. The babies, having woken up, start hollering.

The driver looks uncertain about the road now, and for some reason he has his grandson, a little boy, next to him in his seat. An hour later he stops again, for his own convenience. The sun has set, and it's now obvious that he cannot see well anymore, since he tends to drive over the potholes. The bus has become quiet, the babies are settled. The headlights beam on a partially wet and streaky road ahead, not easy to follow in the dark—a slight distraction in our captain could land us inside a ditch. The conductor, in the seat across, eyes fixed ahead on the road, begins to signal warnings of approaching road bumps by stretching out an arm or banging his hand on the dashboard. We pass a distressed bus pulled over on the side, the passengers spilled out. The young woman next to Joseph on the other side informs him that those people would not spend the night on the highway for fear of witchcraft. There's a lot of superstition in Tabora, where she herself finished high school. Finally, a few electric lamps ahead on the road. It's close to nine when we arrive at the Tabora bus station.

The sight of the meagre settlements on the Tabora road have turned Joseph thoughtful. We are, essentially, on the old slave route. He wonders if the pathetic, reduced state of human life we see reflects the devastation of the slave trade. He is reminded of his own village, which was divided into families along functional lines—shopkeeping, plumbing, carpentry, harvesting, auctioning. There would be a central place for people to gather. There would be children around, and cattle. His area, as much of Kenya, never saw the slave trade.

Am I surprised that the slave trade, on this old slave route, is the ghost we carry on our journey?

There is something pleasant about Tabora, a sense of quiet settledness, a certain self-containment. It was a vital stop on the old east–west caravan route, and is one of the few towns in the country that can be found in the old, precolonial maps. Yet it has hardly any recent urban development. You wouldn't call it pretty—there's no river flowing through it, there are no hills to modulate the landscape, though mango trees abound. Tabora's problem today—why it appears physically neglected, as though development suddenly halted sometime in the 1970s, why you can now go to Mwanza or Kigoma (Ujiji) without stopping here (as you once did)—has to do with national politics, as our taxi driver the next day affirms. Chief Abdallah Fundikira of the Nyamwezi—this is traditionally their territory—had run afoul of the ruling national party, TANU, and founded his own party. He lost, and as a result Tabora was punished. None of the roads leading in and out is paved, therefore during the long rainy season the town is rendered into an island of sorts. But help is on the way now, the Chinese will soon come to build the roads.

At independence Chief Fundikira became a cabinet minister in the new government. Soon after, he was tried for receiving bribes from two Indian merchants in a celebrated court case, an incident which today reeks of politics, for rarely if ever is an eminent politician tried for bribery, let alone for anything else. The two Indians pled guilty, perhaps expecting leniency, but were given the maximum sentence of two years in jail and twenty-four lashes. The chief, however, fought the case using East Africa's most prominent criminal lawyer, Byron Georgiadis of Nairobi, and was acquitted. As Fundikira emerged from the court, he was greeted by a large number of his supporters. I happened to be one of those standing outside the courthouse to witness that hectic scene, a misfit surely, but I had followed the case in our daily newspaper, my interest piqued perhaps from having read too many Perry Mason paperbacks.

The centre of Tabora consists of a main street, on one side of which are a busy bus stand and a large open-air market. The former Indian quarter lies on the other side of the street, with its typical commercial strip. Here, prominently, is the Jamatini, the Khoja khano looking very similar to the one in Dodoma and built during the same euphoric era. Tabora was an important Islamic as well as administrative centre, and the old German boma lies a short drive away from the main street. It's used by the army now, and to get through the gate one must have permission. I tell the adjutant at the gate that I did my National Service some years ago, expecting a favour. He bids us formally to a conference room nearby and in sombre tones asks for our details, including my NS number, which of course I do not have. Suddenly I am reminded of the hair-raising bureaucracy of old, which I have not experienced in decades, and Joseph senses something similar; we eye each other across the large table, dutifully give our names and cell numbers, and depart in a hurry, hoping not to hear from the army. We head out of town towards "Livingstone."

Says our driver, there's not a single white man who leaves his country and doesn't come to see "Livingstone." We, however, have not seen a single white man in town. And the driver doesn't really know who Livingstone was; in his mind, he was some white man who lived at the time of his father. On the way we pass a large but plain white house that belonged to Chief Fundikira, where he is also buried. The driver is chatty, and since on our bus coming in we were told of superstitions and witchcraft in the area, we ask him, "Kuna uganga hapo?" Is there witchcraft here? The answer is strongly in the affirmative.

—*Eh. There is uganga. There are those who do it. They have the knowledge. They can solve problems.*

At our piqued interest, he deflects our query about local practice, but is happy to tell us about elsewhere.

—*But the real ones are in Kigoma. And Sumbawanga. The Waha [people] and the Fipa. They can point a finger at you, and you won't be able to get up. Those guys are more powerful than those of Tanga . . . These ones here [in Tabora], they're deceivers only. Wajanja tu.* Tricksters, amateurs.

He goes on.

—*They [the Kigoma and Sumbawanga magicians] can solve anything. Disease. Business problems. If you want to get rich.*

They can make you rich?

—*They can make you rich. But there are conditions.*

What conditions?

—*They can ask you to kill a dear one. Your child. Or you have to agree to kill your mother.*

And they go after albinos?

—*No albinos in Tabora. But in Sumbawanga they go after albinos. That's what they are good at—magic.*

Have you been to a mganga?

—*No.*

Which cannot be true, surely. But with the slightest nudging, the man has come out in a long spiel, a noticeable nervous edge to him as he speaks. Only recently the albino murders by sorcerers drew a spotlight on the country (though not enough), so that even the president was called upon to condemn it.

"Livingstone" is off the main road, at the end of a rough unpaved trek through lush farmland scattered generously with mango trees, a long, red house with a veranda and a yard in front. The locality is called Kwihira. Stanley was welcomed to this house by a Tabora Arab, Sheikh Syed bin Salim, in 1871 when he first arrived here from the coast, bound for Ujiji on his search for Livingstone. He immediately raised an American flag on its roof.

At the time Tabora boasted some five thousand souls. The eminent citizens of the town were Omani Arabs who wore long white kanzus and caps, and considerably impressed Stanley, and Burton before him, with their grace and generosity. They lived opulently, their houses boasting Persian carpets, beautiful carved doors, and harems. Musa Mzuri was dead when Stanley arrived; the Arabs and their allies were at war with Mirambo, a Nyamwezi warlord who, having united several tribes of the region, now controlled the caravan routes, including the one that went west to Ujiji. Stanley calls him the "African Bonaparte," and also a robber. In vivid detail he describes a battle in which he himself took part on the side of the Arabs and their allies, who, however, after several victories fled ignominiously at the first setback, an ambush by Mirambo. Two weeks later, from Kwihira, Stanley watched Tabora going up in flames.

Stanley found a way to continue on his journey west via a southern route. He found Livingstone at Ujiji, and the two of them explored Lake Tanganyika together before undertaking a rain-soaked journey to Tabora, where Sheikh Salim welcomed Stanley again. A plaque on the outside wall of the house says that Livingstone and Stanley stayed here during February to March 1873; a smaller notice says that Burton and Speke were in Tabora in November 1857. The Arab house where they stayed, however, had been destroyed when Stanley arrived. It is from here, while Burton stayed behind, that Speke made an expedition to Lake Victoria and was inspired to call it the source of the Nile.

Stanley bid Livingstone farewell and departed for the coast on March 14, 1873. Livingstone proceeded west towards the south of Lake Tanganyika, where he died.

There's a museum inside the house, but the caretaker is away at his farm. We return to town.

Back in Tabora we ask around for old houses, ruins, places where the Arabs of old might have lived. Nobody knows about them. There is utter confusion: the past? what past? Livingstone—they tell you—have you been there? We've been there. Did you go to Fundikira? We saw it. Nothing more. We are stumped. Such an old town and yet no sense of its past, which is substantial. There is talk of "Nyamwezi" Arabs and Indians, but we don't see them. Tabora's history has been entirely erased.

Now Joseph informs me that the girl who sat beside him in the bus had asked him, "Why are you interested in those people who put us in chains?"

It's a profound thought. In one's quest for history, in one's obsession with the past, one forgets that there are those who would rather keep it buried. But is that good enough? In the part of the world where I now come from, time is allowed to take its course, and history is revered as record. It is there to teach us about ourselves. Scholarship provides contexts, nuances, altering points of view to learn from. The past is never simply black and white, after all, never entirely good and bad, us and them, victory and defeat. And received memory is too often corrupted.

There must be a chai shop.

After making some inquiries, we find it in the local residential area, a ramshackle storefront run by a middle-aged Khoja couple; there's a counter, four small tables with chairs, a soda fridge. A long corridor leads into the interior where the kitchen and the living quarters are. The sight of us is a wonder for them, but they don't ask who we are. We sit down and are served samosas and bhajias, chai and soda. I see from the written menu on a board that they serve full meals too, and after consulting with Joseph I inform the owners that we will return for our dinner.

Tabora looks like Dar's Kariakoo. A shop in the same row as the chai shop is run by two women, partly Arab, where we go in and banter and bargain, and I come away with a khanga. We cross the main road towards the bus station and find a water-tank shop, a bicycle shop, a spare-parts shop, all of which indicate a cash economy and money. The mode of public transport is the bicycle: you get on one and are taken to your destination. There's a pleasing openness and casual pace to the town, it does not depend on tourists and NGOs. Islam is a presence, but not aggressively so. Our hotel is at the end of a trail on a dirt road, but comfortable and modern, and locally owned; the other guests are local businessmen. On the radio Bongo Flava vies with Swahili taarab. *Bang!* is a music program on TV, with the expected rap and dancing on hormones, the accents shamelessly Americanized, but I saw an interesting clip with tall lanky dudes wearing kanzus and kofias, Islamic style, swaying to music, and women with heads covered with khanga—tongue-in-cheek and stylishly original. Very confident.

The thought occurs that it's music where the creative energies of the country are focused; not in Swahili poetry anymore, unfortunately; and not writing in English, which is too postured thus far.

In the evening we go to that Khoja chai place to have dinner. The couple is out praying at the khano two streets away, and a son is at the till, so we sit down and have bhajias. At a little past eight the couple return and the woman says she can make chicken curry and rice. And roti?—I ask. Yes, with a smile. And in a little while it comes, the chicken tender, the curry tasting as it did back home, long ago in Dar. Now the lady gives vent to her curiosity. (Her husband has gone on inside, the son remains with her.) She has to know. Are you Hindu or Ismaili? she asks. I no longer make these distinctions, but she would not understand. Ismaili, I tell her. We too. I could tell from the photo on the wall, I tell her. She's from Gujarat, a place called Jam-something. Near Jamnagar? Yes. My grandmother came from Jam Jodhpur. Yes, it's close by, she says. She stayed in Dar until ten years ago, for her two daughters' education; now one of them, having attended Muhimbili Hospital, is a doctor at the Aga Khan Hospital, the other works at Standard Bank. The son, I notice, is dark and slim; the woman calls out to his wife, a petite young woman who appears from inside. She's from Bombay, speaks Hindi. (The woman and family speak Kutchi with themselves, Gujarati with me.) They have relations in Toronto. When I've finished, she invites me to wash my hands inside—it's her way of inviting me to her home. I walk inside to a Swahili-style structure—long corridor and rooms on either side. At the back is a dining and sitting space, where her husband and daughter-in-law sit watching TV—one of those Indian soaps that are universally popular. I go through a swinging storm door and wash my hands in a sink. She gives me a towel. Joseph and I depart. I don't even know her name, I tell my friend half in despair, when we're outside.

It's been a moving experience, my own tribal connection, in a dark little Swahili gulley in a little town in Tanzania; and that modesty and simplicity, that mutuality. It's my inspiration.

And yet the thought lingers: why didn't she invite Joseph inside? I was family, he wasn't.

He says that following his circumcision rites at fourteen, he was considered a man. During these rites he was given knowledge of what it meant to be a Bukusu. This was a kind of self-awareness. Now his mother treated him differently, and he had a say over decisions regarding his sisters. For example, in the absence of his father, he could refuse permission to his elder sister to go to a dance, and he did not have to help in the kitchen. Among coastal people, he says, there is a similar rite for girls, in which the instructions imparted cover the subject of sex. Both the novelists Ngugi and Achebe have treated the subject and its conflict with Christianity in their works.

—

At five in the morning we emerge from our hotel into the cool darkness, avoiding muddy potholes. A light wind blows. It's rained in the night and we worry about the onward journey. I recall from my reading that it was the rains that detained Speke and Grant here for weeks. We find our bus, put our bags on our seats, and go wait outside. There seems to be only one other bus preparing to leave at this dawn hour. People slowly trickle into the station, a tout goes around, selling tickets. The sun is rising, the food booths are only now stirring, but there is no hope of tea yet. Tabora keeps to its own pace.

Our bus, an old thing with worn seats, leaves sharply at six. It is not overfull, for which we are thankful. It takes a different, longer route than the one we came on, the road corrugated but not as bad. But very evidently something else is different about this route. It's the vegetation we're passing—burrowing—through, unlike anything I've seen before. Pure, dense jungle, varieties of trees and bushes—thorn, broad-leaved, soft wood, hard wood, short, very tall, some with wonderfully unique shapes—all arranged in a disorder whose intelligence only nature could tell in its bid for coexistence. No mango trees, which one recalls are an import after all. This must be the original African forest. Intermittent foot trails meander off into the dense interior. What kind of people would live in such isolation? The only sign of them are the wooden boxes placed intermittently up the trees, roughly two cubic feet in size, to grow beehives. Once or perhaps twice this dark wooded scene suddenly breaks into a burst of light and a human settlement comes into view by the roadside—huts, corn patches, people, and a scattering of mango trees. The mango tree in this region has a distinct crown, almost perfectly spherical and producing an equally perfect round shade. A mango tree prominently marks the centre of a village, gives form to it, for it is the meeting place. We observe a large meeting of women under a tree. After this relief, the forest again.

Thus, life flourishing, in glorious abundance and variety, oblivious of the sometimes unbearable euphoria of the metropolis.

Finally, near the end of the forest a notice appears, barely visible, written on a weathered, wooden board nailed to a tree, stating what's become obvious, that we've passed a protected area. Now there occur frequent brief stops for pickups and drop-offs; our bus seems to have a complete monopoly on this route. A woman in niqab gets in. A Somali perhaps, but who can tell? A rooster comes on board, and its owner ties its leg to a seat with a long string. It edges down the rows, stealing legroom, and gets prodded gently but firmly forward, the owner sitting conveniently unaware in front.

We arrive in Nzega at around twelve, sore and hungry. The stop is brief, and we have to rush through our chai and chapati (me) and samosas (Joseph). There is an unexpected delay because a policewoman at a checkpoint seizes our driver's licence, before a negotiation releases it.

We are on our way again, this time on tarmac. There occurs now on the landscape, which is otherwise plain, a proliferation of those rock formations called tors. Only here they are spectacular, the elements having contrived to shape them to look precariously, miraculously balanced, one on top of the other. Occasional baobab trees and the ubiquitous mango. Corn seems to be the most common crop, and the population is the most we have seen since Tabora. We pass an innocuous wooden sign for a gold mining company; since there is concern about working conditions at the mines and the pitiful royalties paid to the country, the near-anonymity seems explainable.

Mwanza hits us with a burst of colour and activity—a huge clothes market outside the city, festooned with shirts, pants, dresses, and bedcovers spread out on the ground or hanging on stands. Hotels and guest houses are abundantly advertised; presumably out-of-towners can shop without having to go into the city. There's money here, Joseph says approvingly. The bus stop comes shortly.

Our taxi driver is a man from Kigoma, and moreover from the Wahaa people, famous as those especially skilled in the dark arts. He agrees, in Kigoma there is a lot of magic—uganga—though he hasn't had occasion to come across it. Naturally. Now see how he contradicts himself. Once, he says—the chatterbox unable to resist—he almost got killed. He had picked up an elderly gentleman along with a woman. When she got off, the man immediately brought out his "mguu wa kuku"—chicken leg. A gun, explains Joseph to me with a nod. This was a stickup. Our plucky driver tried out his luck: He said, Go ahead, shoot me, then see what happens to your bullets and to you. Can you see who I am? Do you know where I come from? The bandit could tell, and realizing his error, began to tremble and plead: Come on now, let me go. The driver turned his car around and drove straight to the police station, and ended up receiving a lot of cash from the terrified bandit.

The point of course is not the veracity of the story but the casual belief in witchcraft. The driver, we have noticed, does have distinct features—very dark skin, narrow shaved head—which might have convinced the bandit, if he was real, that he was in the presence of someone special, possibly with "elimu"—knowledge—or access to it.

Mwanza easily distinguishes itself by the number of hotels and restaurants, the new buildings. This is a wealthy city, founded upon an old town. Gold mines are to the south of here, and there is fish in the lake. Smuggled gold has always made a good contribution to the economy. The main thoroughfare is Nyerere Road, starting from the lake and heading into a business section whose old one-storey buildings, going back to the 1930s, remind one of Nairobi's Indian Bazaar. The businesses on this street are still owned by Asians. Farther up, next to the former Lohana Community Hall, the Lohana Hindus having presumably departed en masse, is the Khoja khano, behind a gate inside a large compound. It is an old, distinguished structure, spoilt somewhat by a misfit dome, a crude later addition to give it—one supposes—a more Islamic look. On the street, traffic is brisk; a distinct feature are the three-wheeler short-haul trucks for hire to carry small loads. The dominant mode of public transport consists of the numerous bodabodas, the single-passenger motorcycles. With only the driver wearing a helmet, the ride seems daunting.

Our hotel is a modern though modest building of some six floors in the residential area behind Nyerere Road; to reach it we have to negotiate through a bustling open market occupying two full blocks of a side street. At first we avoid it, for fear of being sucked into the mass of a clamourous consuming humanity and falling prey to a pickpocket or something. Now we easily walk through, mesmerized by the clamour and clash of colours and sounds, the variety of goods on display. I make a list: blue jeans spread out in piles, in a quantity greater perhaps than at any Walmart; T-shirts, dresses, shorts; shoes, suitcases, backpacks, handbags; leather belts and wallets; kitchen items and knickknacks—almost all brought from China, the wholesale merchants travelling all the way to Guangdong to purchase their stuff. And then there are the foods on sale: fruits, vegetables, onions, ginger, popcorn, peanuts, sodas, mishkaki (skewered meat), bread. A dozen small buses wait to fill up, loudspeakers shout announcements, music blares out. I spot a CHADEMA (opposition party) flag outside a stall. This is CHADEMA city.

Upon a rise at the corner of two busy roads, a woman in her thirties, her head covered loosely with a khanga, sits intently before a blazing charcoal stove. She's selling kahawa and sweet bhajias. May we have some coffee? we ask jovially, and she says, Have a seat. We go and sit down on a low wobbly bench for two. Three children are at play nearby, two boys and a girl. It's midafternoon, school must be out. A young man goes around with a birika—kettle—pouring coffee for the various customers—the fruit vendors at the sidewalk who shout their orders out, the shopkeepers across the two streets who send theirs by text. The woman, the children playing around her, mock-fighting with karate kicks, chasing and complaining, singing—"*A goat eats only up to the length of its rope*"—reminds me of my own mother making ends meet at another busy intersection, in a business very different but not more profitable; we always hung around her after school. The price of coffee here? Three little cups for 100 shillings; similar coffee at a tourist hotel, 1,500 shillings or more. Per cup.

But they don't seem to care for chai in Mwanza. It's difficult to find a chai shop, yet surely there must be one? After much inquiry, including cornering a nervous-looking young man sitting on a sidewalk, who replies in English to us and turns out to be an illegal Bangladeshi, we find a rather small "chai" shop called Harish Paan. It serves vegetable samosas, kachoris, bhajias, and "mix" (a version of bhel) over the counter, and is run by an elderly Gujarati couple, the wife sitting at the till by the door. It is a popular place, people come in and go out, mostly men, and the food is cooked elsewhere close by and brought in as needed, since there are no cooking facilities in this narrow space. There are no tables either, just tall stools behind the counter and against a wall. And there is no chai, only soda. The couple are alone, the children have grown up and gone away.

"Thank you, Mama," says Joseph in Swahili as we leave.

"Welcome again, my son," she replies.

What a long way we have come.

On our way back to the hotel through the street market, over a radio blaring music, a Jeep announcing a political meeting over a loudspeaker, we suddenly hear a burst of shouting and cheering from behind the shops and curiously walk into an alley towards the source, and come to a dead end where a man sits at a small table. We are told to pay a fee to go and watch mpira—soccer. It's Saturday afternoon and the English Premier League is on. We pay and enter a long, dark shed, the air thickly pungent with the reek of male human odour and electric with a palpable excitement. Three simultaneous live games are being watched on three TVs by some two hundred men seated in rows on chairs and free with their commentaries and rejoinders. "Give it the boot!" "Go forward, you!" "I told you!" "Now will we listen to you or watch the games?" There are judgment calls, shouts of joy and frustration. A wonderfully raucous atmosphere, the sheer joy of watching football, but at one thousand shillings a ticket this is expensive entertainment for most. But the TVs are flat and wide-screen. How the three matches are mentally processed by the audience is a wonder. They must all have their favourite teams. And there can be no question, Sir Alex Ferguson, Manchester United's manager, is better known than the British prime minister or the Queen.

Passing through the bustling market, Joseph speaks of the "discourse on Africa" in the West. All around us here is abundance of life, moments of joy—which is not to deny there are problems elsewhere. But why don't they show this side of Africa, the sheer exuberance that can also be here? It was impossible for his German colleagues and teachers to accept this idea. Their view of Africa as abjectly poor and starving was unshakeable.

The Sukuma, the predominant tribe in Mwanza, he explains, are short and dark; they have a flattish nose, curved up front. They are related to his own people the Bukusu in Kenya. As we walk around, I look for confirmation of his statement without seeming obvious. The variety in the people we have seen has been a thing of wonder for me ever since we left on this journey; Africans are not simply "Africans"; they are as diverse as Indians. I think, not for the first time, how insular we Asians were, how little we cared to know about the lives of the people among whom we lived. Not that the Africans were aware of the nuances of Asian existence either. Once a Tanzanian African said to me, "I didn't know Asians could have hard lives too."

Says Joseph—

His father would not come to his home, doesn't know where the son lives. No, they have not quarrelled, this is according to custom. He is an adult, has been initiated. Joseph himself would never live with his in-laws, even as a visitor. At his initiation he was instructed that he should see his in-laws at most once a year. When his wife came with him to his father's home, she had to use the neighbour's washroom, even if that meant knocking on the door of an irate man at 3 a.m. For his part Joseph, in this traditional setting, would not get on the same bus as his mother-in-law, even if that meant spending the night at a way station.

But times are changing. According to Kenya customary law, property was inherited only by the male heirs. But the new constitution, which was ratified recently by a majority, is more equitable. There is a palpable excitement in Kenya, Joseph says, people feel it: "Not only are we facing the right direction, we are moving towards it." It's thrilling to be living in Kenya now, which is why he returned from overseas. He supports the incursion of Kenya into southern Somalia, it's supported by the vast majority of people, according to polls. Blood is collected, food sent to families of fallen soldiers. This is an issue over which all sections of the country are united.

The six-storey hotel has a reachable roof terrace, from which the entire city is visible. Mwanza sits in a basin, surrounded by hills and Lake Victoria. It's surprisingly cool and dry in the morning. When I look immediately down at the street below, with its quiet pace of habitation and business, I am reminded again of Uhuru Street in Kariakoo, Dar es Salaam, as it was a long time ago. In fact there is an Uhuru Street nearby and it goes all the way to the lake. The street I am on is Rufiji Street, another Kariakoo name. On the hotel's other side is Nyerere Road; the Khoja khano is clearly visible, with its fake dome.

Later that afternoon we sit for kahawa at our favourite spot, on that shaky wooden bench for two. The corner, we now know, is called the Victoria Hotel Annexe. A troupe of African women in full hijab cross the road purposefully, leaving in their wake a whiff of sweet fragrance. We watch the men bantering with each other, the boys playing; we discuss the meaning of happiness and contentment.

Two men loose on the road—Joseph and I—without those worldly attachments, at least for now, which in Indian spiritual thought go by the name *sansara,* we find ourselves in an atmosphere, a rhythm of sound and life in which we seem utterly at ease. Should I feel a hypocrite, deluded, when I actually live in Canada in a comfort and safety these three children before me can only dream about? I don't. Living in Toronto has its own insecurities, with a fractured being and an in-betweenness that draws me into thoughts such as these, sitting on this corner on a wobbly bench, stifling my euphoria and questioning my belongingness. In Toronto I would ask myself, Am I a real Canadian? What is such a thing? And I would pull out my hyphens.

A young man sitting nearby shouts out to a friend across the street, where there's a strip of shops and a cluster of vendors. "You, Memedi's father!" Memedi's father, in a white T-shirt, looks away as though he's not heard. The men around me laugh. Joseph explains: for Memedi's father, a young man, to admit that he's a father would spoil his chances of hitting on prospective women. Call someone "Mama Rehema!" and she's likely to mutter, "Keep it low. Rehema only."

"Does that mean that philandering is common outside of marriage?"

"Rampant." He grins.

I wonder if that explains his mysterious disappearances some nights. I don't ask. Polygamy, of course, was the order of the day traditionally. Mainstream Churches have been losing support due to their interference in private lives, Joseph says.

Over beer in the hotel patio that night, we get into the giggles. It's time for father jokes.

When he graduated from university, Joseph says, his father proudly took him to the village baraza (meeting) of elders and asked him to give a speech. Joseph began to speak in Bukusu, to his father's chagrin. "Speak big words!" the dad scolded. "What did I send you to school for?" He himself would utter things like, "To your great comportment, I say with much alacrity . . ." And the elders, sitting around, stuffing tobacco into their noses, would look at each other and exclaim with satisfaction, "Educated! Educated!"

There was the time when a young man who had found work in Kisumu, some distance away, would send a three-page letter in English to his father, who couldn't read. A boy would therefore come on a bicycle to Joseph's father with the letter to have it read and translated. Joseph's father, without a qualm, would take out his pen and make corrections and add commentary to the letter, before giving it back with his personal interpretation to the boy to take home.

He had been a liberal as a young man, worked in Nairobi, got married out of tribe to a Kikuyu. He did not believe in religion. His wife, however, had been a staunch Catholic, her family had been among the first to convert. After retiring, back in the village, contemplating inevitable death, the pull of ritual stirred inside the old man. And so he married a young woman thirty years his junior, from his own tribe, who would undergo the traditional rites with him that were required of the elderly. He wore charms. He had two "pure" kids with her, who would perform the required rites for him when he died.

We have excellent lake fish for dinner at the hotel. The next morning we walk at the lakeshore. The area is surprisingly quiet and tidy. Across the road are some expensive homes. There is a mysterious stone monument at the shore, with its brass plaque and inscription removed; the screw holes are still visible. What could have caused the removal, rendering this memorial anonymous? Politics? Theft? Could this be where John Speke stood when he first came to Mwanza and declared the vast lake before him as the source of the Nile? Bobbing on the water are two modern ferry boats that do not run anymore, having been declared unsafe. A conventional ferry comes in and spills out passengers from one of the nearby islands. Across the lake, to my left is the town of Bukoba, where I did the initial (farming) part of my National Service at the age of nineteen, where we worked on a banana plantation, marched and sang and learned discipline, and washed our uniforms and bathed in an ice-cold stream at the end of the day. Across the lake on the right is Musoma, where some of my friends went for their Service, and from where the best ghee used to come to us in Dar. Nyerere's birthplace is not far from there either. One of the largest islands on the lake is Ukerewe, straight ahead. We inquire about times and fares. As I stand at the shore, looking out, I am sorely tempted: out there are Bukoba, Musoma, Ukerewe; and Kisumu in Kenya, where I visited a rich aunt once; and Kampala in Uganda, where I went on a high school trip. Not long after that came Idi Amin. If I went to Kampala, I could return to Dar via Kisumu and Nairobi. How long would that take? But then Joseph, standing a little behind me, tells me in a quiet voice, "Daktari, I think we've gone far enough. We should go back."

And so we go look for a bus back to Dar.

The bus we take early the next morning is from a company called Dar Luxe. It is new and fast, and the seatbelts are a good idea, considering the driving. We reach Ubungo station at ten in the night, sixteen hours after departure. I decide to spend the night at a joint in Sinza, outside Dar, where Joseph usually puts up. There's an open-air bar outside where we have a meal; it's fairly crowded even this late, and a dubbed Chinese soap opera is avidly watched on the TV.

The next morning we take a dala-dala to the city. I put away my luggage in my hotel room and we decide to tour the city—a certain part of it. We trek along Uhuru Street, reach Mehboob Mansion where I grew up—the intersection is surprisingly intact, in spite of the heavy new construction—take the stairs up to the roof terrace on the third floor. I point out a hole in the chimney made by the fire brigade when they came to dispose of the large beehive that had grown inside. Perhaps the bees were drawn to the terrace by my sister's potted jasmine plants. We look down over the boundary wall at the length of Uhuru Street, the aorta of my imagination. I point below at the shops and at the apartments across, tell him about the people who lived and worked there. We then come down and proceed to Msimbazi Street, treat ourselves to cane juice on the way. The entire Kariakoo area has now the feel of an Old Delhi, teeming with people and with every sort of merchandise spilling onto the sidewalks.

We end up at KT Shop, where he simply devours the daal bhajia, kababs, and samosas, saying, "Daktari, I could become a Tanzanian simply for the food." His second wife, a Tanzanian, always complains that Kenyans are far too thin, they don't eat well.

We then say goodbye. He'll be on the plane to Nairobi tomorrow.

What do I recall of this journey?

I picture a vast land, beginning with the familiar coastal plain—green, with large trees, packed villages—ending at the Uluguru Mountains and a bustling Morogoro, then the endless plateau: sparely inhabited, sparsely covered with thorn and bushes, short trees, the occasional baobabs, the mangoes at settlements; small clusters of huts; some subsistence farming. The semi-arid land has grown a green cover due to unusually heavy rains. The placid new capital, Dodoma, the new parliament building, the "mad" hospital, the impressive new university, the earnest young professor. Out of Dodoma, a thrillingly fast ride, we pass suddenly through a hilly region with a stream, a forest, and as rapidly come out into the flat land. Those mysterious geological formations, the tors. As we approach Nzega, the flat roofs turn to V-roofs. The bustle of Nzega, the junction town. The poverty of life, the hazards of the Nzega–Tabora route after a rain, with a partly night-blind driver. The gentle bustle and togetherness of Tabora, the enigma of its neglect; Livingstone and Fundikira; the bhajia shop with the Khoja woman.

The indigenous forest of the alternative Tabora–Nzega route. The richness of the Nzega–Mwanza route, the frequency of the tors, their formations more and more fantastic. Finally Mwanza, the gently bustling city by the great lake: the shore, lined by stones, the mysterious memorial with the inscription removed, the bustling markets, the Indian bazaar on Nyerere Road, the khano with the false dome, and the Hindu temple; sitting on a bench at the kahawa corner, the vendor and her three kids. The bhajia shop of the old man and woman. Stories of witchcraft in Tabora and Mwanza. All the people en route: the Gogo, the Masai (the "doctors" of Dodoma), the Nyamwezi, the Sukuma; the Fipa taxi driver of Mwanza and his "chicken-leg" story, the Nyakyusa-Nyamwezi woman on the bus; the Baganda-Nyasa taxi driver of Tabora; the Indians. And throughout, the stories exchanged between Joseph and me.

12.

Bongoland: Something Is Happening

THEY CALL IT BONGO, OUT OF AFFECTION, out of pride. If you ask a street vendor why he's being obtuse, or a bajaji driver why he just ripped off some poor innocent from upcountry, they're likely to reply, It's Bongoland, learn to survive. There is a certain arrogance to the Bongo folk, a style; a sense of cool or, as they say in Swahili, poa. It's been earned. Over the past few decades Dar es Salaam has seen much: the joy of independence and a popular president, massive street demonstrations and socialist austerity, food lines and spy scandals, a demographic upheaval and an aborted coup, war returnees and a period of banditry; it has matured from a come-tomorrow sleepy-town into a major African city of the region, with an identity to match—seeing itself as different and unique, in the way New York does. There seem to be no bounds here, in modern Dar, no limits to growth or possibility—but while there's some truth to this outlook, much of it is also hype. For Dar retains its essential character, marching to its own casual beat. That is its charm, but also its handicap.

As you come down into the city from the airport, or cross Selander Bridge into the wealthier suburbs of Oyster Bay, Msasani, and Kawe you might easily form the impression that you are in a world where business and IT rule, travelling is by plane, Internet is high speed, money is transferred electronically, the phones are smart—as are the well-bred kids who go to private schools in English. The billboards conveying this message are hip, not as garish as those of, say, Chennai. Dar's English-language newspapers speak the universal language of the world's business pages: stock prices, sovereign bonds, offshore banking, cloud computing, infrastructure development, the GDP (7 percent).

For the first time after many years I feel that a new generation has arrived, ready to take over. They are aware of developments elsewhere in the world, they want to make things happen here. But the older generation is not quite gone: what world is it bequeathing?

First impressions of Dar are soon quashed by the sight of the jammed commuter buses, the beggars on the streets, the vendors, and the idle. And then of course there's the rest of the country behind Bongo. According to a Swahili paper, the World Bank puts Tanzania as the second poorest in the region, with 68 percent of the population earning less than $1.25 per day; 80 percent live on subsistence farming; more than 80 percent spend their nights in total darkness, without electricity. The national debt has tripled in the last few years, standing at 50 percent of the GDP, and the public education system is crippled, the health system rudimentary. In rural areas schools are either empty or overcrowded; there are no teachers or textbooks. The final-year failure rate for the nation's high schools in 2012 was a shocking 60 percent. For those fortunate enough to be connected to the electric grid, there are frequent and frustrating blackouts. There's a thriving business in electricity generators, which you can hear thrumming in all sizes along the top of Morogoro Road.

Three years ago a new word was introduced into the Swahili language: vijisenti, meaning "little cents," that is, mere pennies. It was introduced by a former, highly placed politician who was questioned by the media about the several million dollars found in his bank account during an investigation into corruption. Mere pennies, he replied, arrogantly. The politician was connected with two major scandals, one of them called "Kingston," in which a large contract was handed to a foreign company to fulfill the capital's electricity needs. A fraction of the power was delivered, and thus the power shortage. The American Secretary of State was in town recently and promised help.

The Auditor General reports mass corruption in government: money from pension funds loaned interest-free to politicians and cronies; money allocated for development not released; lavish and unnecessary spending, "embezzlement of public funds . . . outright forgery . . . salary payments to ghost workers. . . ." The list seems endless, and is endlessly and quite wonderfully—you have to have a sense of humour—creative. Says my friend Kumar, a contractor, jestfully, "I can get you a permit to build on the grounds of State House." Someone else repeats an adage to me, apparently a piece of advice that was given in all seriousness to a former president: Corruption is necessary for development.

And this I overhear: We are governed by wahuni, meaning tricksters, and they go about shamelessly sporting a newly acquired title of "Doctor" before their names. When did they get the time to work for their PhDs? It's embarrassing to possess a doctorate now.

The situation is explosive, says Shivji, a professor with a real PhD.

It's explosive, says Charles, a consultant for a foreign NGO.

You look at the desperate-looking, idle taxi drivers—there are hundreds on the streets—and you think, The situation *could* be explosive.

Of course there's hope, says Walter with a sardonic smile. There's always hope. Where can it go from here?

We are at his son Mkuki's flat for a brunch—there are some young people, with a handful of us older folks around. We could be in Toronto or Boston, for the smart, cultured discussion, the wine and good food; Miles Davis in the background. The wine however is Dodoma, which Walter insists is good, others beg to differ. Very soon I feel irrelevant in this company. I'm in the wrong place this Sunday morning—living abroad, an Asian, and of the wrong generation. I'm jet-lagged too, and that could be a metaphor. The young people act young and cool and hip, they talk about jazz—which they rather sweetly assume we don't know about; they speak about tweeting and Facebook visits; having lived abroad they've picked up the mannerisms and phrases. There's a certain studied weariness in them about local conditions, a cool cynicism. I can't tell if they are on display or natural, but we seem to have no place in their world, there is no overlap. I'm being unfair, perhaps, and they simply know each other better.

I think it's Walter who, with a glance at his son, throws a spanner in the runaway exclusivity. The talk turns to writing—Gracie has a well-known column in the *East African*—and the lack of confidence in their age group, a lack of book culture in the country. Can't she compile some of her blogs? Include a sample of local writing in her blogs? Is there a difference between writing a blog and composing a piece of writing as art? Gracie wonders if what they need are a few socialites to bring the artists together, someone who doesn't need to work. A sponsor. I somewhat hesitantly put in that artists traditionally, judging by elsewhere in the world, have been poor, especially when starting out, and movements are created and maintained with much effort and sacrifice. Perhaps—I take a risk—people here are too used to things being done for them? What they need,

I say to myself, is a gentle kick in the backside: Get moving! Don't wait for something, in typical Tanzanian style! Be more like the Kenyans!

Mkuki, who is a graphic designer and commissions artworks, says yes, the foreign NGOs, by paying exorbitantly for commissioned art, have brought the quality down. Artists give the NGOs only what they need to be able to collect funds. A kind of pornography. You can get better art cheaper in South Africa.

The ice is broken. Everyone complains about the Kenyans who come to work in Dar. They are arrogant know-it-alls who stick to each other. The Zimbabweans are so much nicer—and when they speak Swahili they speak like you and I. Not the Kenyans, their Swahili has a rough edge and stands out.

Gracie surprises me by saying that the only racial slur thrown at her in the United States was by some African Americans cruising on South Street in Philadelphia, when they called her a monkey and to go back to the motherland—because she doesn't have straight hair. She was at Bryn Mawr. Omar, who was in Scotland, speaks of soccer rivalry between Azania and Tambaza schools, which turns violent. I could tell them of a time when the rivalry between these two schools was in cricket and academics—but these young folk, I fear, will get distracted and start to tweet to each other.

Walter has a story about Dodoma wine from his days as a junior diplomat in Addis Ababa, and how Tanzania was once the second most favoured nation in China (after Albania), where he got fat because there was no social life there except eating out lavishly. Mkuki has a smile on that says, déjà vu, he's heard it all a dozen times before. Never mind, all is forgiven. Walter brings out a Scotch. I tell Mkuki he should collect his father's reminiscences. He's trying, he replies.

This is modern Dar. Down below is Sea View; a short walk away is the Palm Beach Hotel; this was once an exclusive, almost white area. Only a few days after independence, the manager of the hotel was expelled from the country for a racist comment. These young people don't know that. Their problem is not lack of confidence but ennui. Their resentments are local. Their moment is passing, yet nothing is quite happening for them. They need something to lay a grip on, to be a part of; they need to produce something. It's a cruel thought: we were here before, not as long ago as you like to think. It seems like yesterday. We had ambitions and we pursued them, we took risks, and we gained some and lost some; lost a lot, actually. There was no safety net, no guarantee. Your world is ready-made, you cannot afford to gamble it away for mere ideals or ambitions.

Gracie talks about having been sent to South Africa and being tempted by its many possibilities. How many of these young sophisticates will persist, I wonder, how many will be drawn away? One feels that here is not the creative edge of Bongo; that must lie among those who are closer to the masses, those who make outlandish videos and display them at public halls and inside long-distance buses; and those who write in Swahili, a language that is closer to the heart for everybody and goes deep without fear.

A few days later I sit down with Mkuki at the coffee shop of the Serena. It happens to be his birthday. He gives me his version, the subtext to our Sunday brunch.

All the people you met the other day, he says, are connected with foreign organizations. I could guess that, of course. He admits to the frustration. You return from abroad, you want a certain lifestyle. This is the only way—you consult with foreign organizations, you write reports. A joyless occupation, but the money is good. There's a measure of disappointment when you return. You want to go to an art gallery, listen to serious music. The art scene in its serious sense is almost nonexistent. You see paintings that would not hang in a gallery elsewhere. Those who write in English are a pampered generation, but there's no creativity. They've not lived. Which is why he has greater hopes for Swahili.

Still, he says, you tell yourself you are one of 46 million, what's special about you? You made your decision to return, and you live with it. He did so for the sake of his aging parents. But things are slowly happening. An open mike for poetry that ran for a few months; a session with an author; a proposed prize for Swahili poetry; the discovery of an exciting Swahili poem. It's in music that the greatest creativity lies. The time will come when we will become independent.

Walter calls to wish him a happy birthday, and to seek help with his Mac. He's in London, at the book fair. A friend calls, and the young folks plan a birthday lunch at a high-end restaurant and later a visit to a jazz club. Finally Mkuki says to the waiter, "Take a photo of me with Baba (father)."

"Truly he's your father?" the waiter asks, astonished. He knows me well, for I use the coffee shop as a place to meet and to cool off after my sojourns into town on foot.

"You can say that," Mkuki replies with a laugh.

When he's gone, the waiter tells me, "Truly, the resemblance is uncanny!" In all seriousness.

Genial Jinnah comes by once.

"Where else can you find a place like this?" he says, meaning Dar.

I call him Genial because in the decades I've known him, I've never seen him without that toothy, good-natured grin. I met him once in 1980 in downtown Toronto; we had both recently arrived. Opening his arms wide, he declared, "This is a great country. A beautiful country. You should see it coast to coast!" He had all the intention to stay in the city. A couple of years later, however, he was working in the Middle East. Some more years later he was back in Dar, where he ran a business. Recently he's joined the NGO Brigade, with a white four-by-four and suit and tie, proudly working for the World Development Network, WDN, saving Africa.

I tell him I was at a book reading at a jazz club the other night and the music was good. I was impressed.

He grins. "We have everything here, you'll find all kinds of culture!"

"Really?"

Yes, the cinema that shows Indian films in the city, he explicates, is always full, with kids running around, and plenty of food. All South Indians and recent. I raise my eyebrows. Yes, there are four to five thousand South Indians doing professional jobs in the city. They are good and reliable. The irony in this doesn't strike him. The WDN is doing all sorts of good work, a knight on a white horse saving Central Asia and East Africa. Education crisis? We are working on a curriculum overhaul. Health care? A hospital in Arusha. Relief? Building villages in the south.

"East Africa is a single entity, I try to convince people of that, high school kids need to be told that . . . the West is becoming irrelevant now . . . transnational trade is growing . . ."

But who is "we"? People sitting in Geneva and Paris?

When he's left, I walk over to the hotel reception and pick up a *What's On?* Under "Culture" it shows all the numerous restaurants. In Dar, those who can afford to, eat very well.

Abdu comes by, hurrying on his way to somewhere. He's a filmmaker who's been frustrated by bureaucratic obstacles. An energetic man in his forties, he speaks fast, is always full of ideas, and has recently returned from spending three weeks in India with his father at an Ayurvedic health clinic. Just to get away and be healthy. He regrets how the sense of African-ness and history was lost on his generation and is now completely lost on the younger people. More so in South Africa, where he could be attacked by xenophobes who have not been taught of the role played by Tanzania and the "frontline states" in their liberation.

Gaam—the Indian quarter—is in Bongoland, of course; it was the original Dar es Salaam. But now it sits in its mostly Asian isolation, with a distinct life of its own. Various roads lead into it, though it can be bypassed. There are half a dozen mosques and as many temples, and social life tends to be communal and around the family; bustling by day, at night it turns eerily quiet. The concerns of the folk here would be as far from those of Mkuki and his friends as is possible. Creativity is reserved for business, and perhaps also food.

The realization dawns one day—as I sit at the crowded AT with a bhajia and a cup of chai, the TV showing BBC-format news from an Iranian channel—that there's no music to be heard anymore in public in Gaam. You can hear the azaan—call to prayer—rising up from the several mosques at various times, even in the middle of the night, but no music. Time was when music blared out on the streets, piping down from every home, ranging from Bollywood to western pop, Mukesh to Elvis. Odeon Cinema was close by. Partly, perhaps, this absence of song can be explained by the fact that the technology has changed, rendering music more private; and many homes now are air conditioned, therefore the windows are shuttered. But it's more than that: Gaam no longer looks cheerful, its people don't smile much—in public, at least.

Joseph and I step into Lalji's Travel to buy his ticket to Nairobi; the agency has been recommended by my friend Kumar. The tradition, the adabu, is for the customer to be welcomed with a smile and a "Karibu!" (The reply would be "Starehe" or "Ahsante.") Instead, five black-draped women look warily at us like birds of prey. This is the modern scenario. We make our inquiry and are directed perfunctorily to one of the women, who is Kumar's acquaintance, from whom we purchase our tickets in a brisk transaction. We leave. No smile or welcome, no thank you or goodbye. We feel robbed, of our goodwill and our cheer. We brought business, airplane tickets are not cheap. Lalji's was where I bought my first air ticket out of Dar; the agent who served me paid attention, he smiled, he was friendly. But times have changed, the people have changed. A few days later, pointedly avoiding Lalji's, I bring my business to another travel agent. This time the hijabs are blue and yellow, but the service is as curt. It's only with the African assistant that I can carry out a friendly, normal conversation. I come out thinking, What's with these people?

Life, admittedly, is not easy in Dar. Basic food prices, such as of sugar and flour, keep rising. At the teashops, chai prices have doubled. It would seem that it's only the poor, who suffer the most, who can afford to be cheerful. For the rest, it's a constant battle keeping up with the Abasses and the Samjis—possessing your SUV and a second car, sending kids to private schools, dining out with large families. Habib, a business consultant and Stanford graduate whom I have come to know over the years, hides his anxiety behind a mask of preoccupation. He keeps an impressive office, has kids in exclusive schools, and needs to visit Toronto regularly. Like a common huckster, he hovers around the Serena or the Kilimanjaro, meeting potential contacts—the NGOs, the UN. Mention a name he's not heard of and he'll bring out his notebook to take down a phone number.

But there's something more fundamental that has changed in Gaam, and is perhaps responsible for its new grimness, its lack of song: the people themselves are different, having arrived from the smaller towns to take the place of those who emigrated. The latter were in large part the more liberal Khojas and Hindus, as the names on top of the remaining two-storey buildings indicate; the newcomers followed the Shia faith, which grieves Imam Hussein and his extended family in perpetuity. To my mind, this nature of sombre, obsessive worship, and an orthodoxy influenced by Iran and Iraq and always on the lookout for halal and haram, and proscribing music, is the difference, is the reason why the town that once sang no longer does so. The man who owns Abbas Tea Room is polite but he too never smiles in his shop. It turns out that his daughter, refused permission to marry someone of a lower status, presented him with a fait accompli: a pregnancy. Now the baby is born, and as wedding preparations proceed, all—the entire community—pretend that nothing is amiss, there is no baby. What will happen to it? No wonder they don't sing anymore.

13.

Kigoma and Ujiji: The Long Road

THE END OF THE OLD EAST–WEST CARAVAN ROUTE that began at the Indian Ocean was the town of Ujiji at Lake Tanganyika, which connected to routes in the Congo and all the way to the Atlantic. During the colonial period, however, when Kigoma became the railway terminus, it was developed as the administrative centre and port, and Ujiji was sidelined, much as Bagamoyo, Kilwa, and Lindi were in the east. All four towns were predominantly Muslim and linked to Zanzibar.

It was impossible for me to reach Kigoma by road from Tabora because of the rains, and so back in Dar I have to take a flight, which I do in the company of Shabir, an Asian and a long-time party politician from Kigoma who has new business interests and a daughter in Dar. He picks me up early before sunrise one morning, after his prayer services, to go to the airport. Shabir was recommended by a friend and we met once and discussed my proposed visit to his hometown; since then we have spoken on the cell. He is an energetic, chatty fellow, full of stories. On the way to the airport I ask him to recommend a hotel in Kigoma, to which he says in surprise, "Why a hotel? You're staying with me! Don't worry, my house is almost empty." Just as I had expected, but I had to make sure. To refuse his hospitality would be rude.

Dawn is about to break, the air is cool and damp, and the silent streets under dim overhead lamps have a weirdly alien look. The airport road, the drab old industrial Pugu Road, has been modernized in recent years with smart office buildings and lit show-windows, and in a while it becomes adorned with brightly lit advertising, some of it electronic, atop the buildings. As we check in at the local terminal and show our identities, Shabir startles me by saying casually, "They won't ask for your identity if you are black." He thus reveals a frisson of racial resentment that I've already met elsewhere, but graciously proceeds to explain that a brown person could be from anywhere. Surely a black person too? In the waiting lounge, however, Shabir knows a lot of people, none of them Asian, and when we arrive in Kigoma he alights with a spring in his step and a grin on his face and actually knows *everybody* he sees.

Because I fly into Kigoma, it becomes for me an experience on its own, not the end-of-a-road journey, which is what I had desired. The town lies snugly in a basin formed by the green hills of the plateau and the blue, placid Lake Tanganyika to which it descends. The lake lies inside the great Rift Valley and is the second deepest in the world. Kigoma has one business street, lined with shops of the ubiquitous Indian style, beginning at the rather grand railway station, a legacy of German rule next to the harbour, where an equally ancient steamship, the MV *Liemba*, is docked ready to depart south for Zambia. Kigoma's identity is tied, as it's always been, to its overlooking the Congo and the other side of Africa, just as Dar es Salaam's is tied to the Indian Ocean. The capital, from here, seems far—and actually is, because few can afford an airplane.

My host's home is up on a hill from the main street, accessible via a dirt road that is badly broken so that only a good four-wheeler can make its winding way there, or a pair of healthy, willing legs. As we drive up to the gate, two Alsations are taken away. The house is large with a driveway and a lush garden. Shabir's wife answers the massive door, a sleepy look on her face. Behind her is a high-ceilinged living room, the large flat-screen set to an Indian program, and a raised dining area. The floor and wall panelling are wood. It was obviously built with much optimism for the future; Shabir once ran a hotel from here. I wonder who the clientele would have been besides the politicians.

The daughter, who picked us up, is a chirpy twenty-something who runs the family auto repair shop. Father and daughter discuss business during our ample breakfast served at the large dining table, then Shabir drives me to Ujiji, a few miles away. He has an idea, though I have not put it to him, that I am looking for "history."

History to him, and to others, as I will find out, is something specific and finite, consisting of some quanta of information to be given and accepted, and very kindly he has volunteered to make it possible for me to receive it.

Ujiji, though, comes as a revelation, a breath of the familiar. Its structured layout is immediately striking, a grid of streets with mud and plaster Swahili houses, all having the typical front veranda. The highway through it must have come later, built over an existing local road. There is an implicit togetherness to this town, as Tabora has, as Kilwa Kivinje has, all three, of course, among the oldest towns in the country. In the late nineteenth century Ujiji was a flourishing entrepot in the centre of Africa, trading not only in slaves and ivory, but also fish, fruit, salt, butter, honey, grains, and cattle, in addition to goods brought from Zanzibar, which would have included imported cottons, wire, and beads. The marketplace was on the lakeshore, as Stanley observed when he arrived here and saw men and women from more than a dozen tribes from as far away as Rwanda, "engaged in noisy chaffer and barter." In 1900 the population was ten thousand, far more than today, the important residents being the Arab traders. In 1882 the German traveller (and later governor of the colony) von Wissmann observed some forty dhows on the lake at Ujiji.

An overjoyed Stanley arrived here with his caravan on November 10, 1871, some fifty guns firing in celebration, the American flag ("bendera kizungu") in the lead, the Zanzibari red banner bringing up the rear, having reached at last the end of his quest for Livingstone. "We had awakened Ujiji to the knowledge that a caravan was coming, and the people were witnessed rushing up in hundreds to meet us."

> Then we were surrounded by them: by Wajiji, Wanyamwezi, Wangwana, Warundi, Waguhha, Wamanyuema and

> Arabs, and were almost deafened with the shouts of "Yambo, yambo, bana! Yambo, bana! Yambo, bana!" To all and each of my men the welcome was given.

Stanley pushed through the crowd and went to greet Livingstone outside his house.

The town as it appears today could hardly muster that crowd or level of excitement.

Shabir drops me off at a dingy-looking shop on an unpaved side street. It has an open front, partly blocked, with a step up leading inside, and sells daily essentials to the neighbourhood at the barest retail level—a cup of rice, an onion, a shot of cooking oil. There are items hanging from the lintel, including, rather incongruously, a pair of boy's shorts. What desperate mother would buy a pair of shorts here? There's no room—except to squeeze through—inside the dark interior, but there is a small patio in front. The owner is Mzee Salum, a small, tired-looking man of Omani Arab ancestry with very likely some African blood. He wears a cap, a msuri—a wraparound of soft checked cotton—at the waist, and a shirt, a style of dressing outmoded in Dar by at least a couple of decades, and speaks in that typical high-pitched broken tone as though the native Arabic accent were struggling with the Swahili, which of course he most likely speaks better. Just as Shabir prepares to depart, a largish elderly man hobbles in, Mzee Memedi, partly blind, feet swollen, escorted by Mzee Salum's shop assistant. This is a daily morning chitchat at which I have arrived. Mzee Memedi, because of his age, would be the fount of wisdom. People drop in and leave after respectfully greeting the two men. One of them, however, stays; his help has been sought. I—or Shabir on my behalf—have presented him with a conundrum.

I have been made to sit on a small chair to one side of the patio, Mzee Memedi sits on the ground close to me, and Mzee Salum is on the step at the shop entrance. The third visitor, a younger man, stands.

Mzee Salum, having posed the problem to his friends, now inquires: "Now this historia, how come we don't have it, we were not given it?"

Mzee Memedi in his wiry low voice says: "Our Wazees [elders] only sat us down and told us stories. Or if we cried, they'd look outside and say, 'Fisi [hyena]—where are you?' to scare us . . ."

I find myself in a quandary, squirming as I listen to this exchange kindly put on for my benefit, not knowing how to explain to them my interest—which is not to collect "historia," but to gather anything peripheral to the actual history, for instance how the place—Ujiji—looks today, how people relate to the past, what and how they remember.

The third man puts in: "Nani; nani-nani-nani—I'm racking my brains to think who has this historia . . ."

Finally, having scratched his head, he comes up with a name, "Hababu!" Hababu is Mzee Salum's son and apparently a teacher. Who else would have the historia? But Hababu today does not pick up his phone.

The ancient Mzee Memedi of the thick foot is a smart one. He is a big man with a large head. He has a wry smile on his face, and he seems to know, or at least thinks he knows, exactly what interests me. He is a Manyema, he answers to my query. The Manyema came from eastern Congo, from a region also called Manyema, the etymology of which term is said to imply "flesh-eater" or cannibal. Whether this was true of the Manyema themselves or not, cannibalism was observed in the region at the time. (One of Livingstone's deserters was killed and eaten.) The Manyema region was a lucrative source for slaves and ivory for the Arab and Swahili merchants, such as Tippu Tip, and many Manyema men naturally also joined the forces of the slave traders. The devastation of that area of the Congo has been described by many visitors, and one cannot help but recall the devastation the region has suffered in our own time.

I ask Mzee Memedi, then, "Didn't the Manyema come to Ujiji with Tippu Tip? Where did he put up?"

"You have to ask someone who knows. I'm not going to say what may be half true." He looks around before adding, referring to me with that same wry smile, "He knows what he's looking for, he has to go and find it."

Mzee Salum sounds hopeless as he says, "We need someone with historia."

The wazees finally ask me first to go and have a look at the Livingstone site nearby, while I presume they will continue to rack their brains.

I walk up the highway, and after a short while turn right—as directed—into a road that's rather unusual in that it has been paved with cut stones; it's intact and hardly used by vehicles. The walk is long and straight, a line of houses on either side. A white SUV passes me. On the way people stare curiously and some children call out, "Bye-bye!" assuming I'm a mzungu. Who else but a white man would take a hike by himself in the sun to see Livingstone? I respond in Swahili: "Do I look like a mzungu to you?" "Mwarabu!" a boy replies with a knowing grin. An Arab. "Mhindi," I correct him and continue on my way. Finally I arrive at a fenced compound with a flag mast outside a large single-storey white building. In the outer hall of the building two women sit at a table; there is no one else around. I pay one of them a fee and she comes out with me and indicates the spot on top of a rise where I can see the Livingstone monument. She calls out to someone that one more visitor is arriving.

I climb the rise to come upon three westerners and an Arab girl in hijab sitting attentively on one of two benches before a gesticulating guide. Behind the man is a circular, slightly raised island of lawn contained by a brick border, at the centre of which is the monument to the missionary—a modest white brick structure some four feet high with a plaque. I go and sit on the second bench and pay attention.

In a peculiarly accented English, the man sings out what he must have recited a few thousand times by rote, the story of David Livingstone: birthplace and date, first voyage, marriage, second journey, and the third. He was sitting in his veranda when his faithful servants came running to him, shouting, "Bwana, a white man and a caravan!" Stanley arrived and greeted Dr. Livingstone. The monument marks that meeting place.

According to Stanley, Livingstone was in the company of "the great Arab magnates of Ujiji" and had come out of the veranda to await him. The house is described as having been in the town then. The site now stands isolated, closer to the lakeshore and a little away from Ujiji's present location.

After the recital we prepare to leave. A short distance away from the Livingstone monument is a stone with a plaque on it to commemorate the arrival in Ujiji of Burton and Speke on February 14, 1858. I ask the guide where Tippu Tip (the slave and ivory trader) lived. He says there are some ruins close by in an area called Usagara, at the mango trees. We are invited to see the museum, which is in the inner room of the main building. The museum can kindly be called modest, but it reflects the prevailing attitude to the past: negligent, perfunctory, ignorant. There stands a grotesque, amateurish sculpture of the

"I Presume" moment, and there are some paintings on a wall that could only have been done by school children. Nothing else. No exhibits from the past, no explanations, no history. I ask the white group—an older NGO worker and two interns—for a ride in their vehicle to the main road.

At the road, I pause for a soda before finally arriving back at Mzee Salum's, where I sit down again on the chair. The old man, Mzee Memedi, is more at ease. They all talk about historia, it has gripped their imagination. Hababu can still not be found. I tell the men I saw Livingstone and am satisfied, and listen to them as they recall some past incidents.

Mzee Salum: "That man exposed himself right there and showed us where the Germans whipped his behind. Ah! Viboko!"

Mzee Memedi: "Men were taken to fight [in the First World War], not here but in the south. . . . The slaves were landed at Bangwe [nearby] and brought here where they planted the mango trees."

Mzee Salum, of Omani Arab parentage, looks away, visibly discomfited. Mzee Memedi has that twinkle in his eyes.

The next morning I return in a taxi to Ujiji. The driver has been instructed by Shabir to look after me, and at first he annoys by pointing out the obvious sites along the highway: a girls' school, select government buildings. We pass the formidable-looking headquarters of the security services, away from the road, about which he doesn't say any more. Refugees and illegals are of course a problem here. Finally we reach Ujiji and, passing the Livingstone road, turn right onto the next one, and then left into a trail towards miembeni—the mango trees.

We come to a small cemetery, where I convince a reluctant driver to stop; we alight and ask a passing woman about the graves.

Some locals are buried here, she says, but the graves are being moved. According to the headstones they date from the 1970s, which is ancient enough for the driver. When I say, Not quite, he asks when I was born, and whistles in amazement at my answer. Obviously, to him anyone over thirty is an ancient. We ask the woman about older sites, from the days of slavery. About Tippu Tip the slave trader. She says nothing. But just then an older woman carrying a panga (machete) arrives, wearing an amused look. She knows exactly what I want. "The slaves passed there," she says bluntly, pointing behind her, and we follow her to a shaded area crowded with dark green mango trees and scattered with Swahili-type settlements—houses behind stockades of thatch. The entire neighbourhood looks dark and is eerily quiet, a few women have come out to observe us. And it takes a few moments before I understand, and notice the dirt road that is heading out in front of me straight into the horizon east—to where? "Bagamoyo," the woman says, and grins. The great slave market at the end of the trail.

This, then, is the slave road, planted periodically with mango groves where the caravans rested. It is a stirring site.

We walk back to an area where there is a school. Boys and girls in blue and white uniforms stop their recess play to banter with us. I am called mzungu again, but protest only mildly this time. I have come to the area of the old Arab settlement, where Tippu Tip would have put up, and there are the remains of ruins here—partial walls, brick stumps. Consciously or unconsciously, it's been determined that no trace of the Ujiji Arabs remains. But the canny Tippu Tip did leave a written memoir.

Slavery is not an easy subject to deal with. No one who has seen photographs or read descriptions of a slave raid, and of slaves yoked together in their long march to the market, can fail to be moved by the enormous injustice and cruelty of the practice; or even to feel a trace of guilt—some ancestor could have been involved in the capture or trade of slaves, or owned one or more. But perhaps it's also too easy and safe to invoke these reactions. Slavery, even in Africa, was not always a black-and-white affair. It involved the Indian creditor in Zanzibar, the Arab—and Swahili—trader in the interior, the African tribesmen who captured and sold each other. The freed slave often became a trader himself. Even the European explorer who heartily condemned it in his writings relished the hospitality of the trader—witness Stanley feasting with the Arabs in Tabora and Ujiji. The explorers' caravans included bought slaves. Stanley himself went on to claim Congo in the name of the Belgian king; the horrors of the colonial rule that followed there are now well known.

The life of the famous slave and ivory trader Tippu Tip well illustrates these many facets.

In his portrait, taken in the balcony of his house in Zanzibar, Tippu Tip sits in stately manner, wearing a black robe with embroidered trim over a white kanzu and a turban over his head; there is a ceremonial dagger tucked at the waist, and he supports with one hand a long sword against one leg. He has a full white beard but no moustache. His features are black. A proud man with an ironic smile, shrewd in business, brave and ruthless in battle, he could at once charm and awe his European critics, who had no qualms asking for his assistance.

Tippu Tip, whose actual name was Hamed bin Mohammed, was born in Zanzibar in the first half of the nineteenth century, of Muscati-African parents. He was called Tippu Tip perhaps because his eyelids would twitch, a mannerism sufficient enough in the culture of the coast to garner a mischievous nickname. His mother, daughter of a prosperous Muscat family, was the second wife of his father, Mohammed, whose first wife was the daughter of Fundikira, the Nyamwezi sultan of Tabora and ancestor of the future government minister of independent Tanganyika. The family was thus well connected in both Zanzibar and Tabora. The dreaded Mirambo ("Bonaparte of Africa"), who almost brought the western caravan trade to a halt with his attacks and demands, was his friend and refused to harrass him.

Tippu Tip's grandfather was an enterprising and well-known trader, and so was his father. At the age of eighteen Tippu Tip joined his father in Tabora, and at his insistence was given charge of his own caravan to take from Ujiji across Lake Tanganyika to the Congo. Starting from this apprenticeship he went on to travel extensively from Zanzibar through Ugogo, Tabora, and Ujiji and on to eastern Congo. These journeys lasted several years, criss-crossed large tracts of land, and involved wars and alliances, theft and disease, extortions and payoffs; one of his uncles and some of his men were "devoured" by the natives. All this hardship was undertaken in the name of trade—in slaves, ivory, and anything else—though surely there was also the underlying urge to travel. The caravans could include as many as a few thousand people.

For his last major trading journey, so much prestige had the man already acquired in Zanzibar that the Indian businessmen, the likes of Ladha Damji and Tharia Topan, were falling over their feet to give him credit. That journey lasted more than twelve years, during which Tippu Tip became sultan of a vast area of eastern Congo known as Utetera. When he finally returned to Zanzibar, having been called by the sultan, he was already acknowledged the "uncrowned King of Central Africa." Colonization was in full swing, and soon after his arrival the Belgian government, seeking his influence in their African colony, requested him to return to Central Africa as governor of the province known as the Congo State. Tippu Tip accepted, at the advice of the sultan, who was desperate to maintain some influence in the interior. This time Tippu Tip travelled to the Congo in a ship, via South Africa, and with him was Stanley.

The European explorers are justly renowned for exploring Africa under great hardship; Tippu Tip, however, travelled greater distances for longer periods, and except for his last voyage home, from Tabora to the coast, he travelled on foot. He was a trader, disdaining the vanity and idealism of the explorers and missionaries. Nevertheless he came to the assistance of Livingstone in dire straits, accompanied Stanley on his way to the west coast, as well as Verney Lovett Cameron, on his way to become the first person to cross equatorial Africa, and Hermann von Wissmann, the first German to do so and later the subduer of the coastal insurgencies against the Germans and Governor of Tanganyika.

—

From Ujiji the driver takes me to a place he finds more interesting, where a spring emerges from the ground and the authorities have installed a tap for people to draw water. From here we go to Bangwe, where Mzee Memedi said the slaves were brought from Congo across the lake. Bangwe now is a large beach market, from where boats cross the lake with goods.

I get off on the main street in Kigoma. Mobile-phone booths are scattered about, selling "vocha"—prepaid vouchers—and there are the idle taxi drivers. As I have noticed in Dar, they are an educated, sprightly bunch. How long will these friendly exteriors last, if conditions don't improve? Business is slow on the street, though much of it is wholesale; mattresses are on garish display, ready to be taken away in boats to the Congo, across the lake, where apparently nothing seems to be produced.

On the broken porch of a dingy little restaurant, its interior too dark to be inviting, a man is busy selling kahawa, and I sit down on a bench, if only to view the street bathed in sunlight, watch the slow pace of commercial life. The kahawa is thick and opaque—the coffee is boiled thoroughly in an old, dented saucepan—but it's fresh coffee, not always easy to find, and grown in the region. My newspaper gets shared around, the upcoming new constitution gets discussed. The fellow next to me, looking rather unkempt, and who could be from Burundi, I gather, cannot afford the kahawa—fifty cents. I order for him and he accepts with a casual dignity: I can afford it, he can't, I treat him. He tells me he cannot find a job. He's had eight children, of which four were boys and died; the four girls are prostitutes. And there's a little one, he adds as an afterthought.

Finally I make my way uphill to my host's house—all the time the long slave traders' road to Bagamoyo on my mind. How to respond authentically at this remove in time; yet the image persists, demands. My way to Shabir's is winding and quiet, the road rough, the vegetation mostly grass. In better times this hill would be developed. Down below is the blue water of Lake Tanganyika, the MV *Liemba* waiting to go to Zambia. At a fork I ask a man my way. He walks with me. Everybody knows Shabir.

That evening I go to khano with the family; I do want to see what the Khoja community here is like. It turns out to be tiny, a fragment of the glory it once was. There are fourteen people present, yet a lot of effort has been taken to set up the place, with flowers and incense and food offerings. Three women, including Shabir's wife and daughter, are in salwar-kameez, which is a sign of status but never was the traditional outfit for Asian women in this country. One woman has had her hair dyed a dirty blond. The men are in the traditional casuals of the nation, the Kaunda suit. There are three youths present, all belonging to the mukhi. Afterwards the men and women sit outside in the veranda and banter; Shabir throws in a double entendre. These people have known each other always, have grown up together, and with sinking hearts seen their numbers dwindle. And so the humour is spiked with their unexpressed anxieties.

I ask the mukhi about his business. It's slow, he says, but will pick up. He sells plastic goods; periodically he takes them in a truck to sell in Congo. Isn't that risky? Yes, but we have to do it. He is a small, soft-spoken man with cropped hair, wearing a dark grey Kaunda suit. A man trapped by circumstance, in a geography he doesn't belong to anymore; time passed, took his lifestyle with it, and here he is. The trade he does has a continuity back to the times of Tippu Tip and Stanley, his truck an extension of the caravans; but what future for his boys?

Before heading home we take a drive to Ujiji. We pass Mwanga first, a village where the highway becomes hectic with shopping and street life, shadows fleeting or standing around among lights dim and occasional. There seem to be no bars here. We drive on at a leisurely pace. To our right is the lake, a dull black space with a chain of glowing lights running through it like a strip of gold. These are the fishing boats. The fish will be sold at markets at the ports, some bound for Congo. But there is banditry on the lake too, Congolese pirates robbing fishermen of their outboard motors.

Ujiji is quieter, the nightlife here is of a subdued sort—men gathered or sitting outside their doorways. The streets are dark, people saving on electricity.

We turn around. As we approach Kigoma on the dark road, a row of closed shopfronts to our right, Shabir tells me, "All these shops were owned by Asians once. Every night they would be sitting outside, relaxing, chatting. It was the perfect life, of having enough, wanting little. A few hundred Khojas, a few hundred others."

"What happened?" I ask. "Why did they leave?"

The tale goes back to the late 1960s.

Tejpar Lalji, the town's most prominent businessman and a community elder, Shabir relates, had exceptionally lovely daughters, the eldest just out of her teens. The Regional Commissioner had his eye on her. When Tejpar got wind of this, he sent all his daughters off to Dar. One day Tejpar's nephew happened to cross the road in front of the RC's car as it was passing. The RC came out in a fury, told off the young man, and straightaway had him put behind bars. When the young man's father went to inquire about his son, he too found himself behind bars. Finally, Tejpar Lalji himself paid a visit to the RC, who told him plainly that he wanted to marry his eldest daughter. But my daughters are all in Dar, Tejpar said, which immediately landed *him* in jail. This sounds like an incident from a spaghetti western. There was at that time no free press to resort to, of course, and always fear of intimidation by some political bigwig, especially in the smaller centres of the nation. Dar es Salaam was always far, and every Regional or District Commissioner was a local sultan. Tejpar Lalji decided to move his entire family to Dar, and thus began the exodus.

What amazes me now is how easily, how readily a complete way of life was picked up and folded away like the props of a travelling show. Now in this pitch-dark Kigoma night as we arrive through the gates in Shabir's SUV, as I hear the gates clang behind us and a dog bark and watch the two women precede us to the oversize door of the house, cheered by the family's outing, a gloomy epiphany descends on me. The elegant salwar-kameezes reveal only a longing for elsewhere, where the Laljis have gone. The only place in Kigoma they can wear these bright, beautiful costumes is within the confines of that desolate, gated little khano with its fourteen people that is only a sad reminder of a thriving, hopeful past. Shabir on the other hand completely belongs in the local scene—early tomorrow he heads off by road and lake to the villages for party meetings, and for a few days will brave all the discomforts of rural existence. Meanwhile his wife spends her days at home watching Indian dramas by herself, and at night watches them with her daughter, the two daily discussing the vicissitudes in the lives of Priya or Ram, or some other young Punjabi fantasy creature dreamed up in Bombay, keeping Indian women enthralled from Kigoma to Nairobi to Vancouver. They are a lonely people, with no social life, no friends in town save for that decimated community. The daughter must marry. The frustration and cynicism that the man of the house occasionally throws up fails to convince entirely—I recall the smile on his face as we landed in Kigoma and he jumped out, and I recall how he knows everybody, and they in turn know not only him but remember his father as well. The negativity is contrived perhaps to prepare him to yield to the desires of his family and depart to a future with grandchildren.

14.

The South Coast: A Journey Shortened

EARLY MORNING AT SIX IN DAR, I am waiting anxiously in the front compound of the Serena for Joseph to join me. This is a convenient meeting spot, though all is quiet at this hour, except for the bus traffic slowly picking up outside on Ohio Street. With me is Kumar's impatient driver. Just about when I've given up on Joseph, wondering if it's worth taking on the journey south—to Lindi and farther—on my own, he arrives in a bajaji, calm as ever, and we head off to the bus terminal. It's not Ubungo, as on previous journeys out, but Temeke—a muddy patch of ground with only one other bus waiting to depart. Kumar got me the tickets, not well in advance obviously, because our seats are at the very back, and every speed bump and rough patch is sheer torture. The bus, bearing the woman's name Najma, is old and dark inside, the seats partly torn, and carries a strong body odour. It's not been washed since arriving last night—we are going to a neglected part of the country, after all. Joseph has a smart phone this time, so our chats are shorter, I have to share time with news arriving from Nairobi. It's no surprise he's been so hard to get hold of. Staying close to the coast, we cross a bridge over the mighty Rufiji, which is muddy and swirling, bypass Kilwa, and arrive at Lindi midafternoon.

Our local contact here is Abbas, courtesy of Kumar, and we find him in the cluttered back office of the local petrol station, from where he runs his little empire. He has a spare white beard on the chin, wears a plain bush shirt and trousers, and is ensconced permanently—it appears—in his stuffed chair before a large and ancient wooden desk, dealing with business over the phone as it arises and despatching one of his waiting assistants to take care of it when necessary.

In answer to a query, he tells us cashews are abundant here in the south, the problem is distribution. He gives us the typical Asian story about local inefficiency and waste. During the days of socialism, the government in its wisdom acquired five cashew processing and packaging plants, instead of an experimental one to test the market. The factories could not compete with Indian products and now lie abandoned. He himself runs a water-bottling plant that supplies water to the entire region. He is wealthy, but appears modest and straitened.

His driver gives us a tour of the town. Lindi consists of a lovely beach, behind which is the meagre town centre, and beyond that are the hills. One of the hills is called Mtanda, where the Europeans once lived. Abbas's son has a beautiful house here, but the area looks rather barren, the vegetation consisting of trees and scrub. We pass through Wireless Hill, where the government offices were moved in anticipation of the sea level eventually rising and washing over the old town. Of the town itself there is not much besides small shops and houses on mostly unpaved streets.

Abbas has made reservations for us at a hotel called Adela. My room is called Mosko (for Moscow), Joseph has Cuba, reflecting an outdated political culture. Abbas also tipped us with the name of a restaurant which makes good biriyani, and that's where we head for dinner. The streets are dark and quiet, but for the occasional pedestrian and a lamp in a house or shop. The restaurant is run by a

Somali woman, and she tells us they have run out of biriyani and pilau, so we have rice and curry instead.

What does one do at night in a town like this? From what I know, there used to be a healthy Asian population here; their activities would have centred around the prayer houses. There was an excellent high school in town, with a cricket team to match. Now the few Asians here spend what time they can in Dae. That is where Abbas is headed tomorrow.

In the middle of the night the power goes out, the room turns black and feels unbearably hot and claustrophobic. The next morning at seven we take a bus called "Happy" to Mtwara. On the way, after a stretch of mangrove swamp, we arrive at the town of Mikindani, overlooking a beautiful bay. Mikindani is ancient, and it seems a good idea to stop and look around. We go for chai and chapati at a roadside restaurant and make it known to the boy waiter our interest in the local historical sites. He looks nonplussed, says he'll ask around, but then an elder, neatly dressed in shirt and trousers and a kofia, who's also having chai, offers to take us around.

We cross the road—the small Lindi–Mtwara highway—and walk up a short distance to come to an old ruin. It's extensive, with the remains of several rooms, the broken walls revealing their coral stone, and was a prison once upon a time. There is no information here, but we guess the ruin goes back to German times and must be a little more than a hundred years old.

After passing a modern clinic and a ruling-party office, we come upon a rather large, defunct Khoja Ismaili khano. Across is the Ithnasheri Muslim mosque, which is only occasionally used now, but well kept, and dated the first decade of the twentieth century. Next comes a building under renovation, painted yellow, where—a plaque tells us—David Livingstone stayed in 1860. Johann Krapf had already made a brief stop here in 1850. The Germans came in the 1890s. Opposite the Livingstone house, to one side is the former slave-holding place, according to the guide, and on the other, on a rise, looking out to the bay is the former boma—the German administrative headquarters—now completely renovated and turned into the posh Boma Hotel. We climb up to it from the back, enter a lovely, well-kept garden, go inside from the front door. There is a reception desk here and we are pointed to the poolside, where we order coffee, which is very expensive but excellent, arriving in a French press. There's no one else around the hotel except for the two waiters and the girl at reception. A lot of money has been spent on the hotel, but who comes here?

Our guide tells us that a number of properties have been bought by foreigners. Part of the beach has become private; and from a notice on the road we have already surmised that a boating club is in its infancy. But there's no foreign-looking person in sight today. Perhaps they come on weekends. Our guide's name is Salemani Esmail, and he says he has a farm, and he can always be found at the mosque. He came with his mother from Mozambique.

Mozambique is very much a presence here, as Congo is in Kigoma, Kenya is in Arusha, and the Indian Ocean is in Dar. In Lindi our bajaji driver and the hotel manager were Mozambicans and hardly understandable. All were fluent in Swahili yet there was a hesitancy in their speech that made it hard to comprehend.

A crowded minibus, stopping frequently and with a sick child aboard, brings us to Mtwara at the busy town market. Here we walk around, drink sodas to quench our thirst, and catch a taxi to River Ruvuma, at the Mozambique border.

The drive is over a dirt road and an hour long; the sun is hot, the vegetation mango, coconut, grass. We reach a customs office, where the driver explains his business and then proceeds. We come to the immigration office, where he goes to speak to the officer, a young chubby-faced man in a uniform, reposing on a chair under a tree, who stands up, comes to have a look at us, and says, Proceed; but if you want to see the hippos, see the parks fellow. We proceed.

At the border there's not much to see. The river is wide, and broken up into segments as it slowly makes its way to the sea. At the docked ferry, a truck has been stuck since yesterday, when it tried to come out. A young European couple in a white Land Rover, looking rather worried, bring out a jump cable. Meanwhile those without a vehicle take a boat and it chugs away. It's all slow and easygoing.

We return, wave to the immigration officer, still reclined under the tree, and to a security officer, relaxed inside a kiosk. He was not there before. The driver is a Makonde. If the coast up to Lindi appears ethnically Swahili, in Mtwara it is Makonde. The Makonde are Muslims, at least on the Tanzanian side. They are famous for their characteristic and famous wood carvings, depicting caricatured human figures piled atop each other in various postures that supposedly represent relationships. The Makonde were considered backward because of their prominent face markings and the lip buttons on the women. We used to see many Makonde in Dar when I lived on Uhuru Street; they typically worked as night watchmen, and ours was a short, stocky, and gentle man called Sabini. The driver, a thin, somewhat taciturn young man, tells us the face marks were there to frighten people, but we are not convinced. His name is Livowa. It seems to us that he understands English, though he pretends not to, and he opens up only when we start discussing local development.

There's been considerable resentment directed recently at the offshore drilling in the area that will supposedly bring prosperity to the nation, but of which the locals have yet to see benefits. Harbours run entire nations, Livowa says; we too have a harbour. We have gas, and it's taken to run factories elsewhere. Where are our factories? Joseph and I are aware that there was a riot in Mtwara some months back, when a court building was set on fire. We ask Livowa about it. Our man indicates that he was very much there in the protests.

Joseph asks Livowa about slavery. He snaps, If the market was at Mikindani, who else but Makonde would be taken away? Then he becomes silent. He is angry.

The stendi (bus stand), where we return, is at the bustling Soko Kuu, the great market—which sells grains, spices, fruits and vegetables, clothes, auto spares, bicycles, cooked food and refreshment. This is a cassava area, besides cashew, and we sit down on boxes and treat ourselves to roasted cassava from a street vendor. A stall nearby sells cans of diet Pepsi, Red Bull, and other sodas, which reflects in some way the recent changes in lifestyle due to the offshore drilling that Livowa railed against. Mtwara is also a college town, and rents are high; there are foreigners about, and female students take to prostitution.

We take an evening bus back to Lindi, and arrive just in time for pilau at the Somalis'.

Our plan is to go west to Songea, turn north towards Iringa and Morogoro, and finally arrive in Dar, having made a full circle. It's ambitious, but we're going to try.

We leave Lindi for Masasi, Abbas having informed us that it's a thriving sort of place, a junction. We depart after a breakfast at the station. One section of the road west has been flooded by rains, we are informed upon departure, but the bus driver says not to worry, he can easily drive over the water. The bus—called Buti la Mzungu—"the white man's boot"—is painted all over with a Liverpool Football Club theme, including the picture of a prominent player, and is almost empty when we start. But the driver, sitting back, eating his breakfast, casually picks up whoever steps up to the road and waves him down, and soon we are full beyond capacity. Several times, policemen in immaculate white get in, have a look, greet the passengers and let us go. It would appear that the only real work they do is to keep those uniforms clean and pressed. That the bus carries double or more of the number of passengers allowed doesn't distract them. But there's no cynical comment or complaint about them from the passengers, they are part of the scene.

We arrive at the place where the road has been washed over. The bus stops, instead of driving over the water as promised, and we are told to get out. We are returned a portion of our fare and told to make our way by foot across the water and find a bus to Masasi. There's no choice. And so a walk across the shallow lake, barefoot, pants rolled, through muddy water over a rough and uneven surface. I realize as I totter, trying to avoid potholes, that I need help and acquiesce to a young man's offer to guide me; he even offers to carry me—I firmly decline—and like Gandhi with his hand on a young person's shoulder I cross some three hundred yards of water. Joseph is in slippers and walks unaided, but allows someone to carry his bag. The young men are in peak mood, and tell us jovially that the water sometimes reaches chest height, and once when the level had completely subsided, a crocodile was found at the side of the road. Tall tale or true, a frightening thought in the middle of the crossing. Our helpers are paid, and we find a bus to Masasi and depart.

Masasi is, as promised, a busy, thriving market. It's a cashew centre, where villagers come from the countryside to sell their produce. The highway is lined with guest houses and restaurants, there are a shopping centre and two banks; bajajis, motorbikes, and buses ply the road. The town is a junction for the Tunduru–Songea (west and north), Lindi–Dar (east and north), and Newala–Mtwara (east) routes. Tunduru–Songea beckons, but it's long, and part of the way, we are informed, is under a rainfall. The road is rough, and only four-by-four transports get through, which means sitting at the back in the rain; there are breakdowns and we could spend a night in the forest. And so, bidding farewell to the Tunduru road, eastwards to Newala we go.

Newala. Uncanny: it seems to be nowhere, really. A village between two small towns, a square about a mile from the little bus stop on the highway where we were dropped off, with a single street leading away from it. It has many trees. The bajaji driver who brought us to the hotel, which is out of town, was a distracted teenager. On the way he met a girl, arranged to meet her at the shops later, and his day was made, it seemed, because then on he drove erratically, speeding over bumps and potholes, once almost hitting a tree, and it seemed we'd not arrive in one piece. But we did. The hotel ("gesti" for guest house;

"hoteli" means restaurant here and other places) is a new houselike structure. For our dinner, the folks made us chicken, which was slaughtered and fried, but it was as tough as though tightly wrapped in polythene. After dinner we sit outside on the veranda with beers, chatting; it's cool, dark, clear, and absolutely silent. And I wonder, Is there another world really out there? Or could it all be here, and the other one, with all its buzz and bustle, a mere dream? Could one simply abandon that other one and disappear here, in Newala?

We were supposed to leave Newala at 7 a.m.; we depart at 8:30. The journey is excruciating, over a persistently rough road, with frequent stops, and we are packed with up to sixty or more in a space of thirty, our bodies cramped and sweating. On the way, mango and coconut trees, small cashew plantations, unfenced, indicating joint ownership. Kids playing around, not in school. Young men idling about. There's not much industry or hard work to be seen, but apparently enough to eat. Women move around in bicycles, their heads covered, some in the tight "shuttlecock" style hijab, a few in complete niqab. Muslim women prefer this mode of transport, for privacy, and men use the same "ladies' style" bikes.

Joseph talks about the obsession with education in Kenya, where final examination results are published in the newspapers. He speaks of his pride and sense of accomplishment in having his young son admitted to a private school. Uhuru Kenyatta has been sworn in as president—his smart phone keeps him informed—and he talks about the acrimony the recent Kenya elections have created, the renewed tribal animosity, the discrimination and bullying by the dominant Kikuyu in Nairobi. There is even discussion now, in the periphery of the country, about national disintegration, and about emigration as an option for escape. Strangely, this reminds me of how the Asians once felt. I am also reminded of his optimism of just a year ago, when we travelled to Tabora and Mwanza. Perhaps the dour mood in Kenya is temporary.

Regardless of our frustration, these minibuses are the only modes of transportation, village to village, village to town, they are part of local life and culture. The bus stops for people to buy pumpkins, sitafals, watermelons to take with them to Mtwara. No one except we are in a hurry to get to town and do something. A few times the driver stops the bus and comes out to give quizzical looks at the rear tyres, and we worry. Will we ever make it? One of the passengers has turned into a comic and tells long funny stories. There is hardly any traffic on the road. In the eight hours it takes us to get to Mtwara, we pass eight other motor vehicles. So rare is the traffic on the road that a little boy calls out "Gari! Gari!" as we pass.

During our journey we've seen a bus with "Osama bin Laden" written on the back; another with "Shabab" on it; another with "Air Force One." And a shop sign in Masasi that said, "George Washington DC." This is another reality altogether. There are no newspapers to be seen.

Finally, the bus in its final throes, scrunching and squealing along, we arrive in Mtwara in the evening. After looking around for a suitable hotel, we decide to splurge and stay at a posh one overlooking the ocean, where the watchmen, for decorative purposes partially, are two Masai men. We have dinner on the outdoor patio, by candle lights; in the distance over the dark bay, a circle of lights, indicating the offshore wells and the new prosperity to come.

Early the next day we take a bus back to Dar, asking ourselves, could the Tunduru-Songea route have been any more uncomfortable and tedious? Should we have shown more resilience and kept going and completed the full circle via Songea?

15.

The Southern Highlands: Tukuyu—Neue Langenberg

Ubungo bus terminal once again, teeming at dawn with those who are about to journey and those who will see them go. As I join the bustle, the thought occurs that if India runs on rails, Tanzania runs on highways—and of course on cell phones. The entire country, from Lindi in the southeast at the Mozambique border to Bukoba in the northwest at the Rwanda border, from the Indian Ocean to the three great lakes, is connected, and you can reach almost any place easily from Dar. It's as if suddenly one day the once dormant heart of the socialist nation revived and throbbed, and the country woke up and started humming. In the surreal shadowy darkness lit by occasional vendors' lamps, I meander through the crowds and between the growling behemoths, searching; there's no way to find out which is your carrier amongst the arrayed buses, save by making anxious inquiries. Kiosks and stands sell breakfasts, newspapers, last-minute odds and ends for the traveller, women walk by with breads and cakes to sell, boys with packets of cashews. At a magazine stand two slim books for sale, in Swahili—*I Slept with Satan in Order to Marry* and *He Wants It Here, He Wants It There.* I wonder if Walter Bgoya is aware of this emerging market in smut literature.

And then the buses begin to depart, it seems all at once, squeezing through a bottleneck to enter the main Morogoro Road. From Dar es Salaam, there is only one way out westward by road. The sun is now up and toasty; the bus is air-conditioned. The conductor comes along, hands out candies, then bottles of water, and we are set for our luxury trip.

The landscape is coastal green and lush to start with: the ubiquitous mango and coconut trees, small farms and little markets, boy-vendors running after vehicles selling cashews, mangoes, boiled eggs, termites, bottles of water, cans of soda; the bustle of the way station Chalinze, which was once only a quiet pit stop. There is an abundance of food here, an explosion of smells and colours and shapes amidst the hectic cheerful selling and yelling. The Uluguru range appears in the distance, Morogoro arrives, but the bus terminal is outside the town on the highway, and after a brief, businesslike stop we turn south towards Iringa and climb the highlands.

People still live in mud huts in the countryside; the rest stops on the way are roadside bushes, women going to the left side, men to the right, in the open. There is something earthy and intimate about this, though the fastidious will no doubt demur. The road quietly winds up a mountainside. Close to Iringa comes a spot where we speed by a face of sheer cut rock, a vertical slate, where a gang of school youths evidently stopped to picnic and found the time to write their graffiti. The generous roadside here, before the edge falls off into a valley, is littered with plastics, bottles, and wrappers. Happily this is the only instance of highway vandalism that we see.

Iringa arrives, but the bus does not enter the town. The cool highland climate has always drawn white settlers and expatriates to this area, though they've been a small minority. For many years the local member of parliament was Lady Chesham; her name was often in the newspapers, and that memory now invites images from those sunshine days immediately following independence. We did not know this then: she was born a Philadelphian.

Under British rule, Iringa boasted an English-style, exclusive boarding school called St. Michael's and St. George's School, which became the prestigious Mkwawa High School after independence. One January, at the beginning of the academic year, the Ministry of Education required a few students to be sent from our high school in Dar to Mkwawa in Iringa. When the notice came to our class requesting volunteers, my hand shot up. I didn't even think. Why would I want to leave friends and family and go to bhurr, as we called the hinterland? The restless soul, I suppose, was stirring even then. There was only one other volunteer and we were both accepted; but when I went to the headmaster's office to formalize my transfer, he simply waved me away with a "nenda zako, we"—go away, you—having received a hasty preemptive visit from my physics teacher.

The bus stops and an officious-looking fellow in his mid-thirties gets in and walks down the aisle, then back up. He stops, singles me out, asks for my identification. Who does he think I am? I ask for his ID, he's an immigration officer, and I show him my passport. The bus goes on. It's humiliating to be treated this way. Do I so obviously look like a foreigner? Am I a foreigner? I don't think so. I try to think of circumstances to mitigate this humiliation. My camera, for one thing, marks me out, though I've done my best to keep it out of sight; we are in a part of the country beloved to foreigners, and I'm the only brown man in the bus. There are always explanations.

We are in Hehe country. The Hehe under Chief Mkwawa are famous for their fierce resistance to German colonization. Mkwawa fought for more than seven years. In one encounter, the Germans suffered a particularly heavy defeat during an ambush and lost Major

Zelewsky, who had recently hanged Bushiri on the coast. Every schoolchild learns Mkwawa's name. He was never captured, choosing instead to shoot himself when, on July 19, 1898, he was finally surrounded by German troops. His skull was sent to Germany as a trophy; stipulated to be handed over to the British under the 1919 Treaty of Versailles, it was finally identified among the Bremen Museum's collection of African skulls by the governor of Tanganyika, Sir Edward Twining—with a bullet hole in it—and returned to the family in 1954. One of Dar es Salaam's mayors was a descendant of the chief.

In the heady mid-1960s, this highway going south, skirting mountains, looking down upon deep ravines, and unpaved at the time, was called the Hell Run. White Rhodesia had unilaterally declared its independence from Britain. Black Africa was in a rage. To bypass Rhodesia's blockade of Zambia's access to the Mozambican port of Beira, oil was being trucked all the way from Dar to Lusaka, and copper brought back. Thousands of trucks, originating from as far as Kenya, travelled the route. The pay was high, the road deadly. As *Time* reported, on February 25, 1966 (with a little exaggeration),

> . . . Zambia's single most important source of oil is "the Great North Road" that connects it—sort of—with Tanzania. Winding for more than 1,000 miles through rain forests, game plains and mountain ranges, the road may well be the world's worst international highway. Its dizzy hairpin turns were scraped out and leveled (often with dragged thorn-bushes) by African tribesmen working off their tax debts. Along its flat stretches, the road is little more than a trail of treacherous sand or soap-slick mud. Black, blinding rains and eerie mists make it all but impassable from October to

> May, and the right-of-way is often usurped by two-ton rhinos, herds of elephant and lions basking in the sun.

It's the same road we are on now, though it's paved and much nicer.

Past Iringa the landscape raises those unworldly configurations, the tors, which I already saw on the road to Tabora and Mwanza—heaps of boulders that have all the appearance of having rained down from the heavens. Here individual rocks at the base look as though they simply rolled down from a nearby heap. I recall that they have a rather mundane (and consequently boring) explanation. We pass an area of baobab trees, not single ones as on the coast but hundreds, a weird, ghostly army climbing up the hills like Tolkien's Ents. Later there comes a forest of coniferous trees, recently planted, and a timber mill. The earth becomes red and we pass a prosperous development with quaint little bungalows of red brick.

Finally, the day turns grey and our destination approaches; the fast super-luxury transforms into an aimless local, discharging and picking up passengers at will. Past Mbeya we reach Tukuyu—the final stop and my destination. It's just after nine. I step down into a dark square, the stalls all around beginning to pull up shutters and close; touts approach, speaking English, and I turn them away in Swahili. A vigorous rap song plays on some radio, the lyrics partially in Gujarati and very funny. My friend Mpeli arrives in a beat-up Land Cruiser and we head off to his home.

The next morning I sit outside on the front patio of a country cottage straight out of a fairy tale; the view is spectacular and the rest of the world does not exist. The sun is bright but kind, the earth wet, deep green, and hilly, the air cool and woody. I am reminded a little of Bukoba—where I did my National Service—also on the highlands but in the northwest, and also green and wet. There too the preeminent vegetation was banana and the mornings glistened. This looks like a place to retire in, which Mpeli's mother, whom we call Mama, has done. Water is supplied by a stream and piped. Electricity is both solar and mains—but the latter is frequently off, as it is most of today.

Consider the problems, though. The pipes need to be maintained but neighbours cannot get the money together. The road to the main highway is unpaved and so broken that it's an agony to drive on; voluntary work is available to fix it but the cost of equipment and supplies comes to about ten thousand dollars. And so, in Tanzanian style, they await donations. A Japanese lady is fondly remembered for her generosity, which made it possible for a portion of the road to be repaired.

Mama is a quiet, graceful woman, always appropriately dressed. Her husband was permanent secretary in the government immediately following independence, and for a time the high commissioner to Great Britain, and so she's been around, and was present during some of the key moments in the nation's history—the army mutiny of 1964 and the brief disappearance of the president, the Zanzibar revolution the same year, the Uganda coup, the war against Idi Amin in 1981. She was prominent in the women's movement. All these she casually mentions. She could be in the city, where the sophisticates of her generation reside, but she prefers the simple country life in this cool weather. She is fluent in Swahili, Nyakyusa—her mother tongue and the language of this area—and English, and before every meal says a simple grace in Swahili. The family are members of the Moravian Christian order, and she visits the local church, a few minutes away by car, on Sunday. The meals come in several courses: meat stew, banana, rice, spinach or cabbage, and once, for my benefit, chapatis. The latter are rather coarse, but since they are made specially for me, I finish them over several meals. Breakfast: banana, cooked banana, pineapple, bread with margarine.

The house has a large estate that provides plenty of banana, avocado, maharage beans, and vegetables; these could be sold for profit but there are no proper facilities or cooperatives locally to market the stuff. On the roads you see trucks filling up with banana bunches, on their way to Dar. TAZARA, the railway which was built in the 1970s with Chinese assistance to link Tanzania and Zambia and provide the latter access to a port, passed through Mbeya and was a godbless. But it is now more or less defunct, and Dar seems farther away. The bus rides are long and only wealthy businessmen can afford to fly. Mpeli, the ambassador's son, takes the bus whenever he visits the capital. It is difficult to maintain a more civilized life—hot water, food varieties, fresh meat, plumbing. The bathroom I use has a tub and telephone shower; but the latter leaks profusely and supplies for the fixture are not available even in Dar. A massive plumbing job awaits. Every evening a large wood stove is lighted outside the house to supply the hot water. Sunset is a little after six and there is barely light to read in most rooms. The fireplace gets lit as we breakfast. It all looks romantic, but it's difficult too.

Tukuyu is a small, quiet town consisting essentially of a main street and a few smaller roads. It has the look it must have had fifty years ago, minus the Asians who ran the shops. On the main street is a typical Indian-style market strip, with one-storey buildings of cement brick, painted white or yellow. There's a certain ghostly feel to the street; the shops look meagre and dull and tentative. One easily imagines the well-stocked outlets of yesteryear run by the Indian men and their wives, their children playing marbles or tag or cricket outside. A neighbourhood, a community. It's gone.

The old boma is up the red hill from the main street; it has been rebuilt and houses the council office, though the thick ramparts of the former fortified structure are still visible over part of a concrete side-wall and near the front entrance. A man approaches, chatty and digressive, and informs us that there used to be a canon or two in place outside the boma, brought by the Germans, who had come here after first settling at a place called Masoko by a lake—which has the miraculous feature that come rain or drought, the water level never changes. The Germans had fled the mosquitoes of Masoko, preferring the higher ground of Tukuyu, where they used forced native labour to build the boma. They called this town Neue Langenburg.

After five separate handshakes with the informant, a cousin of Mpeli's mother and reluctant to leave us, we drive off in the Land Cruiser on a rough road in search of Masoko, jerking painfully in our seats. The way is down, in the direction of Lake Nyasa to the southeast, the landscape formed of undulating hills with farms, here and there a simple roadside village. In the distance, the green-coated Mount Rungwe, head in the clouds at ten thousand feet; the streams we cross all head down the Rift Valley to feed Lake Nyasa. It occurs to me that it's impossible to starve here, provided you have a bit of land; and perhaps even if you don't have it. We pass farms growing banana, avocado, maharage, occasional mango and palm, tea, coffee, cocoa.

Holding desperately on to my seat, I am treated to Mpeli's business schemes. His family has farmland, and he's contemplating a chocolate factory for—of course—the western market. I tell him my objection: the market is cornered, and westerners, partial to Swiss and Belgian, are not likely to buy chocolates made in Africa. He's looking for investors, and I am reminded that to an African, anyone with Indian roots is a businessman or has business connections. He may be right. Perhaps he thinks I might have the money to invest. I don't. I let the idea pass. Here is another one: developing electronic readers for school textbooks, with foreign assistance, naturally. Meanwhile this cheerful man, overeducated in England, earns a sporadic living as a translator.

The roadside through this glorious abundance is well peopled, but the traffic is only pedestrian. Life proceeds at walking pace—or remains stationary—under a cool sun. We pass women drying cocoa beans, men paused on the road to gaze pensively at us. Several times we slow to ask for directions, once we stop at a little market and have sodas—chai and mandazi having run out. The people are helpful and chatty, unwilling to let go of a conversation—which often ends with the Nyakyusa word *ndaaga*, generously stretched out, that carries a spectrum of meanings, used to show sympathy, to bid welcome and farewell, to show thanks. Finally we take a hidden turning past a bridge over a beautiful, burbling, stone-banked river, onto a dirt track. A long line of neatly dressed women, carrying baggages on their heads, comes walking in the opposite direction, returning from church. It's Sunday. Up on a hill, right at the corner where we've turned, are the red-brick ruins we've come to look at; we decide to return to them later. Farther along the track, at the church from where the women have spilled out, we stop and park, then follow on foot a gently sloping trail that leads to the miraculous lake that Mpeli's sticky relative had spoken about. It's inside a crater and has no overground streams feeding or draining it. It's a beautiful, still lake, the only activity on it some young men, bathing and washing clothes at the shore.

We drive back up and pause at the ruins. Situated atop a rise, overlooking the lake, this is where the German colonialists first set up in the area. It's a good, scenic location for an administrative headquarters, were it not for the mosquitoes. Parts of the original red-brick structure have been built over and extended, and show signs of occupation. The original walls, where present, are thick, the windows and doors are arched. This is it, a bit of local history.

Back in Tukuyu we sit out on the porch of a rather pleasant but empty restaurant on the main street and have instant coffee, with roasted corn brought to us by a street vendor. Before us are the former Indian buildings with their stucco facades that date them to the 1960s. Their names, which would have been at the top, have been erased—evidence of the venom that socialism could release—but I can read "Ladha" faintly on one of them. I wonder if it belonged to the family whose son came to study at my high school in Dar, and whom I met in London recently after several decades. Upon his arrival at our school he had introduced himself as the most handsome boy of Tukuyu, causing a ripple of merriment and teasing. There is also the Makanji Mansion, the only name that has been allowed to stay, because the letters stand up on the top edge of the terrace wall to become a decorative landmark. The town is quiet, with low-energy activity—the muhogo seller, the corn seller, the newspaper vendor, and our quiet café. The sun shines brightly and it's still a beautiful day.

Early morning at the house, sitting outside at the porch set—round table, four chairs—I am reminded of the casual style of life we termed or thought of as "European." Who in today's frantic Dar, European or otherwise, can afford this leisure? It takes all one can do simply to keep up a lifestyle, even a modest one. Leisure is bought and timed, parcelled. It rained all last night, vigorously, and this morning the outside looks engorged. Some worker singing nearby, a birdcall, insect chirps. And this is the dry season, Mpeli says with satisfaction. But Mbeya, an hour away, can get really dry, they've seriously cut down trees there, including something called the Mbeya Forest. I tell him of the area in Dar es Salaam behind our former primary school, which was all woods once, with mango and coconut trees and lantana bushes. Not a tree left now.

Mpeli and I often talk of "then" and "now," how the spirit of Uhuru (independence) is gone, how it's every man and woman for themselves. It's by now an old African complaint, of course—the betrayal after independence—and the subject of several important novels, but that doesn't make it less real. There is a contradiction here, also, for it was the enthusiasm of the post-independence period followed by socialist zeal that destroyed much, including the education system and the lamented Mbeya Forest.

The Moravian Christian mission is a large property off the highway and on the slope of Rungwe, not far from Tukuyu. The road is rough but thankfully short. As soon as we park and alight, under a large tree, out of the vehicle that's been following us emerges a tall, sharply dressed man in black trousers, black jacket, and white pointed shoes. He could be mistaken for a night club operator but is in fact the chief executive of the mission. He looks anxious because his wife collapsed in the bathroom earlier this morning and he has to head back; but first he takes us to his office, inside a long, white, iron-roofed house. He tells me he recently visited Canada and gives me a brief history of the mission. He points out on the wall the framed photos of all the previous executives of the Moravian mission, starting with the Germans who founded it, followed by the British, and then the Africans. One of his predecessors left him a sword symbolizing, I suppose, his role as a soldier of Christ. Was it ever used as a weapon?

I don't ask. After more polite talk, the executive takes me to the new Rungwe Archive and Museum Centre building next door.

The Moravian Church, according to a 1957 handbook at the museum, is a Protestant order officially called the Church Order of the Unitas Fratrum. It was founded in 1457 in Bohemia (in the present-day Czech Republic). In 1620 or thereabouts when Roman Catholicism was in its ascendancy, the Moravian Church was completely suppressed; its members went underground and dispersed. It re-emerged a hundred years later in present-day Germany.

On March 31, 1891, four missionaries left the Moravian centre in Herrnhut, Germany, and arrived at the mouth of the Zambezi River (in present-day Zimbabwe), from where they embarked on a long journey north. The Berlin conference under the auspices of Bismarck had recently taken place and the scramble for Africa was well underway. The missionaries had to take the longer route because of troubles on the coast in German East Africa (Tanganyika), then seething with resistance. They stopped at Kapugi, at the Free Church of Scotland mission (which does not seem to exist now), where Dr. Kerr Cross who was in charge welcomed them and recommended that they go up to Rungwe. Two of the missionaries, Meyer and Richard, arrived at Rungwe Hills and were welcomed by thirteen-year-old Chief Mwakapalila on August 21, 1891. The place was consecrated and a church built. Richard stayed here until 1903, Meyer until 1916. The vision which that wandering German missionary, Johann Krapf, dreamt only fifty years before, of Christian missions "spreading the Gospel throughout the benighted region round Lake Niassa," and beyond, it would appear, has came true. The Moravian mission proselytizes actively, and currently Tanzania boasts the largest number of Moravians in the world. The Rungwe Mission oversees activities on the coast and in Zanzibar, as well as in Malawi. There are a high school in Rungwe, a new university in Mbeya, and three girls' hostels built specifically so that schoolgirls do not have to travel long distances and suffer molestation.

The Archive and Museum Centre is a new red-brick building with a pretty garden in front. The archivist is a young man, a bony lad called Mohamed Ayub Junior. It turns out, however, that records from German times are missing; it is possible that the missionaries removed them during the First World War. In fact there is nothing here from before 1927 that I can see. Junior—as the archivist calls himself—is aware of this lacuna. When the director comes around to inquire how I'm doing, I inform him of the missing years and he makes a show of mild surprise. Details such as these don't appear to bother him. He repeats that he was in Canada not long ago, and later asks if I can find something for his son there. On a small shelf in the office there is a *Life of Bismarck*, a German–Nyamwezi dictionary a hundred years old, and a Latin word book from the same period. Among the correspondence, a long and polite letter from a young man to the Church in the 1950s asks it to prepare for the country's independence, in its outlook and its leadership. The young man turns out to be Mpeli's father.

A walking tour with Junior. It's still pleasantly cool and sunny outside, in the distance are the hills and forests, and in this haven in their midst all is neat, picture-clean, and quiet; the gardens are tended and the lawns mowed, the few small buildings are well preserved. We cross a stream over a quaint bridge of cut logs, walk past the modern church, a red-brick affair, then past the site of the first church, where there's only a little shop now with a few young men sitting around, and reach the old cemetery. There are not more than twenty headstones on an uneven ground, some recently placed. But there are some child graves from German times. Most of the European expatriates, it would seem, were able to return home, but some had to leave their dead offspring behind. We proceed to the place where Meyer and Richard first pitched their tents, but the path is steep and covered with wet leaves, so we turn back. There's a natural spring which supplies free water to the area. It was used to run a generator not long ago, supplying the area with electricity, before the national electric company convinced the Church authorities to switch over; the generator fell to disuse and pillage. Now the mission has to deal with outages, like the rest of the country, and not everyone gets electricity, as they used to.

I ask Junior if he had trouble getting his job, with a name like Mohamed. He says his father is a Muslim, his mother a Christian. And he himself? He has a choice. And he'll choose to be a Christian? Yes, but he's not yet told his father, who's travelling. And his name—has he picked a new one? He's the first-born, he says, so he can't change his name, which is why he's adopted "Junior." Ingenious, though what will the Church fathers say? Christian–Muslim coexistence in a family is not unusual; it's in the nature of Tanzanian society to accept and live with others' beliefs. The animosity and suspicion of recent times is due to outside influence—the Christian evangelists from America promising miracle cures, the Muslim fundamentalists promising the same, while also proliferating mosques.

The museum, housed in a single room, is small but impressive. The display consists of Nyakyusa weapons (mostly spears), traditional constumes, and historical photographs. Men and women, when the Europeans first came, wore a metal ring around the waist from which a cloth went around the crotch. The history of the Church is told pictorially by means of the photographs and detailed captions. There's no mention of the boma—now the district office—down the road, though I understand that the grandfather of the chief executive was shot to death by the Germans.

What was the relationship of the Church to the boma? How did they each respond to the European War? What was the Nyakyusa response to the Church initially? A large number joined it. Membership did bring benefits, in the form of schooling and good jobs, and the Church has been ready to go with the times. It's a pity that critical information about the early, formative years is missing; it could not all have been destroyed, perhaps it lies scattered around in foreign archives. Mpeli is of the opinion that recent foreign visitors have been pilfering papers. It's not hard to do so. The century-old Nyamwezi–German dictionary waits to be taken home by some bibliophile.

16.

The Southern Highlands: Mbeya

THE ROAD TO MBEYA IS SMOOTH AND HILLY AND LIVELY, the wayside markets more densely packed the closer we get to the town. There's an abundance of carpentry shops, since wood is aplenty. We see heaps of bananas and tomatoes for sale, we pass stands of eucalyptus and fir trees. The police checkpoints are an irritant, and surely there to keep the force occupied, and take bribes, as many people will say; they do let you know that the government is always watching. Mbeya is a dusty, sprawled-out town; the side roads for the most part are dirt-surface and back-breaking. In the past, I'm told, there was a large golf course in town belonging to the Mbeya Club—but in the interest of egalitarianism when capitalist "bloodsuckers" were despised, it was put to disuse and sold, and now, with capitalism back in favour again, the land is commercial and residential. There are an impressive number of colleges in Mbeya, including the new Moravian university, Teofilo Kisanji University (TEKU), at the outskirts. It is our first stop.

The campus, tucked behind neat boundary walls, is small but impressive; the road to it is rough, the ride pure torture. The programs offered by the university are education, business, technology, and theology. A class has been let out, and a rush of young people emerges outside into the sunshine, the scene is heartwarming and familiar. I'm not sure why Mpeli has brought me here, except for me to look at the campus and for us both to pay respects to the vice-chancellor. There's a lull in the day's activity in the administrative block, due to a power outage, and the place is dark when we arrive. The vice-chancellor's office is modest; we meet a tall and very urbane man with whom we talk about this and that—my event the next day at the Mbeya Club, books, and publishing.

The road into Mbeya clamours with business. This is the "new," booming Mbeya, outside the older town. We stop at a liquor store in a two-storey building, whose owner is the sponsor of my event. An unassuming man with a brisk manner and a sense of humour, not a Nyakyusa, I guess. He studied in the Soviet Union and is married to a Ukrainian. He gives me his take on why academics are inept at business: they follow rules without sense. He comes to stand with us outside his store as we depart, and he points to a tall building under construction next door. It will soon be completed, he says, though without the necessary permits; an academic would still be waiting for permission. There is a lesson or two in this example that I cannot quite untangle.

We put up at a decent but modest hotel called the Karibuni, run by a European evangelical Christian who broke away from the Rungwe Moravians. Part of the premises is rented out to another European group, on a mission to translate the Bible into all the languages of Tanzania. "God speaks your language!" proclaims the back of one of their white four-wheelers. The Christians have targeted this and other areas with all the ardour of the space race of a few decades ago, but I am also reminded of the ardour and ambition of the intrepid German missionary Johann Krapf who came long before them. My room is clean and efficiently furnished, though the overhead lamp is hidden behind the mosquito-net canopy, and the towel provided would make a horse flinch—a form of Christian penitence perhaps.

As I write this, in the dining hall, where—a rare treat—the coffee is ground on site and brewed in a percolator, a Russian channel describes how the Russians repelled the Germans during the Second World War. The chef comes out to chat and regrets the flight of so many Indians from the country—he worked for an Indian family in Tanga and names some gourmet dishes he used to prepare.

Felix and I first meet at a place called Garden Café, which only partly lives up to its name with its charming outdoor ambience, for it serves no coffee, only beer. There is always a wariness, I've noticed, in Africans outside of Dar es Salaam when they meet an Asian (who might well be a businessman), especially one who now lives abroad. But when I tell Felix that I am from Uhuru Street, he grins. I have credentials. Many people today—Asian or African—would balk at the thought of visiting the tumult of the Kariakoo area of Dar es Salaam. And when I tell him I did National Service in Kaboya, outside Bukoba, we break the ice completely. This means that like him I sweated in the countryside "building the nation" in the heyday of patriotism and Nyerere, a school graduate humbled to suffer abuse at the hands of the uneducated sergeants. Not many today carry that badge. Immediately we start exchanging National Service anecdotes. Like all such stories, even when told in Toronto—and they often are—they are accompanied by irrepressible laughter at the comic situations encountered during our service to the nation. He did his service in Ruvu, where the roars of lions in the night were enough to deter you from going AWOL, more than the fear of the sergeants' brutal punishment were you to get caught.

Felix is an investigative journalist with perhaps the hardest-hitting Swahili paper in the country. He has many tales of corruption and abuses that happen in the countryside and are not reported; he has become a sort of ombudsman of last resort for the desperate. Two of his stories are particularly disturbing because, told in his unassuming manner, free from rhetoric and high-mindedness, they show in pure form the helplessness of those who live away from the centres of power and wealth.

He was brought into the first story by a telephone call from villagers at a uranium mining location. A South African manager had hired a local man to lure teenage girls to him, and then he raped them. In the most recent occurrence the girl had been pregnant and had been raped anally. Do something, they told Felix. Have you gone to the police? he asked. Are you kidding, came the retort. You think they don't know? Felix then called some local authorities—he's not merely a reporter, he has connections—and gave them an ultimatum: if they did not do something about the situation he would release the story. The pimp was arrested, the South African got into his car and fled in the night, but was recognized hiding away at a hotel during the day and was caught. It would have been easy to kill him, Felix says. People's justice.

The second story is similar but involves Chinese miners in another area who had been molesting local women. If they are not stopped, the villagers warned, we will kill every Chinese in sight. These threats are not empty. There have been cases of vigilante justice reported in the newspapers, where villagers have killed bandits whom they had themselves captured. In one recent case bandits had already killed four people before one of them was apprehended and promptly dispatched to his maker.

I ask Felix if he will accompany me to Kyela, on Lake Nyasa, close to the Malawi border. He agrees. Kyela is his hometown, though he grew up partly in Zanzibar and has travelled to every corner of the country, which explains his cosmopolitan outlook. And his knowledge of Uhuru Street.

We leave by bus the next morning at around ten. Our route goes directly south, taking us past a countryside that already looks familiar. We speed past wheat, maize, and banana plantations before entering a rice area. The vegetation changes from thick and green forest and farmland to grass and thorn, palm and mango, the temperature steadily rising. We are descending into the great Rift Valley, and Lake Nyasa, to the discerning eye, is visible in the haze. (But not to me.) Felix takes pains to point out how rich the country is, how enterprising the people are; and yet how poor. There's a communal feel to this bus journey, a measure of intimacy. Men and women are shouting into phones, the radio is blaring; two clucking chickens in a cage in the centre aisle are our co-passengers. The music is an eclectic mix: South African, rap, and suddenly, to my astonishment, *la-la-la* and a Bollywood love duet in Hindi and nobody bats an eyelid, then a Swahili spiritual praising Bwana Yesu, Lord Jesus, at which a friendly argument erupts behind me. Where is this Bwana Yesu, jeers a young upstart, to which a woman answers robustly, He's everywhere, don't you see him—here! there!—and she dances in her seat. Police checkpoints once again, the familiar irritants, rude interruptions to the rhythm of the journey. A cop gets into the bus and unctuously addresses the passengers, If you have any complaints, you should let me know, I am here to serve you—do you hear me? Like he is believed.

We pass a stretch of road called Uwanda wa Ndege, or "airport," a downhill bend where speeding vehicles would fly off the curve into the valley below; now there are speed bumps to prevent such deadly accidents. Another patch of road is the site of a recent oil tanker crash; the local residents rushed to the toppled tank to help themselves to the oil, while someone thought it smarter to steal the battery, which sparked. Some forty people were killed in the explosion. As a reporter Felix had to go and view the gruesome remains of charred bodies; for months afterwards the mere sight of meat turned his stomach. He points to a coal-mining site in the distance, developed by the Chinese, subsequently sold to a politician's relative, and now more or less defunct. It would have generated 3MW of power. It has been proposed now to let the Chinese run it. Finally we are down inside the valley, and arrive at Kyela and get off on the main road, where Felix's brother runs a hotel and restaurant. We find him inside a large barnlike hall, relaxing at a table with two other men. Business looks dull. It's around noontime, the place is empty. I'm asked if I wish to stay the night, and I say no. We have sodas, the talk is politics. The local MP has been investigating corruption, and the men believe there have been attempts on his life.

Kyela is a thriving rice market. In the milling area, a large and busy square surrounded by shops, rice is spread out on the ground to dry, people free to walk on it, trucks to pass over; heaps of bags wait to be taken away, while a loud and cheerful bunch of women wait around for their rice to return from the mills. The town is compact, with a frontier feel to it. The Malawi border is close by and easily crossed. Kyela is known for Malawi marijuana—the best, they say—and sugar, and street vendors walk by calling out biscuits from Blantyre. On the main road, buses come and go, and the side streets are busy with shops, restaurants, guest houses, and hotels. After walking around the town, and treating ourselves to a simple meal of soda and roasted muhogo, we depart on one of several buses clamouring for custom; but not before witnessing a fight between competing bus conductors.

You think the constant police presence on the highways is an irritant, placed there by a harassing government; but when your bus stops on the highway and you are summarily transferred to another one, which then keeps piling up passengers and dropping them off regardless of space and safety, and it's getting late and dark and there's no electricity anywhere, you feel you need them to check the runaway overcrowding and violation of contract—but where are they now, these police? One of them finally appears at a stop, gets in, looks around; the conductor quietly takes him outside to the side of the bus and returns, and we are off. A bribe has been paid. Of course, to be fair, this overcrowded bus in the dark, chickens included, unsafe as it is, is the only means by which many people can get home.

We departed Kyela at four, arrive at the Mbeya bus station at close to nine; a car ride would have taken us not more than two hours.

An SMS from Mpeli says there's no electricity at the Karibuni, there's a blackout, and therefore I should go to the Mbeya Hotel, which is what I do. I find him sitting near reception with his laptop, preparing notes for the TEKU board meeting the next day. Such are the frustrations of getting things done.

In 1958, a "tourist" arrived in Mbeya, and wrote about it as follows:

> Mbeya is a little English garden-suburb with no particular reason for existence. It was built in the 1930s as a Provincial capital at the time when gold was mined there. Now there is a little aerodrome and a collection of red roofs among

> conifers and eucalyptus trees, a bank, a post office, a police station. There is also an hotel, named after a non-existent railway, where at that time, it was reputed, there lurked some disgruntled English journalists who had been forbidden entrance to Nyasaland. . . .

The visitor was Evelyn Waugh, travelling from Mombasa to Rhodesia, mostly by road. He had already visited Tanga, Dar, and Kilwa. Back in Dar, he was driven to Iringa in a Mercedes, and from there came to Mbeya in a Land Rover, where he stayed with a Mrs. Newman, who forbade him to stay at the Railway Hotel with its disreputable clientele.

That hotel was posh and European by local standards, serving such exotic delectables as oxtail soup, roast beef, and peas. It is now called the Mbeya Hotel and is owned by Khoja Ismailis—a large photo of the Aga Khan is displayed in the office—who've done well with it. There's a porch, parking, and a garden. The bar is decent, the food is mostly Indian and excellent; no wonder it's crowded this evening. The manager looks like a recent immigrant, speaking Hindi or Urdu with the owners, who are themselves Gujarati-speakers. At a table nearby sit some foreign construction workers; at another some young Indian men discuss schools, safety, the virtues of Mbeya compared with those of Arusha as places to settle. These are the new Indian entrepreneurs, a world apart from my ancestors who came in dhotis and turbans a hundred years ago; these young men are trim and fit, they wear smart casuals and carry laptops and briefcases and represent the multinationals of a new India. And they are the foreigners.

The next day, starting from Mbeya Hotel I take a walk through the old town. It's quaint and quiet, with the typical strips of one-storey buildings with businesses; a plain Hindu temple, the priest or caretaker sitting idly outside—infinitely remote from the bustle of India. On the other side of Karume Avenue are the wealthy houses, where the Europeans, and perhaps Waugh's Mrs. Newman, must have stayed. The Khoja prayer house has nothing to distinguish it, yet it's impossible to miss on Jamatkhana Road.

A few years ago, that intrepid American traveller Paul Theroux came by Mbeya. He found it "a habitable ruin." In his travelogue *Dark Star Safari,* he went on to write,

> In a town like Mbeya I understood the sense of futility. . . . In such towns I felt: no achievements, no successes, the place is only bigger and darker and worse. I began to fantasize that the Africa I travelled through was often like a parallel universe, the dark star image in my mind, in which everyone existed as a sort of shadow counterpart of someone in the brighter world.

In other words, a dark continent. How do you explain to a fleet-footed traveller, who speeds through a place like the Road Runner, ignorant of the language and knowing nobody locally, and with naive arrogance reports to his brighter world about it, that there is *life* here, and all that living entails? That the people who live here are not shadows or mere creatures but human; all you need to do is touch them.

My session at the Mbeya Club goes well. The club was once exclusive, of course, and one easily imagines the snooker table, the card tables, liveried waiters, the bar. Mpeli repeats that it once had the best golf course south of the Sahara. What remains now is an underutilized stub of a building. There are some forty to fifty people present, which is surprising for this dark, cool night when the town looks essentially dead; the food has been donated, as have the drinks. Among the audience are a handful of foreign workers in the medical field, including a young Ethiopian American woman, who explains to me why she is rootless and back in Africa. I read for the audience a story about the trauma of a boy leaving home to go to America; it's an old one, set at a time when going away was a daunting process portending a perhaps permanent exile, but it has a completeness, and a relevance even today, I think. It tells in fictionalized form how I myself went away. Then I say what I have said many times before, why it's important to tell our own stories, write our own history. I prove my credentials because I don't come as an outsider, or speak as one; I am from Uhuru Street, now living in Canada. The Street runs through my veins.

There are many questions, there is overall a great deal of satisfaction. We should have more meetings like this one, goes out the cry.

Early the next morning Mpeli takes me to the bus station; on the way he gives me a tour of the town. We are early and take breakfast at a stall, tea and chapati—which is fried and what I would call a paratha—then we say goodbye, and I leave for Dar.

The bus is an "express," which means that it does not stop on the way, except for a few rest stops beside bushes, and a quick stop for meals, when we are told to be back in ten minutes, to bring the food with us if necessary. We rush back with fried chicken, cassava, rice, chips. As usual, a candy and a bottle of water from the conductor, and later a soda. There are two television screens to show movies; the intrusion is annoying on one hand, but the local productions are also instructive and amusing, with a very distinctive local humour, and therefore easily engage the passengers. In one, a blustering, bullying man learns that he cannot push around his office-working wife anymore; by the time she's finished with him, he's begging her for attention. The characters live wealthy lifestyles in well-furnished homes, though far from the opulent extravaganzas of Indian film and TV. The women are young and pretty, wear western dresses and have straightened hair. On the other hand many of the women and girls I have seen in Dar and on this trip have beautiful and intricate cornrows, displaying a fashion taking off in just the opposite direction.

It takes thirteen hours to get to Ubungo station in Dar. And then two more hours of traffic to get to my host's house.

17.

Book, Medicine, and Spirit

In Dar es Salaam one morning, the Asian owner of the hotel in Oyster Bay where I happened to be staying, Mr. Solanki, asked me if I wished to consult a mganga—there was an African wunderkid who had shown amazing powers in solving all kinds of problems and bringing good luck. I would be well advised to see him.

Ashok Solanki, a short rotund man in his forties, wearing a grey Kaunda suit, belonged to the Kumbhad, or potter—a so-called "lower"—Indian caste, whose community used to live in the poor, self-contained neighbourhood of Dar es Salaam called the Kumbhad wadi. Here in an enclosed compound in a corner of downtown they had their rather basic residences, no more than shacks, where they produced assorted earthenware, which they would take around in pull-carts to sell in the Asian streets of the city. Their red clay pots were used for storing boiled water for drinking, and their rounded, shallow pans—the tawas—for baking chapatis. As children we would sometimes be cajoled during the holidays to go to Kumbhad wadi and fetch clumps of wet clay to play with and keep ourselves busy. In the heyday of socialism, the late President Nyerere paid a visit to this Kumbhad village and praised its communal, self-help style of living.

The daily paper printed a photo of that visit and the potters became famous. Where other Asians were often caricatured as capitalist exploiters, bloodsuckers with long straws (though most eked out a living in small trade), here were the true and exemplary socialists living right in our midst.

Since that time, I discovered, many of the potters had done well economically and moved into other, more profitable businesses; some became mechanics, others drove taxis. The old Kumbhad wadi neighbourhood was now occupied by a few apartment buildings, though it was still set apart. Solanki himself was in construction and owner of the Karibu, one of the leading hotels in the city, in Oyster Bay; his daughter attended the exclusive International School, which had invited me to Dar and put me up at the hotel. That morning, Solanki, having introduced himself, had taken me to his office and treated me to chai. He had proudly pointed to the photo, hanging on a wall, of that famous presidential visit to the Kumbhad wadi. After some chitchat, he recommended to me the wunderkid, the boy-mganga, whose name was Sheikh Sharriff. All my troubles would go away. Did I look so troubled? But I was curious. Was it from such help that Ashok Solanki had gone from potter's son to local tycoon? He had already consulted Sheikh Sharriff before, he told me, now he needed more advice before starting on a new venture.

The next morning when I came down, Solanki had already left; obviously his business with Sheikh Sharriff was urgent, not to mention too private for my ears. But later his driver was ready with a Mercedes to take me. On the way, on a tape recording I was treated to the life story of the boy—his ominous birth, the miracles he had performed. He had begun to speak when he was only nine months old, all of a sudden, when he reminded his mother of a vow she had made when pregnant with him, that she would take him to a mosque. Both his parents were Christians, his father was a former policeman. The boy refused the name they gave him, Fidelis. He also refused the names that various Muslim sheikhs offered, and preferred to call himself Sheikh Sharriff. He had since gathered a large following.

The driver took me to Temeke, into a neighbourhood with houses of the traditional type—plastered mud walls, tin roof, a front porch supported by an upright or two. Coconut and mango trees were scattered over the neighbourhood, giving shade from the sun; the ground was sand. We parked under a tree, and as we approached a house, a gathering of about thirty people was being dismissed outside with a prayer; the driver pointed out Sheikh Sharriff, a little boy of about seven wearing kanzu and cap and barefoot, trotting away by himself. The driver spoke to the father, a tall and burly man, who replied brusquely, "Wait," and strode away to the house, which had two entrances. We followed and were told by someone to sit and wait in one of the two corridors leading inside, where we met the boy's two older brothers, attired traditionally like the father and the boy. After a while we were instructed to proceed into the second corridor, which we did through the backyard and entered one of the rooms. It was empty, but soon two charcoal braziers were brought and placed on the ground. This was going to be a private session. It occurred to me that the family wouldn't want too many Asians to be seen here: Asians meant money, and presumably corruption.

Sheikh Sharriff shuffled in, preoccupied with two toy cars he was clutching in his hands. Very much a shy little boy. Behind him walked his father. I could sense that my beard perturbed the father—he seemed suspicious, perhaps, that I was an orthodox Muslim (nothing could be further from the truth) who might denounce his prodigy and call out the sheikhs. The boy's lack of attention embarrassed him.

A small number of men had now come inside to watch the proceedings.

"Sharriff," said the dad, "these are the people who help us. Pray for them."

Sharriff was playing with the cars. One of his brothers stepped up and took them from him. Then the father told the driver and me to reflect on our problems and needs, and he opened two of the packets of incense we had brought and sprinkled the contents onto the braziers. A scented smoke arose. The other packets were emptied into a partly full bottle. There was something remarkably bare-bones about this ritual, as though this were the mere outline, a postmodern enactment of an opera ordinarily more elaborate and complete.

Sharriff was asked to begin. Looking distractedly at the ground, he mumbled the name of a sura of the Quran, and either "three" or "five."

This was hardly the articulate precocious child I had been told about and heard about in the cassette recorder, the wonderful young African Jesus who carried out serious discussions with elders in the mosques and performed miracles. As a brother recited the prescribed Quranic verse, all the men having raised both their hands in prayer, the boy began playing with a timing mechanism he had produced from somewhere, pressing it to move the digits. After three recitals, the men stopped, and the mechanism was taken away from the boy, who commanded, "More." "You said three times," said the brother. "Two more," the child replied, sounding wilful. The verse was recited, and the litte sheikh named another sura, which was also recited. The session was over.

The driver put some money into the boy's hands, who without looking at it gave it to his father. I put a bill into the little hands, and it too went to the father.

There was something to ponder in that small episode; from the outset it reflected comprehensively the complexities of Dar es Salaam's multicultural, multiracial society, throwing up as well some delicious ironies and coincidences. Solanki's resorting to the Temeke boy's famous powers broke at once the traditional barriers to Asian-African and Hindu-Muslim interactions. Perhaps his "lower" caste background made that easy. Caste discrimination was still very much in existence in Dar, as I was soon to find out. The boy's family itself combined Christian and Muslim faiths, the boy having been fashioned by his minders into a caricatured Muslim Jesus. When I was asked during my session with him to think about my "shida," my problem, I had brought to my mind a recent injury, which had recently received the services of a young Toronto physiotherapist of Tanzanian background. Did I believe in the boy's powers? Hardly. I had long put my faith entirely on the rational. I could afford to, of course; others had to rely on miracles.

As we drove back from Temeke to Oyster Bay in the Mercedes, I saw displayed on the sides of bus shelters garish posters announcing a revival meeting, to be attended by pastors from Kenya, Uganda, and Canada, and calling on the public to bring their sick, blind, and lame to be prayed for.

I never found out if Sheikh Sharriff's prayers had helped Solanki in his endeavours. In fact I never saw the hotel-owner again. But soon after that episode, when I had moved from his luxury hotel to the familiar and cheap, though mean-spirited Flamingo Guest House in Gaam, I came across an angry letter in the national daily that named Ashok Solanki and a few others as members of an Asian "mafia" that had "bought" the government but whose days were surely numbered. He had made his millions, it was said in the city, using the goodwill that the potter caste had gathered in the past due to their exemplary "socialist" living and the famous presidential visit. These days, as I had found out, he resorted to other help. Perhaps he ended up in England, where part of his family had already moved.

Uganga is the Swahili term for magic or sorcery of whatever sort and the practitioner is called a mganga. In the past, regular medical doctors were also known as mganga, before daktari became common. The word mchawi is sometimes used for the sinister sort of magic; and the Muslim mganga is also called a maalim.

There are various forms of sorcery. There is the magic of the Book, involving the Quran; there is the magic of the medicine, involving potions, sometimes obtained in gruesome manner; and there is magic involving sacrifices. All these may overlap—why stop at one means? Potions are often made using parts of murder victims. There is good magic and bad magic.

Living abroad, it is easy to forget how common are the beliefs in witchcraft even today, how much a part of life they once were in your own life—when you feared passing by a cemetery or walking under a tree at night in case a djinn got you and you were transformed into an albino, or became possessed and acted strangely, and needed the services of a maalim or mganga. Djinns and spirits supposedly stayed on trees, especially the dreadful-looking baobab that looked as if its head were buried in the ground; they wandered out at dusk, the time known as maghrab, which could be both holy and sinister. Asian children were commonly threatened with bogeymen who could take you away—in Kilwa there was said to be an old woman who set traps for children. You could come under a spell, cast by some mganga, through a drink or some other means. The outcome of a football match could be blamed on a wicked spell:

rematches have been demanded on the basis of a rooster having ominously crossed a field before a game.

All this sounds amusing and primitive. But only a few years ago came grisly reports of albinos being abducted and hacked to death by sorcerers' agents, their body parts used for magical purposes as far away as the Congo. Victims included babies and family men; a man had offered to sell his albino wife. Tanzania has an inordinately high number of albinos. The incidents involving their murders and hacking received large coverage, especially from the BBC, and Tanzania's president made a speech condemning such sinister crimes. The police subsequently exhibited an albino skin at one of their stations to demonstrate how terrible the crime was. This begs the question: did the people need convincing?

One day in the 1950s, at dusk in the Muslim month of Ramadan, a coven of four sorcerers held a meeting in the village of Mteniyapa in the coastal region. They were the senior sorcerer called Bwana Shambi and three women: Binti Jizia, the planner of their misdeeds, Binti Hanifu, a young woman, and Binti Ramadhani, an older woman and their weakest link. Bwana Shambi sounded frustrated that day. Listen, he said to the three women gathered around him. We must perform a rite to bring us good fortune; enough time has passed, and we suffer. For what? At once Binti Jizia pounced upon the young Binti Hanifu: It's your turn now, she said, you've done nothing for us. Bring us a victim if you want the benefits from this coven. It's as simple as that—no free rides, pay up. When Binti Hanifu demurred, Binti Jizia pressed on, And your victim must be someone close to you—your child, or a sibling. Just anyone won't do. Bring them soon.

With this ultimatum given, the four went their ways.

The next day was Saturday. Just as Bwana Shambi was passing Binti Jizia's house, she came out. I am looking for you, she said. Bwana Shambi, feeling listless that day, said querulously, Binti Jizia, you are our planner. Tell Binti Hanifu to give us her sister—if not, let herself be sacrificed.

On Wednesday the four of them sat and waited in their secret place, which was towards the sea. Binti Ramadhani had already had qualms about the plan, and she had come unwillingly. As they waited, Salima, Binti Hanifu's younger sister, who was also Binti Ramadhani's daughter-in-law, left her house, pulled by the power of sorcery set in motion by the evil four. As she walked through the village, entranced and barely in her own mind, she was observed by a few of the villagers. She left the village behind and approached the four sorcerers.

Grab her, cried Bwana Shambi as Salima arrived, whereupon Binti Hanifu grasped her sister and pulled her down, saying to the others, Now I've settled my debts to you, I owe you nothing. The other three sorcerers rubbed Salima with medicines, and as she lost her strength and became faint, knowing her end was near, she said the Shahada, her confession of faith: There is no God but God. The four sorcerers left her there, trussed up, planning to come back for her that night.

At sunset a cry went out that Salima was missing, and the next morning a frantic search began, in which the four sorcerers also participated, though they had already killed the girl in the night and placed the body in a derelict hut to make it appear that it had collapsed over her. When the body was found, it was clear that the girl had been murdered. A part of her tongue had been cut and taken away. The police were called, and it was also decided to call the famous magician Nguvumali.

This story of the four sorcerers and the murder of Salima in a small village has been narrated in a long epic poem of 393 four-line verses, *Swifa ya Nguvumali*, by Hasani bin Ismail, an ode to the powers of the most famous magician in the country during that decade. The poem has been translated by Peter Lienhardt, with an excellent introduction.

Nguvumali came from a village in the Kilwa region, though he often came to Dar es Salaam for his work and would be cheered by the crowds. He used plant or herbal magic, and so successful were his methods that on certain occasions he was consulted by the police to solve murders. He died in 1957, when the bus in which he was travelling from Kilwa to Dar overturned. The *Tanganyika Standard*, the English-language daily, called him "a white witch doctor working on the side of law and order rather than with any evil or ulterior motives."

The story told in the epic is somewhat anticlimactic. When the police arrive, Binti Ramadhani confesses, naming not only her accomplices but many others, and dies from remorse. Nguvumali arrives in the village, summons all the suspects named by Binti Ramadhani; he dons his special clothes and puts on his necklaces, as do his assistants. Twelve hundred people from the area gather around to watch the magician at work. After doing a dance he brings out his charms, his herbs, and other medicines. He gives a medicine to the suspects to drink. The three guilty sorcerers feel its effects immediately, but not the others. Bwana Shambi's eyes pop out, his nose drips, his face changes. He starts talking and confesses to many misdeeds. He then asks to be taken to his hut. Among the objects that he shows them is a portion of a tongue. The two women meanwhile are confessing volubly. The guilty three are finally handed over to the policemen, who are from the Luo and Nyamwezi tribes and beat them up mercilessly. Later Bwana Shambi recants. And when the three sorcerers are brought to court, they each receive a sentence of less than a year for witchcraft, there being insufficient evidence of murder.

Years later, in 1990, Nguvumali's son, named Matoroka, was practising sorcery using his father's name and would visit Dar es Salaam periodically to collect money that was placed at his father's grave. And two more decades later there occur the grisly albino murders, and a taxi driver in Tabora tells me casually that a mganga can make me rich, but for that to happen I have to sacrifice someone dear to me.

But most waganga are there to solve ordinary problems believed to be caused by spirits and spells, or cure illnesses that cannot be cured by ordinary medicines. When I was young, there were a couple of Asian women who were called on to "strip" away jaundice, which they did using a certain secret ritual requiring water, a brass bowl, a needle, and special prayers; this ritual was learned during the festival of Diwali and the women healers could be Khoja or Hindu. Asians also consulted the Muslim maalim for cases of spirit possession.

As I write this, a man in a remote northeastern village of Tanzania, affectionately known as the Babu (grandfather) of Loliondo, claims to cure all illnesses, including AIDS and cancer, with his herbal potion. Ambilikile Mwasapile, as the man is called, is a former Lutheran pastor who received his formula in a dream. Hundreds, if not thousands, go to see him every day in hired minibuses from as far away as Nyeri in Kenya. The queues waiting for him are claimed to be miles long. There they sit before the elder and receive "the cup"—and are cured, so they say. He charges the equivalent of thirty-three cents for a cup, some of the proceeds of which he donates to the Church. But a bus ride over the rough terrain to Loliondo costs as much as forty dollars. In all seriousness, a newspaper report criticizes the Babu for not having a medical degree. Suppose he did have one? The government has set up a task force to evaluate the situation. Not surprisingly, even government ministers are said to have taken the Babu's cup.

When I was in Kilwa, one morning I inquired of Mwana Hamisi, our young waitress at the Island View Hotel, if she knew of any mgangas in the area. Kilwa, like any old town on the coast, had its reputation as a place of the supernatural. And it easily had the look of one. Nights were pitch-dark and empty but for the occasional subdued, disembodied voices; there were old graves scattered around town, some of them mysterious and abandoned; and the baobab trees looked suitably grim. As a man of these parts, however rational I've made myself to be, a man of science who sees death as mere corporal disintegration into the elements, someone who's tangled and tangoed with complex mathematical formulas that explain intriguing features of atomic nuclei—of which we are all made—in all honesty I could not in Kilwa's dark night help that little supernatural shiver, the skin prickling at the slightest suggestive brush from the breeze at night.

That evening as my companion and I were quietly finishing our meal, our visit to Kilwa having come to a close, the chef—a short, stout man wearing the white jacket of his profession—came over from the kitchen and told me somewhat furtively to be ready the next day at 3 p.m., if I wished to see a mganga. I said I would be ready. I did not know what to expect, but the temptation was too great, and my friend's presence emboldened me.

At the appointed hour, the three of us and our venerable kofia-clad driver (who it appeared had been informed of our mission) headed off on Masoko's main and only paved road, from which, just past the small airfield, we turned into a track winding over a grassy landscape. After a short, bumpy ride we arrived at a small settlement of typical Swahili houses. The last house, somewhat more solidly built than the others, looked away from them and was our destination. There the chef asked us to remove our shoes on the porch, which we did, and we stepped inside.

The house opened into a large room, on the floor of which sat a collection of women, perhaps twenty in number, all looking patient and subdued, ready to wait forever if necessary. We were in a consultancy. To the left the room led into a short corridor, at the end of which, leaning against the front wall, sat the mganga, the maalim, speaking in a voice rich and mellifluous, but pleasantly edged. He was a man in his forties, small and wiry, with a chocolate skin, wearing shirt and trousers and a kofia. Before him sat a woman, between them glowed a brazier. While he spoke, with mechanical deftness he executed symbols or characters on an aluminum tray using his forefinger and an orange solution as ink. What he wrote looked like an Arabic formula, possibly from the Quran. Having finished each tray he would set it aside and pick up another one. Room was made for my friend and me to sit against the wall across from him. Finally he sent off a bunch of finished trays to the main room, where the women poured water on them and drank the solution.

Throughout the process a benign but firm smile lit up the man's face and his inscription-writing was fluid and automatic. The woman in front of him having got up, he invited the one beside him to come forward and asked her what ailed her. A husband not paying attention. He sprinkled some incense on the brazier, the smoke billowed out, and he asked her to repeat after him: *I am Fatuma, daughter of Binti Yusuf, I beg you, Almighty God, to remove my problem and help me . . .* When she finished he gave her an inscribed tray into which he poured water; the writing dissolved and she drank from the yellow solution; he poured what remained over her head. She stood up to go.

It was my turn. He asked my name, my mother's name, and then my shida—my problem, which I had practised beforehand: I was a writer, I told him, but recently whenever I sat down to write my mind went blank. This was a recent affliction, I added. All the time I spoke he carried on his writing, his questions put to me in a bantering, teasing manner. When I had finished he gave his diagnosis. You are possessed by some air spirit, he said. It was perhaps sent to you by a no-gooder. It may have been around and got into you while you were walking. It is not going to come out by the pills of the wazungus—the whites. It has made you weak. It will affect your virility. That is your problem.

I didn't know what to say. I had invented my problem, therefore I couldn't look desperate. Perhaps he guessed. My friend and I were the only non-Africans there, though we spoke Swahili; and my problem was not the kind that would come his way. He must know too that we were from the tourist hotel. Nonchalantly he returned to his writing and said, Who's next? A woman came forward and sat before him and underwent the procedure. She was depressed. When she had left, the maalim turned to me and asked, Well, what do you say? As I fumbled for a response, not knowing what was expected of me, the chef came to my rescue. But he's come for the cure. You should give him the cure. I agreed promptly, and was asked to come and sit closer, across from the maalim, and to spread my legs, the brazier hot before me. Sprinkling incense on the glowing coals, as instructed, as the choking smoke billowed out, I recited after the maalim, *Mwenyezi Mungu, I beg that my problem goes away, that I am able to write well*—and more that I can't recall. Then my friend did the same, asking for my cure but with more eloquence than I had managed, clearly affected by the ritual. His grandfather, he had already informed me, had been a maalim in Bagamoyo.

And then the maalim took my hand in his hands, saying, Let this man's problem go away, let him write well, let it come to his head; if the problem is caused by a person, let that person come to no good; if that person is on a plane, let it fall; if he is in a car, let it break; if the problem is caused by a jinn, take it away; if it is caused by you, My Lord, let it escape from him . . .

On and on he recited, in that warm, fluid, yet edgy drone, now reading in Swahili and Arabic from a tattered book in his hand, giving me the full treatment. A tall man came and sat down beside him, picked up another tattered book and went full blast reciting some Arabic prayer, so that the two rich and full voices, one higher than the other, filled the room and there seemed no conclusion in sight. The second man could have been in his thirties; he had a short scruffy beard and a grave look, and also wore trousers, but with a T-shirt with a logo on it.

While this ritual proceeded, a woman in the main room seemed to enter a trance, rolling her eyes and groaning. The maalim continued, all the while holding my hand, his plea on my behalf sounding more urgent, counterpointed by the second voice, and I thought, This will never end, and my knees are hurting, and I struggled to suppress a sudden burst of giggling at the predicament I had put myself in. The maalim would throw the occasional look at me, hoping perhaps that I would also enter a trance.

Finally, at long last, the two men stopped, and we said together, Alhamdu lillahi rabb al alameen. Praise be to the Creator of all beings.

Now the maalim put an inscribed tray in my hand, gave me a glass of water. I poured it into the tray, producing an orange solution, which I then poured into the glass I found in my hand. Drink it, the maalim commanded. I took a sip—tasteless—and said, I can't drink more, pour it on me. There was a pause. The chef and my friend explained to the maalim that my stomach was delicate and there was a journey the next day—which was irrelevent, of course, if the water was blessed—whereupon the maalim poured the water over my head and sprinkled it on my face and body with some force. More orange water was produced and poured into a bottle for me to take away.

We walked out to the porch, where I was given two small bundles of cut roots to be boiled into a tea and consumed. An ugly black ball of gooey stuff was handed me from which to take up pinches and rub on my body.

We paid the maalim handsomely, took photos with him, and departed. The chef, our agent, also received his commission.

18.

Zanzibar: Island in the Sun

From the sea it appears as one has read and heard about it, and consequently imagined it, and yet the breath catches when it appears glimmering in the distance. On the continent it's the endless expanse of the land that impresses, here it's the sea and the sky, and the small island in their midst. A row of short white buildings in a light haze; it's been likened to a chain of pearls, though the buildings are not all the same nor all white. The sea is blue and green, parted by the hull of the speeding ferry leaving a frothy wake behind, and the sun is hot overhead. By compulsion or instinct, tourist cameras have appeared and click away. Perhaps it's what one brings to the scene, but there's a sense that here and now time has slowed, if not stopped altogether. That statement needs much qualification, nothing is so simple, this sleepy-looking isle has stories to tell and connections round the world and is rife with contradictions. It's a conundrum in the sun. A young man has left me in charge of his backpack and disappeared, and as I stare at it, I get worried; it's what the world has become. After a long time he returns, I sigh gently with relief and ask him which of the two prominent buildings before us is the palace. He points it out.

Growing up in Dar es Salaam, to us Zanzibar—"Unguja" in Swahili, "Jangbar" to the Indians—was Easygoing Isle, close enough that it was thought our best swimmers could easily reach it. Actually it was some fifty miles away, and you got there by steamship or dhow, there was no ferry. But few of us mainlanders ventured there. It was too much of the past when we all looked to the future.

There's a story Zanzibaris like to tell—and similarly other people on the coast—to explain their pace of life.

A fisherman lies stretched out on the beach, relaxing, when a tourist—a white man, to be precise—strolls by.

"Relaxing?" asks the tourist.

"I caught my fish and sold it," replies our local.

The tourist looks doubtful. "Really? No more fish in the sea?"

"I caught what I needed."

Like many a foreigner who comes to these parts, the tourist wants to help, to advise.

"If you caught more fish wouldn't you earn more money?"

"Yes . . . And then?" asks the fisherman, looking confused.

"You could save money, and put it in a bank. And then, after some time, with all your money saved in the bank you could buy a bigger boat and catch a whole lot of fish. Make a lot of money!"

Our man looks seriously doubtful. "And then what?"

"Why, you could let others do the work!"

"Aha! I see. And what would *I* do?"

"Why, you would relax . . . !"

The Zanzibari says nothing and the tourist walks away.

In Dar es Salaam, there were many Zanzibaris—Jangbari, we called them—people who were born on the island and had moved to the mainland. There was always something upbeat about these people—a certain lively sense of common identity and wholeness that must come from living on a small island. You could identify Zanzibari Asians by their forthright manner, their sense of high drama, and the rather sweet Kutchi-Swahili they spoke that the rest of us enjoyed imitating. It sounded something like this: Nimekuja *gharé* yako, nil-iona *vado-vado-taado*; basi nime *dharé* umekwenda *baaré*. This means, I came to your house, I saw a big-big padlock; and so I thought you had gone out. (The words in italics are in Kutchi.) Not only the nouns, the verbs too got replaced and inflected. Two of my Zanzibari aunts were dramatists par excellence. Fatu Masi, having had a pre-monition of her death, went around wishing goodbyes to the entire extended family. Bai, she said to my mother, my time has come; the two embraced. As expected, Fatu Masi died many years later and left a lot of memories. And big-hipped Fatu Mami, whose father was a fearsome exorcist, once at the Odeon sprang up angrily to her feet in the midst of a movie, exclaiming, "Allah!" thereby startling the entire theatre. This, to voice her objection to the goings-on of a scene. And moments later, satisfied that nothing was amiss, she sank down back to her seat, saying, "I see!"

Long after the heinous excesses of the Zanzibar revolution of 1964 and its repressive aftermath, and long after the union of Zanzibar and Tanganyika that became the United Republic of Tanzania, the Zanzibari sense of self persists in a way in which a Dar one doesn't, the latter easily being subsumed into the larger Tanzanian identity. Zanzibaris, regardless of race, will affirm that the unification of their island with the mainland stole away their Zanzibar. (Though mainlanders are likely to retort, "But when there is trouble in the islands, it is to Dar that you will run!") The irony is that in the past Zanzibar had ruled the mainland coast, and dominated much of the hinterland. Zanzibar was a multiethnic cosmopolis when the mainland boasted at most a few small towns. Therefore today Zanzibaris tend to be anxious about their history, culture, and traditions, lest they be lost or forgotten. Memoirs and histories of Zanzibar, both amateur and professional, buzz over the Internet, contributed by former citizens of the island now living on every continent.

Before it gained prominence, however, for much of the second millennium of the common era Zanzibar had been a minor island entity, and it was Kilwa, Mombasa, Malindi, and Mozambique that thrived as major Indian Ocean ports. In 1330 the Moroccan traveller Ibn Battuta, after completing his pilgrimage in Mecca, sailed from Aden down the African coast to Mogadishu then on to Mombasa and Kilwa; he does not mention Zanzibar. Nor does John Milton in *Paradise Lost* (1667), though his angel Michael points out Kilwa, Mombasa, and Malindi to the exiled Adam. Milton's knowledge of the Indian Ocean world would have come from Portuguese accounts of their voyages. Vasco da Gama had in fact bypassed Zanzibar on his way to India in 1498, sailing to the east of it; on his return trip a year later, however, he did sail into the channel between the island and the mainland, and anchor offshore, where the ruler of Zanzibar sent him refreshments.

In later years, Zanzibar became a tributary to an ascendant Portugal. It is known that the Portuguese built a chapel and a small factory during their period of dominance, which lasted until 1698, when the Omanis of Muscat wrested control of the East African coast and made it a part of their own Indian Ocean empire. They constructed a fort on the site of the chapel. In 1832 Seyyid Said, the sultan of Oman, made the momentous decision to move his capital from Muscat to Zanzibar, changing forever the fortunes of the island and the mainland across. By the mid-nineteenth century, under the Omanis, Zanzibar had become a major Indian Ocean entrepot, a "great mart . . . the Bagdad, the Ipahan, the Stamboul, if you like, of East Africa," as declaimed H.M. Stanley in 1872. Stanley, a reporter for the *New York Herald*, did tend to exaggerate. He had arrived in Zanzibar to begin his search for Livingstone. He described his first sight of the island, seen from the harbour, thus:

> Towards the south, above the sea line of the horizon, there appeared the naked masts of several large ships, and towards the east of these a dense mass of white, flat-topped houses. This was Zanzibar . . . which soon resolved itself into a pretty large and compact city, with all the characteristics of Arab architecture. Above some of the largest houses lining the bay front of the city streamed the blood-red banner of the Sultan, Syed Burghash, and the flags of the American, English, North German Confederation, and

> French Consulates. In the harbour were thirteen large ships, four Zanzibar men-of-war, one English man-of-war, the *Nymphe*, two American, one French, one Portuguese, two English, and one German merchantmen, besides numerous dhows . . . traders between India, the Persian Gulf, and Zanzibar.

With great exuberance Stanley goes on to describe the town of Zanzibar, its tumultuous "crooked, narrow lanes" with the "red-turbaned" "Banyans" in the Indian quarter outside their stores, which sold anything from cloth and raw cotton to ivory to crockery and hardware; the African quarter, its people sitting outside their huts; Europeans strolling along in the evenings on "Nazi-Moya" [Mnazi Mmoja] with "languid, moribund steps to inhale the sweet air that glides over the sea"; and the Arabs.

For centuries, as the Portuguese had already observed when they arrived on the scene, Indians from Gujarat had been a small but significant presence all along the East African coast. In the later-nineteenth and early-twentieth centuries, however, they came to Zanzibar in greater numbers, driven away by the droughts in their native land and attracted to the Eldorado of Africa. In the 1920s many of the Khoja Ismailis, who were the largest Indian community in Zanzibar, upon advice from their leader moved to the mainland of Tanganyika and Kenya. Legend has it that a bloodshed had been prophesied for the island that was fulfilled in the revolution of 1964. Whatever the case, it was wise to move to the mainland, even though it must have seemed then a cultural nullity; but Zanzibar had reached its saturation, whereas the mainland, recently colonized by the European powers, promised greater opportunities and a vast space for new immigrants to move into. Dar es Salaam, initiated as an escape or a resort by Zanzibar's Sultan Majid, and later developed by the Germans, was a small town of a few thousand people at the turn of the twentieth century; today it has close to four million. The entire island of Zanzibar on the other hand can boast a little more than a million people; it has stagnated, and if it has any attraction today, it is as a romantic getaway of short duration. Many of the Indian families of Dar and Mombasa came originally from Zanzibar following that prophecy, or advice or command. My maternal grandparents, originally from Jamnagar and Porbandar, were among them.

My taxi driver is an Asian, a big heavy-set man who speaks to me in Swahili. He is known as Suli, he says, and then elaborates, Suleman. Everyone knows him. How nice, I think. Two people of Indian origin driving a bargain, conversing in Swahili. It turns out that Suli speaks nothing but Swahili. He takes me to my hotel in Stone Town, the old city behind the beach. This is an area of hotels, tourist shops, restaurants, and government offices, but it's quiet; motor traffic is spare, the touts numerous and listless; business is slow, one of them tells me later, begging me to go see the dolphins.

I was informed in Dar about a restaurant on the island that serves absolutely the best biriyani; it's called, somewhat improbably, Passing Show, and that's where I head off for lunch. Walking along the shore, past the old fort (site of the seventeenth-century Portuguese chapel), the museum called the House of Wonders, the Sultans' Palace, and the "Old Dispensary" (the Jubilee Hospital built to commemorate Queen Victoria's Golden Jubilee in 1887), I reach the harbour and godowns, where the quiet road bends and suddenly transforms into a busy street. Here, at one edge of Stone Town, I find the restaurant, a joint run by Arabs for working people. There are a couple of tourists or expatriates about. The food is good, the biriyani of the familiar Kutchi variety—meat or chicken cooked with browned onions and gharam masala and served over yellow-specked rice; and it amazes me again how a dish that once was an Asian specialty for occasions like weddings and festivals has become so commonplace. The yellow in the rice, however, is food colour and not saffron, a luxury that the patrons of the Passing Show can hardly expect or afford. Banana stew, curry, pilau, ugali, and chapati are also served here. Zanzibar may seem stagnant, but it maintains a delightful sense of the authentic. How more satisfying this local fare than the chicken and soggy chips, or the globally standard "North Indian" so common in Dar!

Zanzibar is an elongated green island spanning roughly fifty miles north to south and twenty miles at its widest. On its west side on a small triangular peninsula, facing the mainland, lies Zanzibar Stone Town, the commercial and political centre of the island and its tourist town, where the ferry unloads daily visitors. Except for a connecting neck of land to the south, some three hundred yards wide, Stone Town used to be separated from the rest of the island by a creek, "Pwani Ndogo," which at high tide would be crossed by a boat. It was filled in the early twentieth century and is where the old Creek Road, now the bustling Benjamin Mkapa Road, runs. The area across the creek is still called Ngambo, "the other side." It was the poorer section, with mud and thatch dwellings—very much like Dar's Kariakoo, where Indian stores served a mainly African clientele.

The maze of narrow streets in the ancient Stone Town makes navigation seem daunting, but its geometry is best grasped when one realizes that—as in other old cities—it is made up of distinct little neighbourhoods, each with a suggestive, picturesque name: Shangani (at the sands), the area close to the tip of the peninsula;

Gerezani (at the old fort), farther along the shore; Forodhani, still farther down; Sokomhogo (the cassava market, that is, the people's market), which lies behind Shangani; farther inland one finds Kajificheni (hide yourselves); Hamamni (at the Persian baths); Darajani (at the crossing, near the former creek).

Shangani is now the heart of the tourist area, with its hotels, curio shops, and hungry touts; at its tip, in a leafy enclave away from the crowds and the shops, the luxurious Serena Inn occupies pride of place, next to (according to an 1892 German map) the site of the old British Consulate—which was described by Richard Burton as "a large solid pile, coloured like a twelfth-cake, and shaped like a claret chest, [lying] on its side, comfortably splashed by the sea." Burton stayed here in December 1856 at the beginning of his East African adventures, when he explored Zanzibar before heading off to the mainland. The Consul was an ailing Atkins Hamerton.

Farther up from the Serena is the location of the former American Consulate. As early as 1833, the Americans had concluded a trading treaty with Zanzibar, and in 1837 the United States was the first foreign power to open a consulate, more than a decade before Britain did. By the mid-nineteenth century the United States was Zanzibar's biggest trading partner, exporting predominantly coarse but durable cotton cloth from New England, known locally as marikani, and importing ivory and copal. The American civil war ruined that trade, and marikani started coming from India. During the European colonial era that ended in the 1960s, American presence in East Africa was minimal. The American Consulate in Zanzibar was closed in 1915. It was reopened in 1961, at the height of the Cold War.

All around Shangani were located the other European consulates and trading companies. This compact breast-shaped peninsula, with its nipple at the British Consulate, was the springboard for the colonization of East Africa. Here the missionaries and the explorers first came and prepared themselves for their journeys to the mainland, the reports of which so shaped public opinion at home; and here the European warships came to loom and threaten, one of them ultimately bombarding the hapless Sultan's Palace in August 1896, in what the British proudly called "the shortest war in history," lasting thirty-eight minutes.

Walking northeast along the shore from this nipple, perhaps after a cold beer at the Serena, we come to the old fort or Gereza to the right, behind which used to be the principal market, the Soko Kuu. The fort now houses a few rudimentary tourist kiosks. Farther up along the road come the Palace and the Beit al Ajaib, the House of Wonders, which is a museum. Opposite is the promenade called Forodhani, beyond which is the old Customs House, once the busiest part of town and now the place where the ferries and ships arrive, marked by a prominent heap of containers.

Richard Burton, impressed by the market behind the fort, uses it to describe his impression of the town's population:

> Motley is the name of the crowd. One officer in the service of His Highness [the Sultan] stalks down the market followed by a Hieland tail [whip], proudly, as if he were the lord of the three Arabias. Negroes who dislike the whip clear out like hawk-frightened pigeons. A yellow man, with short, thin beard, and high, meagre, and impassive features, he is well-dressed and gorgeously armed . . .
>
> Right meek by the side of the Arab's fierceness appears the Banyan, the local Jew. These men are Bhatias from Cutch [Kutch] in western India; unarmed burghers, with placid, satisfied countenances, and plump, sleek, rounded

> forms, suggestive of happy, well-to-do cows. Their skins are smoother and their complexions are lighter than the Arabs'. . . . They wear the long moustachio, not the beard, and a Chinese pig-tail is allowed to spring from the poll of the carefully shaven head. These top-knots are folded, when the owners are fully dressed, under high turbans of purple or crimson stuff, edged with gold.

So much for the happy cows in their turbans. There are also at this market the Baluchi mercenaries, "comely brown [men] with regular features" and flowing, henna-dyed beards, sporting long-barrelled matchlocks; as well, "the wildest and most picturesque figures . . . the half-breeds from the western shores of the Persian Gulf. . . . Their elf-like locks fall in masses over unclean, saffron-stained shirts [kanzus]." They wear heavy swords over their shoulders and daggers at their waists, and their whips "await immediate use."

Burton goes on with full hyperbolic gusto,

> Add half a dozen pale-skinned Khojas, tricky-faced men with evil eyes, treacherous smiles, fit for the descendants of the "Assassins," straight, silky beards, forked after the fashion of ancient Rustam, and armed with Chinese umbrellas. Complete the group by throwing in a European—how ghastly appears his blanched face, and how frightful his tight garb!

Burton, a British secret agent a few years before, had intrigued with the first Aga Khan in Persia, not a happy experience for him, and is under the misapprehension that the Khojas (who follow the

Aga Khans) were Persian in origin; they were in fact Indians, cousins of the Kutchi Bhatias, the "Banyans." But whatever value one gives to this portrayal of the island's inhabitants, one still takes away a sense of its tumult and diversity, and the arrogance of the Zanzibari Arab, not to mention the white man, in this case the Englishman who observes and reports.

Forodhani is the grassy plain next to the harbour, across from the palace, where townspeople and tourists come in the evenings to shoot the breeze, and young people come for overt trysts. Formerly a part of the palace establishment, the ground was laid waste by the British bombardment in the Anglo–Zanzibar (thirty-eight-minute) "war" and became a public space, where for decades now a nightly food court has indulged the public with sizzling snacks. Vendors arrive at dusk and set up their stalls, offering grilled meat and seafood, breads, fruit juices, and sodas. The smoky dark, lit up with sporadic lamps, the charcoal fires, and the quiet chatter of people strolling about combine to produce a uniquely Zanzibari ambience reflective of its attitude to life. There's no hurry. Recently the park was renovated with paved paths, stone benches, a bandstand, thick bounding walls to sit on, and rows of built-up stalls for the vendors. It looks clean and pretty and perhaps a bit touristy, but Zanzibaris are grateful; tourists are needed to boost the economy.

All the young visitors who were on the ferry with me this morning are here, what else is there to do in Zanzibar but wander about on this beautiful, balmy evening? Out in the distance a ferry takes on its last batch of passengers for the mainland; farther away a container ship lies in apparent coma. A bunch of touts appear, call out in English and Italian—"Amici!"—to the young Europeans hovering around in small groups, many of them actually Italian. Caution on their minds, they are hesitant initially to savour the food so abundantly and aromatically on display. But then gradually one by one and then all together they yield. The grills are crowded, the vendors sound relieved.

I have arranged to meet here Abdul Sheriff, local intellectual and historian, the author of several books on Zanzibar. A quiet, unassuming man in his mid-sixties, he went to university in Berkeley and London. Later he taught at the University of Dar es Salaam, where he was one among the intellectual crowd during the heyday of the 1970s. Returning to his native Zanzibar, for a few years he curated the House of Wonders, the rather impressive though underfunded museum of Swahili and coastal history, across the road from where we now stroll on Forodhani. His edited book, *The History and Conservation of Zanzibar Stone Town*, is studded with gems of information. His *Slaves, Spices & Ivory in Zanzibar* is a detailed analysis of the growth of Zanzibar as a commercial hub in the nineteenth century. Until recently, when he retired, he ran the Zanzibar Indian Ocean Research Institute. Funding was difficult, he says, dependent on foreign agencies, which preferred to donate to high-profile charities. The study of the Indian Ocean zone is not sexy enough. Poverty and disease are always more attractive.

We get our mishkakis, he with a naan, and I with a chapati, and sit on the seawall, partly facing the harbour. A few small boats are about, nothing else. Sea traffic is much less than it was in the time of Burton and Stanley, more than a hundred years ago. This island has only memories left, and Stone Town is one such memory. Abdul's current project concerns the proposed new constitution for the Tanzanian Union, and he is involved in public discussions about it. The Union government is keen to push it through as quickly as possible. The present constitution, describing Zanzibar's relations with the mainland, he says, was forced upon the island in the shotgun marriage of 1964, only a few months after the revolution. Now Zanzibaris want a better deal, on the model of the American federal system.

We find ourselves talking of our respective communities, the Ithnasheris and the Ismailis. They were initially a single community of Khojas, which split up in the late nineteenth century in India, and then again later in Africa, on grounds of religious practice. The split in Zanzibar, with repurcussions on the mainland, was bitter and sometimes violent; it divided many families. Such was the bitterness that Ismailis were forbidden even to accept water from an Ithnasheri house. That is saying a lot. And the colour black was frowned upon because it was identified with the "enemy." It is all embarrassing now. As young people who had not seen the bitterness of the conflict, this attitude in our elders was curious, producing a slight niggling in the mind, a portent of the greater doubts that would in time arrive.

He walks me back to my hotel on Kenyatta Avenue.

The jamatkhana, the Khoja khano, on Jamatini Street was built in 1905, apparently on the site of an earlier, nineteenth-century structure. It is a light yellow rectangular building flush with its neighbours in the old section of town called Kiponda. The windows are arched and barred, the massive front door is typically Zanzibari, carved and studded. There is a carved trim on the outer wall, but none of the geometrical calligraphic affectations that seem to be de rigeur nowadays. There is no dome. This was the East African headquarters of the Khojas, and the area was called the Khoja Circle. The khano would have been crowded once, hundreds coming to pray every day, at dawn and dusk. Visitors would be welcomed. The tycoons Tharia Topan and Sewa Haji would have received pleadings and homage.

As plain and dignified as the outside is, the inside is magnificent in a baroque sort of way, with intricately carved woodwork on the wall panellings, trellises, railings, and columns, and massive ancient-looking chandeliers hanging low from the ceilings. And like all old buildings in Zanzibar, this one has its own ghosts.

The last time I went to the Zanzibar khano, I counted seventeen people.

19.

Zanzibar: The Revolution

It was January 12, 1964. In Dar es Salaam, schools had reopened after the month-long holidays, the hot season was at its height, and the mangoes were ripe. Almost exactly a month before, Tanganyika had become a republic, refusing a British governor general and formal ties to the Crown; also a month ago Kenya had gained independence from Britain, and so had Zanzibar. It was an exciting time. They would tell us in school, You are the future. And so we believed. But that Sunday morning we woke up to a bizarre piece of news. There had been a revolution in Zanzibar. Those who listened to Radio Zanzibar heard the thundering voice of "the Field Marshall," in a Swahili that sounded Kenyan or Ugandan, announcing the overthrow: "Wake up, you imperialists, there is no longer an imperialist government on this island. This is now the government of the freedom fighters. . . ." All these terms were foreign to us. A revolution in our backyard, in sleepy, peaceful old Zanzibar. It is impossible to describe the impact of this news. Disbelief, confusion, rumour. What did a revolution look like? Other countries had revolutions. But here? And what did it mean to our world? Zanzibar was a different country, an insignificant place, a stopover for our grandparents. The overriding fear when news of the violence had somehow drifted across the channel into Dar was, Can the revolution come here, to Tanganyika? Where will we run?

Zanzibar—easygoing isle on one hand, and on the other, the place of perhaps the bloodiest revolution on the continent. It is a conundrum. To this day many Zanzibaris remain stunned by the fact, the violence, the suddenness of the revolution. It appears relaxed even now: the streets are mostly safe and life is slow, the sun shines and the blue sea is accessible to enjoy, the dressing is casual, the kahawa seller comes by with his kettle, at Sugra Bai's people of all races will sit in a plain room in a humble abode in an alley for a snack of tasty bhajia mix, there remains a sense of humour. Yet sporadic—though much smaller—violence does take place. Perhaps Zanzibaris, the poor ones, hide their resentments well most of the time. Or perhaps—this can hardly be satisfactory—one simply accepts the puzzle that is Zanzibar.

What brought about this upheaval? There's no denying that beneath the placid surface of island life there has lurked the memory of a historical racial grievance: many of the Africans were the descendants of slaves. To feed that resentment, the seeds of a revolt had already been planted in the flawed general election that was a gift of the British to the friendly Sultan of Zanzibar before they lowered their flag and departed. At independence, Zanzibar found itself with a coalition government—formed by the Zanzibar Nationalist Party (ZNP) and the Pemba People's Party (PPP), both dominated by the Arabs—with Sultan Jamshed as the constitutional monarch. (Pemba is the smaller island to the north, considered politically a part of Zanzibar.) The ZNP and PPP were "moderate" parties; moreover, a constitutional monarchy suited the British, for they had been the patrons of the sultans and their senior partners since the nineteenth century. The colonial powers had sponsored such mixed-race "moderate" parties in other countries as well, and failed, for the simple reason that history was against them. The Africans did not want a partnership with the minorities who had dominated them in the ruling and social hierarchy, and would continue to dominate given the chance. The predominantly African parties were the Afro-Shirazi Party (ASP) and the Umma party, the latter formed by disaffected socialist members of the ZNP and now banned.

At independence there were approximately 230,000 Africans, 50,000 Arabs, and 20,000 Asians on the island. As expected, the majority of the popular vote was captured by the Afro-Shirazi Party, the ASP; and yet the ZNP–PPP coalition managed to obtain the greater number of seats and formed the government. There was something manifestly unfair about this outcome. The wealthier ZNP could buy votes; the distribution of constituencies was questionable; and there were charges of vote-rigging.

The revolution began at around three in the morning and was over within the day. A few hundred "freedom-fighters" armed with rudimentary weapons—spears, machetes, bows and arrows, tire irons—managed to overcome two police stations and capture their weapons, and to take over the radio station. Their numbers swelled, and quickly a violent rampage spread across the island. Soon after the attacks began, the Zanzibari prime minister requested British troops, based in Kenya, to intervene. The British government refused, despite American recommendation. Early in the morning the sultan, the prime minister, and members of the cabinet quietly fled in the royal yacht, stopping in Dar before flying off to England. What remained was the lingering aftermath. The world had changed.

The revolution was shockingly bloody, most of the violence directed against the Arabs, some against the Asians. It is surprising how many people today will casually mention having witnessed a murder, a rape, a beating. Don Petterson, an official at the U.S. Consulate at the time, describes a scene witnessed by some frightened Americans crowded inside the living room of a house:

> [They] could see African men furtively making their way through the trees . . . heading for nearby houses, the homes of Arab families. The Africans were dressed for the most part in shorts and short-sleeve shirts and carried an assortment of weapons: sharp-bladed pangas (machetes), spears, and knives.
>
> . . . suddenly, the quiet was broken by shouts, and the armed men could be seen rushing the nearest neighbouring house. The shouting was now joined by screams. The American onlookers saw a bearded Arab man dragged out of the doorway of the house. Struck by a panga, he fell to the ground, nearly decapitated. They saw no further violence, but the screaming within the house continued for several minutes. Afterwards, the attackers herded the disheveled women and three children. . . .

And in its January 24, 1964 issue, *Time* observed,

> An air of weird unreality hung over the sleepy, sun-baked capital of the world's newest "people's republic." Cuban-trained "freedom fighters" sporting Fidelista beards and berets stalked the narrow twisting streets. Carloads of whooping blacks careered through the Arab and Indian

> quarters, looting and shooting. Radios blared ominous messages of doom and death. From the hood of one car dangled a grisly trophy: the testicles of a murdered Arab.

Arab bodies would be seen on the roads, testicles stuffed into their mouths. Women's breasts were cut off. Estimates of Arab deaths range from a few hundred to 20,000. Pettersen's estimate is 5,000 Arabs, one in ten, with many others wounded. The systematic, selective, and continuous killing seemed to western observers an attempt at genocide, long before Rwanda. There were many rapes. As Asian boys would repeat in Dar, in a grotesque attempt at humour, "they"—the Zanzibaris—had duriani in the morning, biriyani in the afternoon, and an Arabiani at night, the latter referring to an Arab woman. Recalling this repugnant line, I try in vain to understand the teenage mind that would utter it. I am relieved I did not speak it, remember distinctly a feeling of distaste, a queasiness. Our home had four girls and my mother. Our own Khoja community of Zanzibar, we heard, had gathered frightened in the khano, seeking safety in numbers and the sanctuary of a prayer house. They seem to have suffered minimally in physical terms, though according to some people today the violence against Asians was under-reported. I recall that in the khanos of Dar there were special prayers said every day at noon for our people on the island.

How to explain this violence in an island long considered calm and peaceful, with a common identity so strong even to this day? I once put this question to a few Zanzibari friends; there was no satisfactory response. One muttered, "Racism . . . Rwanda," surely hopelessly inadequate and inaccurate, except perhaps revealing the residual bitterness. Another simply said the obvious, that the common faith, Islam, and its fraternity were momentarily forgotten during the violence. Few will recall, unless prodded, the blunt racism, the racial hierarchy that preceded the revolution: Africans at the bottom and treated with contempt, then the Asians and Arabs and the whites. The Arabs had come as rulers, they were for the most part the elite, owning plantations and the higher positions in the civil service. Among the Africans, on the other hand, there would still have been those who remembered the days of slavery.

But this purely race-based explanation is perhaps a little too clean. There were, after all, many African families among the elite. And often in Zanzibar there is no clean division between Arabs and Africans: the "Shirazi" of the revolutionary Afro-Shirazi Party is a conscious acknowledgement of Middle Eastern roots. Many so-called Africans have Arab blood, and vice versa. Even the sultans had black wives. But the mobs that went around hacking with their pangas seemed to know their victims. The point has been made that many of the revolutionaries were from the mainland, for whom the racial division was indeed clear-cut.

In the days and months following the revolution, a time of anarchy and, for some, pure terror, thousands of Arabs were expelled, thousands were put in camps. Plantations and properties were confiscated, corporal punishments meted out. But the revolutionaries had instructions not to harm whites; British warships lurked not far away, the British troops in Kenya were on alert.

Who were the leaders of the coup, and how was it organized? There has remained a cloud of mystery surrounding the details, aided by deliberate obfuscation, historical erasure, and propaganda. The new president of Zanzibar was the leader of the ASP, Sheikh Abeid Karume, an uneducated, unsophisticated man, often dismissed as a former fisherman; could he have led the revolution, as it was ultimately claimed? Or was it truly the "Field Marshall" who had proclaimed the revolution and for a few days was its voice on the radio? His name was John Okello and he was from Uganda. From the outset there was suspicion of Cuban and Soviet involvement, and the Americans in that heyday of the Cold War were quick to see in Zanzibar, East Africa's own Cuba and a communist triumph. The new vice-president was Abdallah Kassim Hanga, educated in Moscow, where he had married a Russian woman. The minister of external affairs was Abdulrahman Babu, a left-wing intellectual who had also travelled to communist countries, and, according to *Time*, "Africa's most brilliant and ugliest politician." There is, however, no evidence of communist involvement in the coup, but the Warsaw Pact countries immediately recognized the new government, while an anxious West waited.

Official Tanzanian government records have attempted to erase John Okello's role in the revolution. An "authoritative story of the Zanzibar Revolution" appeared on its first anniversary in the propagandist daily *The Nationalist,* published in Dar es Salaam. It is a shamelessly biased and inaccurate account, in which John Okello's name is not even mentioned. Nor is he mentioned during the annual commemorations of the revolution. Yet there can be no doubt that he was a key leader and spokesman. Few who lived through those tumultous weeks can forget that voice on the radio; or the attention he garnered and the apprehensions he generated throughout East Africa. Not only the local but also the international media kept track of him. There exist published photos of Okello with the presidents of Kenya and Tanzania, and I recall the fears and rumours that spread in Dar when he came visiting, and went on to Nairobi, that he had come to instigate new revolutions. The *New York Times* clearly affirmed Okello's leadership in the revolution, and an article on

March 1, 1964, was headed "Kenya on Alert in Okello's Visit; Nairobi Wary." Don Petterson of the U.S. Consulate mentions Okello as a key figure; so does the Polish writer Ryszard Kapuściński, who apparently spent a few days immediately following December 12 in Zanzibar. (His account is in other ways quite fanciful.) John Okello wrote up his own version of events in *Revolution in Zanzibar.* It is a straightforward account with minute details about the planning of the coup, that regardless of the naïveté of the author, has a certain ring of truth. How much truth it actually contains is impossible to say.

John Okello was born in Uganda in 1937 in the Lango tribe and baptized, significantly for the calling he would take upon himself, with the Christian name Gideon. As a young man, having lost both parents, he travelled in Uganda and Kenya, working at different jobs—he was, variously, house servant, tailor, carpenter, mason, labourer, and street vendor. He was deeply influenced by the Bible and affected by the lowly treatment of Africans by Europeans and Asians (the latter of whom, he admits, also often came to his assistance). He says he became fluent in Swahili. (Though in the 1950s, we must remember, the level of the language in Kenya and Uganda, except for the Kenya coast, was rather crude even by Asian standards.) In Nairobi he was sent to jail for two years for an "alleged" sexual offence. Upon his release he proceeded to Machakos and on to Mombasa, where he arrived in February 1958. There, he recalls, he resented in particular being called "boy" and "mtumwa" (slave) by the Asians and Arabs, and he had a dream, in which a voice told him, "You will not die. God has given you the power to redeem the prisoners and the slaves, and you will make those who cannot understand to understand." In June 1959, hearing of better prospects on the island of Pemba, he left illegally by dhow for that destination. With him were some new Kenyan friends.

In Pemba, Okello became involved in politics, joining the youth wing of the ZNP, later abandoning it for the more African-supported ASP; he started a brick-making business and became involved in organizing workers. He gave political speeches. And he had another dream: "God the Almighty has anointed you with clean oil. . . . With power from Almighty God you will help redeem your black brothers from slavery. God will give you more wisdom, courage and power to do this." After the General Election of 1961, in which the two parties supported by Arabs and wealthy Asians won a majority of the seats, he became disillusioned and began to think of an armed struggle. Given to quotations from the Bible, he sought inspiration in these words from St James: "Go now, you rich men, weep and howl for your miseries that shall come upon you. . . ."

Okello arrived on Zanzibar island in February 1963. And after the disappointment of the July 1963 election for the government of independent Zanzibar, in which ASP again lost, he began organizing workers and members of the ASP youth towards an armed revolt. He called secret meetings, organized weapons training, planned strategies. In all this, he says, he did not involve Abeid Karume, in order to save him from arrest in case his plans were found out. What his actual relationship was with Karume before the revolution, we don't know.

Okello gives detailed information about the planning and the meetings, some of which involved large numbers of people. It is hard to believe that with so many youths of his party involved, Karume would be unaware of what was going on; but then the government in power was also in the dark. It is also interesting to note that the core group of fighters, according to Okello, had more men from the mainland than indigenous Zanzibaris. The delusions of this young man who heard voices from God are evident; we cannot help but feel that he exaggerates, and writing from a prison after three tumultuous years, some of his accounts would be inaccurate. Okello seems to have believed that the Arabs had planned a genocide of Africans: "All male African babies would be killed, and African girls would be forced to marry or submit to Arabs. . . ."

The revolt, as described by Okello, has a distinctly African-Christian ritualistic component to it. Before the fighting began, he had two dreams. In the first of these, God asked him to step into the river at Mtoni and pick up a black, white, and red stone and perform a ritual. In the second dream he was asked to sacrifice a black cat and a black dog and mix their blood and brains and the powdered stone in a pot. Afterwards all the recruits passed over this grisly mixture and took an oath. The oath, the water dipping, and Okello's instructions and injunctions to his fighters regarding food and contact with women are reminiscent of other African wars, for example, Maji Maji in mainland Tanzania and Mau Mau in Kenya. His rules on the conduct of war sound eerie: "Never in any situation rape women whose husbands have been killed or detained. No soldier may rape or even touch a virgin girl. . . ." We can assume what was allowed or even encouraged.

Here was a demented, naive, and sensitive young man, restless, religious, and deeply wounded by the racism he saw and experienced. There can be no doubt that for a period of a few weeks this unlikely person managed to take East Africa by storm, by emerging as a leader in the Zanzibar revolution. Many of us are confused, even wounded, products of colonialism, in our culture, our politics, our responses to racism. It is possible to see in this lonely, wandering John Okello an extreme manifestation of this confusion.

Once the revolution got underway, a madness consumed him.

His arbitrariness and cruelty are legendary by now. Seif Sharif Hamad, in his biography, describes:

> Okello started the punishment of caning and whipping people . . . [he] liked, in particular, to humiliate Arabs from Oman. . . . [He] rounded up Arabs and ordered them to sing [a revolutionary song] . . . and then he would order their beards to be shaved without water, just dry. I personally saw this take place.
>
> . . . he really frightened people. When Okello arrived in Pemba, he moved with a contingent of heavily armed followers in about three Land Rovers.

This account of course implicitly acknowledges Okello's role in the revolution. Another account, by Ali Sultan Issa, a member of the ZNP and later the Umma Party, dismisses reports of Okello's dominant role in the revolution as "rubbish." But, an avowed Marxist, Issa was in China when the revolution began, arriving in Zanzibar two weeks later on January 25, having taken two days off for shopping in Hong Kong with his wife. Arriving in Zanzibar, he was immediately dispatched to Pemba. His hearsay account of how the revolution began is hardly reliable.

A CIA report, written in 1965 and released in 2010 as *Zanzibar: The Hundred Days' Revolution*, suggests but does not affirm that Karume and Hanga were the leaders of the revolution. No details of what role this leadership took or how the planning occurred are given. The report moreover has no references and is out of date, having been written long before the books by Petterson, Okello, and others appeared. If Karume were involved in the planning, surely details would be available to become part of the history and folklore of the revolution?

A full, authoritative account of the Zanzibar revolution, then, continues to remain elusive.

Under Karume, a repressive regime was in place. The Asian and Arab minorities especially lived in constant fear. Properties and businesses were confiscated. Favouritism and outright theft by the leaders was the order of the day and people were afraid to speak out, to complain or criticize. There were disappearances, mass detentions, public floggings, and abductions of women and girls that were tantamount to rape. "During Karume's time," writes Hamad, in a statement corroborated by many, with the naming of names, "people had no security in their homes because if they had a beautiful wife or daughter, she could be taken and forced to sleep with a big shot." Many people, women and children first, were smuggled out in boats by means of bribery.

From a global perspective, this tiny spice island in the Indian Ocean had caught the spotlight as a place of contention between the Communists and the West. The worry for Britain, the recently departed colonial ruler, and America, democracy's somewhat shortsighted crusader, was that the coup was the stepping-stone for the spread of communism into East Africa. They were watching Abdulrahman Babu, in particular, with an obsession, seeing Karume and Nyerere as friendly and moderate. Don Petterson gives a clear picture of American concerns about Babu:

> [The State Department], taking for granted that "for practical purposes" Babu was a "Communist and may lead Zanzibar into Commie camp," wondered how Karume

> could be convinced of this and how Babu's power could be "drastically reduced or eliminated."
>
> In their view it was imperative that Babu be removed from his position of growing power.
>
> Karume, they believed, did not see the danger. And if he did come to see Babu as a threat, he himself would not have the means or capacity to deal with Babu and his supporters. . . . [T]he way to get Karume to see the danger would be through the East African leaders. Kenyatta was the key. . . .

One of the people who expressed this latter opinion, in a cable to Washington, was the American ambassador to Kenya, William Attwood, who would himself soon produce a book, *The Reds and the Blacks* (1967), about the Communist threat in Africa. It would be banned in Kenya, which is surprising since Kenyatta was an avowed friend of the United States. In a rather candid account of his career as a diplomat, in *The Twilight Struggle* (1989), Attwood blithely admits that several Kenyan members of the cabinet were on the payroll of the Americans. Those of us who come from small countries can only muse later in life how such casually described machinations not only changed the course of our countries but also determined our own personal lives: why we are here and not there.

And Okello? He was a loose canon on the scene, one who genuinely believed that it was his mission to liberate not only Zanzibar but also South Africa, Mozambique, and the African countries still under colonial rule. On one hand he respected Karume, the new president, on the other he would set conditions on the presidency. He was the one who sent Karume to safety on the eve of the revolution, and the one who invited him back. He was also aware that as a

Christian in a predominantly Muslim nation, his position could not last. He mentions receiving anonymous letters of threat. But his image was large, his speech populist, and the three East African presidents, Nyerere, Kenyatta, and Obote were nervous.

On January 19, Okello paid a visit to Dar es Salaam for medical treatment, apparently in a plane sent for him by Nyerere; he met Nyerere and members of the cabinet, and he was in Dar when early the next morning the Tanganyka African Rifles went on a mutiny. This only fed rumours of Okello's nefarious influence, but he says that he only placated the mutineers, telling them that they were going about their protests the wrong way. This was a scary moment in Dar es Salaam, especially for the Asians, after the violence of Zanzibar. People on the streets, watching defiant-looking soldiers speeding by in open army trucks, quickly started a free-for-all, a fujo, breaking down doors and looting shops. I recall my mother frantically praying, pulling her tasbih, at the same time warning us kids at the windows not to peep out. The mutiny was quickly quelled with the aid of British commandos.

The next month Okello visited Uganda and Kenya. According to the *New York Times* of February 29, Kenya went on emergency alert. "Prime Minister Jomo Kenyatta and his closest associates were said to fear that a coup might be in preparation." On his way to Nairobi airport to catch his flight back to Zanzibar, Okello says, he was whisked away to "a large office building in the city centre." There he met a nervous trio of Nyerere, Kenyatta, and Obote, who interviewed him about the situation in Zanzibar.

Okello proved too strong a medicine, and he was very soon sidelined. Lied to and betrayed by the East African leaders, he was asked once to accompany Karume to a meeting in Dar es Salaam, where Nyerere pointedly ignored him and had him escorted to

Kenya, from where he was post-haste deported to Uganda. He had little money on him. Ironically, as he says, "The ousted Sultan fled to Britain, where he is living comfortably. He had been paid £200,000 by the Colonial Office . . . as compensation. . . . I was expelled from Zanzibar as an unwanted person without a cent."

Ironies abound in this postcolonial drama. Within three months of the revolution, Tanganyika and Zanzibar formed a union, the United Republic of Tanzania; apparently, Nyerere had tamed Zanzibar, as the West had desired. Calling Nyerere a statesman, *Time*, in its May 1, 1964 issue, declared jubilantly, in its florid style, "Last week, with scarcely a twitch of his toothbrush mustache, Nyerere swallowed—whole—the People's Republic of Zanzibar."

> A strong adherent of African nonalignment, Nyerere shared the fears of Western leaders that Zanzibar, since its savage coup last January against the old Arab ruling crowd, was sliding into the Communist camp. Early last month, Nyerere sent Foreign Minister Oscar Kambona winging across the 23-mile channel that separates the two countries with an ultimatum: unless Zanzibar halted its leftward slither, Tanganyika would dissociate itself. . . .

But Tanzania in a couple of years was one of the staunchest allies of the Communist Bloc, in particular China, which built the Tanzania–Zambia railway line when the World Bank denied assistance. Chinese goods flooded the Tanzanian market (as they do now under different conditions). And Tanzanians visited in droves the Chinese trade fair in Dar, on the Mnazi Mmoja ground; many even saw the opera *The East Is Red*. Tanzania consistently supported China's bid for admission to the United Nations, and when it was finally admitted in 1971, the Tanzanian ambassador, Salim, as the world press reported, "danced a victory jig." One might well ask who swallowed whom. And Babu, whom the British and Americans had feared as a "Commie," and might perhaps even have had assassinated, went on to live his last years in London. "Friendly" Karume turned out to be a brutal dictator, an embarrassment, who soon after he had forcibly married a sixteen-year-old girl, was assassinated. Today we know more about Okello than Karume, whose Wikipedia entry is almost barren. Many believe that he was in fact a mainlander, born in Malawi. Until the Zanzibar authorities release archival material—newspaper reports, radio transcripts, photographs, whatever remains—Okello's account is all we have of the details of the Zanzibar revolution.

20.

Zanzibar: The Sweet and the Smelly

One day a funny smell hit Uhuru Street in Dar es Salaam. It was cloyingly sweet, and extremely repulsive to the young folk. My mother however immediately recognized the foreign odour with a smile. It was duriani, a fruit found in many parts of the tropics, including Zanzibar, but unusual in Dar. A vendor had brought a basketful for sale. We ran from it. Zanzibaris love duriani, and my mother was born in Zanzibar. Apparently the islanders don't react to the smell the way others do. But it repelled enough people on our street that we never saw it again.

Whenever I bring up the issue of race with Zanzibaris, often the first response is an uncomfortable silence; the next one might be a subtle change of subject. I wonder if it's the smell they are afraid of. Zanzibari Asians feel, perhaps with some truth, that important nuances will be lost if their island life is not properly understood. In 2009 a BBC report on the revolution created an uproar of protest. Zanzibar was never simple.

It is, foremost, a small island. Stone Town and the part of Ngambo (the "other" and formerly poorer area) adjoining it are tiny compared to the expanse of any modern city. In pre-revolution days the families living here, closely packed together in the maze of narrow streets, had known each other for decades, and were known by nicknames that are in use even today. It was difficult to keep secrets when you could get the story of a family through several sources, when you could eavesdrop from your window or balcony. News and rumours about the revolution had spread from balcony to balcony, window to window in ripples.

The Internet has created a virtual Zanzibar in which the exiles speak to each other, sharing information, keeping sweet memories alive, all in Swahili and English. They write about the various community festivals they would attend, the cricket matches at Mnazi Mmoja, the promenades at Forodhani where boys and girls threw flirtatious looks at each other, how the old sultan wearing his robe and turban, driven by a liveried chauffeur in the open state car, would wave at the people on the roads. They talk about the festivities of Imam Ali's birthday, how the scouts marched through the streets, throwing salutes at the mosques. They recall the processions of the communities at their festivals—the Goans, the Khoja Ithnashiris, the Khoja Ismailis, the Bohras, the Hindus of various castes; the Yemeni kahawa sellers with their tall urns and tiny cups which they clattered together to announce their arrival, the snack places—Masi's bhajia, Abedi's "mix," Adnan's mbatata (potato), Maruki's halwa; the street vendors they knew by name; all the island's fruits, including, yes, duriani. They will tell you of how on New Year's Eve they would go and stand in front of the English Club at Shangani and watch the elegantly dressed "European" couples go inside, and listen to the music and imagine the dancing. From the ships in the harbour and the hotels too would come strains of music, the entire Shangani seashore thrumming with lively jazz.

"There was absolute harmony and peace," writes former islander Abdulrazak Fazal wistfully in a blog.

> At dusk the loud siren would traditionally go off and the fluttering red flag in the backyard of the Sultan's palace descended from its mast. The azan (call for prayers) from the mosques and the church and temple bells sounded from each and every corner. The public servant with his long wooden rod went from one street to another lighting street lamps. Zanzibar by night though dim was inviolable and had its serenity, sanctity and also liveliness.

These are the sweet stories of pre-revolution Zanzibar, sad and nostalgic. But there is a smell, and that smell has to do with race. But race in Zanzibar, as anywhere in a mixed society, is not simple; people lived peacefully and intimately for the most part, and many Zanzibaris were of mixed origin. In his book, *Race, Revolution, and the Struggle for Human Rights in Zanzibar*, Thomas Burgess writes,

> It is easy, however, to overstate such divisions within colonial Zanzibari society. Allegiance to Islam was overwhelming, creating something of a spiritual brotherhood. There were large numbers of poor Arabs and South Asians, as well as Africans who owned considerable numbers of clove trees. Each of the communities also experienced its own sharp divisions. . . .
>
> Africans were divided by ethnic identity. Former slaves in both Unguja [Zanzibar] and Pemba sought inclusion in island society by acquiring land and by adopting the dress

> and manners of wealthier islanders. They sometimes adopted ethnic markers, such as Swahili, Hadimu, and Shirazi, which obscured their slave origins and identified them as free and established members of coastal society. . . .

Still, the question persists, Why the orgy of violence directed primarily towards one identifiable race? Despite the mixing of races, the ambiguity of origins, and the class differences that could override race and religion, the division of the population into Africans, Asians, and Arabs existed and still does. The key word in Burgess's observation is the uncomfortable *slave.* Slaves were retained in Zanzibar due to the growth of the clove industry in the nineteenth century; slaves were also used domestically. Reliable population estimates do not exist, but Zanzibar rarely had a non-slave population of more than 50,000. Burton's estimate for 1857 was 25,000. It's an astonishing fact then that during that period there were 60,000 to 100,000 slaves on the island. In 1860, 3,000 slaves were emancipated from the Indians. How could that memory not have irked any African, of whatever description? The underclass remained, throughout, "African." And who, beyond a certain age, could in all honesty have forgotten the treatment of servants everywhere in East Africa?

In 1857, Richard Burton undertook a tour of Zanzibar town. He describes the African quarter in the "East End" thus, in his book *Zanzibar*:

> As we go eastward all such signs of civilization vanish; sun and the wind are the only engineers, and the frequent green and black puddles, like those of the filthy Ghetto, or the Jews' quarter, in Damascus, argue a preponderance of

> black population. Here . . . the festering impurities render strolling a task that requires some resolution, and the streets are unfit for a decent (white) woman to walk through.

This area would have included Ngambo, across the creek, where the poorer Indians had yet to arrive in significant numbers in the early twentieth century.

There are two prominent museums on the seafront, the Bait al Ajaib, House of Wonders, and the People's (formerly Sultan's) Palace. The former, built in the later 1800s by the third Omani sultan, the ambitious Seyyid Barghash, is a large and tall white building; inside, the central courtyard is open up to the roof, with tall slim columns supporting the balconies, which run around the second and third floors. It's a museum of coastal art and culture, displaying photographs and artifacts with useful annotations. The lighting is poor everywhere and the place has a somewhat shabby, neglected look, surviving as it does on the most meagre budget. There's much on show; the only regret is that there could be much more.

The People's Palace next door, built in the eighteenth century, contains exhibits relating to the sultans, including large, impressive portraits of most of them. This building too has a central courtyard. Of some interest is the royal receiving room, on the front side of the second floor. A large chandelier hangs over an oriental carpet; at one end of the room is the padded royal chair with armrests, looking upon two padded benches facing each other. A door opens to a balcony, which looks out upon the sea in front and the city from the sides. Across the courtyard on the opposite side of the second floor is the sultana's receiving room, similarly appointed. This was evidently the royal house of a very modest, a minor sultanate. One suspects, however, that much of whatever remained in the palace when the last sultan fled on the royal yacht on the day of the revolution was stolen.

The Omanis arrived in Zanzibar relatively recently, in the seventeenth century, displacing the Portuguese. The earlier history of the island remains somewhat murky.

During the first millennium, Zanzibar island had consisted of separate African fishing and farming communities, following which, starting from the eleventh century, came an era when settlers arrived on the East African coast from Arabia and Persia—according to tradition, the city of Shiraz—and founded the thriving city states Kilwa, Malindi, and others. Shangani (Stone Town) was a minor entity, though Unguja Ukuu to the south, as an eleventh-century map shows, was an important Shirazi city. (Excavations indicate that Unguja Ukuu was a major African community as far back as AD 500, trading with the mainland.) With the arrival of the Portuguese on the Indian Ocean in 1498, life all along the coast, from Mozambique to Somalia, round the Arabian Peninsula and on to India, underwent a dramatic change. In 1507 the Portuguese had already occupied Muscat, the capital of Oman. By 1509, with the defeat of a massive Muslim fleet off the western coast of India, their dominance over the Indian Ocean was complete.

In the following century, however, Portuguese power waned and in 1650 the Omanis expelled them from their territory. Omani naval prowess was considerable and they continued their offensive south until finally by 1698 they had wrested control of the entire East African coast as far as Kilwa. They failed to take Mozambique, according to a story related by Burton, only due to the treachery of the local "Banyans" (Indians). The last ruler of Zanzibar under

Portuguese hegemony was Queen Fatuma, whose palace is believed to be in Shangani on the site of Bait al Ajaib.

The Omanis belonged to the Ibadi sect of Islam, a minority distinct from the Sunnis and Shias, holding the belief that any person could be the rightful head of the Muslims. The Omani leader had thus a religious authority by tradition and was called the Imam. With greater global ambitions, however, the imams adopted the secular title of sultan. In 1827–28 Sultan Seyyid Said moved his capital from Oman to Zanzibar. The emergence of Zanzibar from a minor polity into the major Indian Ocean entrepot that it became has been attributed to his liberal trade policies and friendly relations with foreign businesses.

Almost all of the precolonial observations of Zanzibar come to us from foreign visitors—the explorers, tourists, businessmen, and government representatives who were charmed by it, but limited by their prejudices. However, one of the most fascinating accounts of the island comes from a native, Seyyid Said's daughter Princess Salamah bint Said (b. 1844), who caused a major scandal by eloping with a German merchant; soon becoming a widow, she went on to write her memoir under the name Emily Ruete.

Memoirs of an Arabian Princess from Zanzibar, published in Germany in 1886, gives us an intimate portrait of palace life as well as glimpses into island custom. Seyyid Said is remembered as a white-bearded kindly father and a devout and just sultan. (Burton considers him friendly, liberal, extremely superstitious, and not a good military general.) He had a number of wives of various nationalities, the principal among them a fearsome lady from the royal house of Oman, and a multitude of concubines. There were thirty-six children. Salamah's mother was a Circassian. The language of the court was Arabic, though in the sultan's absence Swahili, Persian, Circassian, Turkish, Nubian, and Abyssinian might all be spoken at once. There was an abundance of food, similarly eclectic, and "every day thirty or forty or even fifty men brought loads of fruit on their backs." The expensive and fair Circassian wives refused to sit with the dusky Ethiopians, and their offspring were called "cats" because of their blue eyes. The girls of the palace were educated in reading (from the Quran), the boys learned to write as well. And although Oman was the "motherland," there was no desire by the young people to visit it, a remarkable, nineteenth-century instance of generational differences among immigrants and their growing alienation from the homeland:

> Not many of us, in fact, cared to visit Oman, whose conceited women liked to treat natives of Zanzibar as inferiors. Members of our family born in Oman would exhibit this attitude toward their Zanzibar relations, assuming that we must resemble Negroes from having been brought up among them. Our most obvious patent of degradation was our speaking another language [Swahili] besides Arabic.

Oman was ruled in the sultan's stead by his eldest son Tueni, and every few years the sultan visited Oman. Salamah recalls his departure in 1853, when "a hush seemed to fall on the house." He stayed away two long years, but ships plied regularly between Oman and Zanzibar and brought news and gifts from him. Finally one day a ship brought the glad tidings that the sultan was returning, and there was much anticipation. Weeks passed but he failed to arrive. His son Majid took a ship and went to look for him. One morning at prayer time, the fleet was sighted, but the ships all flew mourning flags, and the islanders knew that their sultan had died. The year was 1856. Contrary to Islamic custom, the body had not been buried immediately at sea but brought to Zanzibar by his son Barghash, who had accompanied him.

A problem of succession arose. Should the Omani empire fall to the eldest son, Tueni, in Muscat, or Majid, in Zanzibar? It was decided, through British intercession, that Oman and other northern territories went to Tueni, while the East African coast (some 960 miles of it) and Zanzibar went to the fourth son, Seyyid Majid. Majid cuts a dashing figure in his full-length portrait at the Palace Museum. According to his sister Salamah, he was afflicted by seizures. He liked animals and kept fighting-cocks, and like his father he was friendly to foreigners; it was in his frigate that Burton and Speke left for the mainland to begin their East African Expedition. Majid is also credited with the founding of Dar es Salaam, which he named and began to construct but did not finish. And it was during his reign that Salamah eloped with the German Rudolph Ruete, escaping in the British warship appropriately called the *Highflyer.* He died in 1870.

Majid was followed by the heavy-set Barghash, who had twice in the past attempted to seize the throne from his brother. After the second attempt was foiled with the aid of British marines, he was sent into exile in Bombay, escorted by the redoubtable Indian merchant Tharia Topan. European colonial intentions were now overt, and British protection was becoming essential to Zanzibar.

In 1885, Princess Salamah, now Emily Ruete and a widow with three children, arrived in Zanzibar to claim her inheritance and reconcile with her family. There were four German men-of-war in the harbour, in addition to the *Bismarck.* Emily Ruete was a German subject. Her brother refused to see her, and the British consul-general apparently made no efforts to help. As she puts it, "Everyone familiar with Zanzibar is fully aware that the Sultan rules but in small things, whereas the British consul-general manages the rest."

The *Memoir* is a spirited account, feminist in tone and well ahead of Salamah's times, and while critical of some Zanzibari ways, especially superstitions, she stalwartly defends Islam with a keen understanding of the faith and does not hesitate to challenge western customs. She had become a Christian in Germany, but we wonder if, with the spiritual knowledge she shows of her native faith, she did not remember Allah in private. At the end, expressing intense disappointment in her visit to Zanzibar, she sounds sad and even shrill. While saying how the islanders welcomed her, often in secret, she cannot help displaying her prejudices. Indians, whom she calls "blackfeet," are despised: they are crafty "spies," always devious and untrustworthy. "Negroes are very lazy" and she doubts if slavery would be completely abolished. (She is astute enough to inform us that many westerners did keep slaves in Zanzibar, often using them for more difficult labour.)

We might dismiss her prejudices simply as the attitudes of her times, were we not to recall the ignominous and timely escape from the island of her royal house only seventy-eight years later and the bloodbath of the revolution.

Kassam, a Zanzibari Asian, now lives in Toronto. He is a quiet and thoughtful man, a successful business consultant, with a large family. His wife is Goan, from Dar. In that considered, distant gaze he has, he often sees, I suspect, memories of Zanzibar. He grew up in Ngambo, the poorer and more bustling, and mainly African section on the other side of Creek Road; nevertheless he attended the prestigious King George VI Secondary School, with high-achievers of all races. Among his classmates was the novelist Abdulrazak Gurnah.

He shows me a senior class photograph on his smartphone. Arab, Asian, and African boys stare out intently at the camera. A youth member of the left-wing Umma Party, Kassam was at an ASP (Afro-Shirazi Party) fete on the eve of the revolution, when someone whispered to him that there might be trouble in the town later that night and he should go home early. Revolution was announced early next morning by crowds mobbing outside on the Asian street of Ngambo. People barricaded themselves inside their houses. He remembers a bullet zinging past him as he made a dash for the police station to get help. It was useless. The next day he was outside the Raha Leo Community Centre, where all the Asians had been commanded to gather, perhaps to receive a hectoring from John Okello. There he was recognized by someone as an Umma Party cadre and handed a rifle—which he surrendered when everyone else did, a few days later.

After the revolution, Kassam stayed on in Zanzibar and did his National Service by teaching at a school. Upon completion he asked permission—there was now a tightly controlled totalitarian state in place—to go to the U.K. to study medicine. He was refused. When he complained of favouritism, he soon found himself under surveillance, and his principal at school was questioned about him. He was warned against shooting off his mouth. At this time his father, running a shop in Dar es Salaam, died and Kassam found himself on the mainland supporting his siblings. He met his future wife, and they moved to Toronto. For many people from Dar or Nairobi, that would be the end of their African story. But Kassam is a Zanzibari. Once when I visited him at his house in Toronto, he called up his aunt in London to ask for a recipe for lamb chops; they spoke in Swahili. He returns frequently to Zanzibar and has had the primary school where he taught repaired and extended. He sends books there.

When I next visit Zanzibar, Kassam is there too, arranging for the opening of his renovated school by the vice-president of the country, and he proudly takes me there to show it. It is in the Unguja Ukuu area, to the southeast of the island, a lovely small school shaped like an open rectangle with classrooms all around, freshly painted, water pipes installed, the old desks back in place. It needs to be cleaned up to be occupied. On our way back we go to see the ruins of the ancient town of Unguja Ukuu. All that remains are a few brick stumps. A businessman has had the area cleared for construction. The following day Kassam takes me on a tour.

Starting from Shangani we walk towards Soko Muhogo—the former people's market, now with modest shops and residences—and pass by the old Kutchi Bhatia community centre, a ramshackle house with a compound, now closed off; squatters have recently been removed from the site. Here the likes of the businessman Ladha Damji, custom collector to the sultan and facilitator to European travellers, would have attended for prayer and community gatherings. Next, Kassam shows me a large, gated apartment complex, consisting of twenty-seven flats on its three floors. This was where once the Golaranas lived. Their name literally means "slaves (or servants) to the king," and they were low-caste Indians who did lowly jobs. The complex is a slum now, with a cluttered compound, and it's variously occupied. From here we go to an Ithnasheri community mosque—a two-storey stone building, elaborately laid out with a prayer hall, a hall for community feasts, a kitchen, a place for shoes and to wash feet. Outside the prayer hall are pietistic sayings and prayers, and photos of holy men, including those of the ayatollahs Khomeini and Khamanei. This was the second Ithnasheri mosque on the island, and it was the one Kassam used to attend. He shows me the wall where his father once sat. The Ithnasheris proselytize actively, and this mosque now happens to be the prayer house of the African Ithnasheris. We reach the Portuguese Gate, and sit down under a tree across from it and ask for a couple of coconuts to be cut. It's March and sweltering.

Proceeding to Mnazi Mmoja ground, past the Hamamni (Persian Baths) area, we turn into Benjamin Mkapa—formerly Creek—Road, to reach Kassam's old primary school. It looks old but solid, a two-storey affair with an open square courtyard where we come to stand with an attendant; familiar-sounding choruses come buzzing out in all directions from the classrooms—the sound inside any school. There's an impressive assembly hall with a stage. This is now a high school, running two sessions of 1,500 kids, in the morning and afternoon.

We go to Ngambo, crossing at Darajani, an endlessly long street of shops, with residences on top, and thick with shoppers and mere idlers. The shops are owned by Arabs and a few Asians. Most Asians of course left after the revolution. People greet my friend warmly, calling out across the narrow street, "Weh, Tunda!" using the old family nickname, by which everybody still knows him. These are people he has known, or their children; people who never went away. This was the street, these the gulleys leading out, where he played as a child. He pokes his head everywhere. As I watch him in his typical island casuals, striding here and striding there, greeting this fellow and then that one, cheerful and loud, I can't help wondering, Is this the same man—so formal in Toronto, speaking English, consulting his calendar, receiving business proposals on his smartphone, driving a sleek black Audi? Which one is real?

This street is also where all the Khojas lived, he tells me; and this street, I realize, is where my mother was born. There were lots of rapes here, he tells me with a nod. Nothing more need be said.

An old fellow in kanzu and kofia stops him for a chat. Kassam recently gave him a smartphone. It apparently does not work. I'll give you another one, Kassam says. Does it have Bluetooth? the mzee asks.

We cross the old Creek Road again and tour the fish and meat market, stop for sodas once more, and there meet the veteran muhogo-seller Mamedi. His claim to fame is that he knows about all the old Hindi films, their stories, and the stories behind their making. As he tends to the muhogo on the grill, turning and picking out pieces for customers, he talks about the classics *Boot Polish* and *Awara.* How the fire in *Mother India* was real, after which Nargis, the star, married Sunil Dutt; how she later financed the films of the legendary Raj Kapoor, with whom she had an affair.

One person who did not leave after the revolution is Mr. Chagpar, my friend Habib's father. "You ask me why I stayed," he tells me. "I stayed in order to recoup what I lost." I don't quite believe this, because he seems so completely a Zanzibari, and I cannot see him surviving in the stiff formality of Nairobi, where his wife went away with the kids and later divorced him. He is a tall and dark well-built man wearing a cotton jacket and a red fez. His office, next to the Khoja khano, is a medium-sized cluttered shopfront, in which he sits behind a large desk. The ceiling is high and he has built a loft, to which he can repair for his privacy. So completely a man of the place, who's stayed here through thick and thin and on familiar terms with everybody, he is also a raconteur of a somewhat cynical bent, with many stories to tell, most of which he says are so sensitive that he will leave them for posterity.

He had owned a petrol station. Early morning on the day of the revolution one of his workers phoned to tell him not to come to the station, there was trouble in town. Chagpar called up the mukhi, the Khoja headman, and started walking towards the khano. As he approached it he saw on the quiet, narrow street a woman coming towards him, very obviously in grief. Her two sons had just been killed before her eyes. He and the mukhi put up a few people in the khano, then after a day or so the others arrived and the khano filled up to become a shelter in God's house.

He says, dramatically, "Don't ask me what I saw during the revolution, ask what I didn't see. Murder, rape, you name it—everything happened."

His favourite story is about how he was made an army major by Karume, the new president of Zanzibar (and vice-president of Tanzania).

Abeid Karume was somewhat of a laughingstock among the educated on the mainland. *Time* had likened him in build to the boxer Sonny Liston, whom the handsome and sharp-witted Muhammad Ali had just beaten. There were schoolboy jokes about his impromptu utterings, and he was clearly an embarrassment to Nyerere, the Union president, a sophisticated man educated at Edinburgh and a translator of Shakespeare. But Karume was a canny politician.

One day some policemen came to Chagpar's office and told him, "Come, the president wants to see you."

A summons like that could mean jail, or execution; he could disappear. Fearfully, Chagpar followed the men and got into their car. At State House, where he was taken, he sat at a table and waited nervously. Then Karume strode in with his underlings.

"Waswahili ni wezi," Karume said bluntly to Chagpar's face. The Waswahili—the local Africans—are thieves. This is a stereotype some Asians might have used.

"But I never said that!" Chagpar protested, utterly shocked.

"All of them are thieves!"

"I didn't say that, Your Excellency. I swear by the Almightly, I didn't say that."

"You didn't say it, *I* say it! Give him orange juice," Karume commanded.

Chagpar was given orange juice.

It turned out that money was being pilfered from the army, and Karume wanted Chagpar, an Asian, to keep the army's accounts. Chagpar said he was not an army person. "You are now a major," Karume declared.

A bizarre story and typical of the times, of the randomness of the leaders and the fears of the minorities. It was Karume who introduced an amendment to the Marriage Act to force Asian girls to marry Africans; these men were usually elderly and connected to the government. A girl as young as fifteen or sixteen had only to catch the eye of a passing elderly bigwig for a marriage offer to arrive. Refusal of such a proposal was punishable by a fine or imprisonment and possibly a corporal punishment of twenty-four strokes of the cane. But this was mere legalese, much more could happen to a family if it refused the offer. In response to the act, families married off their girls posthaste to boys through the usual family and community connections; many girls escaped by boat to Dar. The case became notorious because four of the girls so coerced were Iranians, of whom one committed suicide. The intention of the act, Chagpar says, was to increase racial integration. Soon we will become like Cuba, Karume told him, where you cannot distinguish among the races. One wonders.

"When we read *Animal Farm* in school we thought it was just a funny story about animals. Well, after the revolution I understood that book, because Zanzibar had become Animal Farm. Everything was upside-down."

Chagpar had to undergo military training, and his instructors were Russians. Because he knew English, he was also their interpreter. Soon he was making a fat salary. He recalls personally putting people on boats to escape to the mainland.

Not far from my hotel on Kenyatta Road is the old English Club, a large boxlike structure. Next to it is the old German Consulate. Behind these stands the stylish and expensive Serena Inn, where today's foreign delegations put up. The nightly cultural entertainment and menus of local food at the Serena promise to be good, though the lengths of human flesh stretched out inert by the pool tend to discourage any thought of lingering there over a beer or coffee. Close by is Vuga Road, which has some interesting traditional-style buildings with white facades, balconies, and arched windows. Most impressive is the court building, now dilapidated but still in use, an example of what the historian Abdul Sheriff calls Saracenic architecture—with arched doorways and windows, verandas and balconies, dark wooden trimming, and raised domes—a style in fact introduced by a British official named J.H. Sinclair. An example of this style farther down the road is the old Aga Khan School, now part

of the local university. Close by is the new Majestic Cinema; the old one, burnt down in a fire, was also in the Saracenic style, the new one is a pastiche art deco structure in typical twentieth-century cinema style.

The bloodletting of the revolution therefore has not carried over into a violence against the past in the form of its monuments and architecture. Zanzibar remains a puzzle. Unlike Dar es Salaam, Zanzibar's Stone Town has preserved its distinct physical character. Its economic power is gone, the political landscape has altered, yet the island thrives on its historical and cultural connections, in the same way, I am reminded, that Shimla, the former British summer capital of India, does. Zanzibar now hosts film, book, and music festivals. It promotes traditional taarab music—when the ancient diva, "the Queen of Taarab" Bi Kidude, died recently, the entire coastal region of the nation mourned. And Zanzibar likes to tell its stories. Of course it's also moved closer to Oman, where everyone—one is told—has links to Zanzibar, and Swahili is the second language.

Dar es Salaam, in contrast, is a market that keeps on growing as it destroys and alters the cityscape. It seems to remember nothing.

A friend has arranged to have a car take me to Kizimkazi, a village near the southern tip of the island. We pass on a quiet road through a forested region to reach the village—a scattering of houses—at the edge of which in the midst of farmland is its famous mosque, built in 1107 and still in use, except for the Friday prayer. Today is Friday and 1 p.m., the caretaker is praying at the village's other mosque. He arrives on his bicycle to open this ancient one for us. It is a square white building with a green, corrugated, and sloping double-roof. The inside has three original fat pillars, newly plastered and painted green and white. The front—the qibla—is also original, with a row of Kufic inscriptions on the line of bricks above that give the date of the mosque's construction, by settlers believed to have come from Iran. Unfortunately the inscriptions have been oil-painted over, a prettifying defacement much lamented by historians. Because the mosque has been in continuous use, it has seen regular renovation, and that is the reason why it doesn't look typically ancient.

On the way back we cross over to the southeastern coast of the isle, to an area called Makunduchi. Here Muslim Indians from the Kumbhad (potter) caste had settled in the nineteenth or early twentieth century, becoming completely accultured to native life. (The Kumbhads of Dar es Salaam, in contrast, are Hindus.) Already in 1925 it was observed that the Kumbhads of Makunduchi, called Makumbaro, spoke Kihadimu, the local Swahili dialect, as fluently as the local Africans, called the Hadimu and considered indigenous. The Makumbaro were from Kutch and Kathiawad, in Gujarat, and were the only people on the island who used the camel for transportation. There were thirty families in the area. Kihadimu was very distinct from Kiswahili (Swahili) and for an outsider took some effort to understand, as we find even now when we stop to ask if there are any Makumbaro around. After a few queries, we are directed to a house that's one among a cluster, well built and plastered; outside in the yard two children, who look of mixed race, are at play. We knock and are met by an Asian man wearing shorts and an open shirt, who greets us warmly in Swahili, welcomes us to join him for a lunch of rice, stew, and mango. We decline politely. He says that all the Makumbaro have moved to the towns; they used to run shops. This must have been, presumably, after they gave up their traditional occupation of working with clay.

As we drive back, we pass on the highway signboards indicating tourist restaurants, which are closer to the water and not obviously visible; and men in white kanzus and kofias walking back casually from Friday prayers. It is a quiet, tranquil scene, ours the only vehicle for long stretches of the road, which is often shaded by the trees. When we reach the town I treat the driver to a lunch at Passing Show, where they have run out of pilau and banana, so we opt for chicken and fish biriyanis.

Two men in their sixties, one of whom, Shiraz, left forty-eight years ago for the U.K., soon after the revolution, at the age of sixteen. His Swahili is halting and accented. The other, Sadru, left more than thirty years ago for Toronto. Both have children and families abroad; Shiraz is divorced from his English wife, Sadru is widowed. And now—this is a typically Zanzibari attitude—they both feel utterly at home here, where they run a much-appreciated dental clinic. Shiraz is a long-experienced dentist from Brighton, Sadru is the manager. They have converted a storage room into a consultancy, having had it cleaned and painted and installed with a dentist's long chair and other equipment. Judging by the looks on the patients' faces as they wait outside to be called, these two men are a godsend. As I arrive, a root canal is in progress.

A woman in her sixties lies on the chair, mouth open. Shiraz instructs an assistant, a qualified young graduate; Sadru stands by with the cement for the filling. A generator rattles away somewhere; mains electricity is unreliable. Sadru usually takes care of the business end, banking and buying supplies. He also lectures the patients on dental care while they wait. The clinic charges what the patient can afford to pay. European prices for Europeans, though, to make ends meet. Some donations come from Toronto. The men work hard, five and a half days a week, plus a half-day to take care of business.

They live on the first floor of a traditional-style white house off the main drag that is Kenyatta Avenue, not far from the practice. All around them, NGO residences, SUVs parked outside. The building is owned by an old Khoja family. Shiraz is a Bohra, Sadru an Ithnasheri. Shiraz, who has acquired his accent and mannerisms from the U.K., doesn't practise his faith anymore, but one day, he says, he went to pay his respects to the local Bohra mulla, who received him cordially—which community doesn't appreciate a doctor or dentist in its midst? Shiraz had put on a kofia for the occasion, out of respect. But having met the mulla, as he came out of the room he was accosted by a young man for not wearing the traditional Bohra hat. (I didn't even know that such a thing existed.) There were more youthful fanatics waiting as Shiraz came out of the building, threatening to beat him up for his effrontery. He looks nonplussed as he narrates this, and I ask, But why did you bother to go? The answer, though he does not put it this way, is simple: it's not so easy to break off one's traditional ties completely. Reason says one thing, the heart pulls the other way.

It is Saturday night, and the anniversary of the Prophet's death, so Sadru dresses up, cologne and all, and goes to his mosque. He returns late, past midnight, having paid a visit to an Arab friend. She went to school with him, he says.

As boys both Shiraz and Sadru witnessed at close hand the violence of the Zanzibar revolution. Shiraz was smuggled out on a boat at night and after reaching Dar, ended up in Tanga at his married sister's. Sadru was sent off to Dar by his brother. And yet here they are, home in a way, living out their senior years in the place where they grew up, still belonging to it. It's not that they are not aware of race; they are, as everyone here is; their attitudes regarding efficiency and punctuality have also altered. But Zanzibar is a small place and different peoples have lived together for centuries. Memories of the aberration and nightmare that was the 1964 revolution remain but are being set aside to continue on with the simple process of living. The people are Zanzibaris first. Regardless of their politics, the overwhelming majority being Muslims, they all bow to Mecca during prayers, and on the Prophet's birthday and during the Eids they all come out to celebrate. Islam—in principle—does not distinguish between races. The first person to make the call to prayer in Mecca was a black man named Bilal.

21.

The Old Warriors: Dar es Salaam Again

THEY SOUND WISTFUL OR CYNICAL, disappointed or resigned, the aging leftists of Dar who engaged with zeal with the new Africa, indeed the new world that had emerged in the 1960s; now passing middle age most are doing very well, for who in his right mind—there are a few—would try to live by their old idealist codes now that socialism is gone and there's a free-for-all? For this meeting with some of them, I requested less food and more chat, having observed that those who can afford to, eat and eat. We meet at the Patel Brotherhood Club, an assortment of Asians—the term is too broad, just as "African" is—on the lawn of the old club house, which has been converted into an open-air restaurant. Of the club—tucked away in the midst of Gaam—a vestige remains. It had snooker and card tables, a dart board, and tennis courts; the cricket team was respectable. There are five of us today, the other four being Nadir, Harko, Chauhan, and Muzu. Nadir and Harko met in England in the 1970s, radicals ripened in Tanzania and coming out for African causes. Harko regales us with a humorous tale in which he stood before an almost all-black audience in London, to speak out against Idi Amin, when the audience evidently supported the dictator and his anti-Asian rhetoric. Against all advice, Harko spoke his mind. His message was that Amin was bad for Africa and Africans, leave aside the Asians (who had been told to leave the country). Much to his bewilderment he received a standing ovation. He is an ebullient, quick-witted personality, who adventured in India—spending time with the Naxalite-Maoists—and the U.K., before returning to socialist Tanzania, where he became the English-language editor of the state-owned Tanzania Publishing House (TPH). This is where the question of race comes in.

There was a hint of it when I happened to mention earlier that in German times a few Asians had been hanged for supporting African resistance. And Harko said, briefly, "That should come in handy in the future."

I remind Muzu, a professional photographer and an artist, about my first meeting with him, more than a decade ago, when I had been invited to Dar to spend two weeks at the International School, where his wife was employed. One afternoon I was asked to speak to a group of professionals in town, and at the meeting I had noted, indiscreetly and perhaps ungraciously, my surprise to see that all of them were Asians and no African was present. There was an uproar—who was I to judge them, coming from abroad. I still debate with myself if I should have been more prudent and refrained from that comment. I was being naive, but I had also hit a nerve. My offence was that these were the educated, progressive elite, and I had embarrassed them.

Now Nadir says, "How come when Africans talk of integration they only speak of intermarriage. It all comes down to fucking."

"There is the attraction of the exotic," I mention.

But Harko's daughter is marrying an African Tanzanian, whom she met in the U.S., and the couple are returning home for the wedding. "We explained to them the possible problems, and then it was their wish," says the father.

Still on the subject of intermarriage, Chauhan, who is a businessman, and his wife are from different castes. There was so much opposition to their union, they had to elope. This was forty years ago. Now one of their sons is married to a Swede.

The subject is dropped.

Nadir is an architect. "We are all controlled by our wives," he says. "But I don't mind. And my wife doesn't follow me around, doesn't ask where I've been. Today I feel like drinking." He is also an artist; one occupation gives him a handsome living, the other his passion.

We start with beer and move on to Scotch. They like to talk of wines here and drink it, but their expertise is beer and Scotch. The food is prawns, mishkaki, chicken, naan. Abundance.

The race question. Harko says, when an opening came up for the general manager at the TPH, he was the obvious choice. But he knew he would not get the post. There were rumblings against that idea. An Asian in a top publishing post, a sensitive one at the gates of culture in a socialist African country. And so he himself suggested the name of Walter Bgoya, who was working in the foreign office at the time, having just been sent down from the embassy in Addis Ababa for misbehaving. Harko went into business. And thus began Walter's long career in publishing, and Harko's rise in wealth.

We've perhaps had too much, it's almost midnight, and ours is the only table left occupied. But Nadir wants to make a long night of it, therefore three of us decide to go to Harko's house. Muzu, always in control, decides he has had enough and goes home.

Harko lives in Oyster Bay, behind the Canadian high commissioner. We drive to his house in a large SUV with all possible extras, a car like which only one other person owns in Dar, he tells me. But, "Frankly," he continues, "I was happier when I was younger." When he returned to Tanzania, he was one of a political discussion group that met regularly, and included the country's future president Benjamin Mkapa, as well as Walter Bgoya. Now he owns one of the country's biggest fish-processing and exporting companies, and is on the way to moving into the chicken business. He does not quite fit into the role of a chicken and fish magnate, doesn't much talk about the business. He obviously still thinks left, which is what's responsible for his cynical humour. He visits India frequently, the music on the car is Indian—there is now in our generation an unabashed acceptance of Indian heritage without a feeling of betrayal. We arrive at the house, which as befits the area has a forbidding gate with guards, but there are no German shepherds. It's a large, modern house with a pool, and was designed by Nadir. We sit outside by the pool so as not to disturb Harko's wife and continue our imbibing until 3 a.m., when Harko, still remarkably alert, drives me to my hotel.

Harko is a Hindu, his wife is Ithnasheri Muslim. Nadir is a Khoja Ismaili, his wife is also Ithnasheri, sister of the leftist intellectual Hassan at Makerere. Hassan's former wife is Fawzi; his current wife is a famous film director. Hassan, Shivji, and Abdul of Zanzibar are long-standing friends. And so they are all connected.

Nadir's house, where I visit him one evening a few days later, is also in an exclusive area by the sea, and is designed by himself, naturally. He is a tall, soft-spoken man, who makes the cutting remark without Harko's bite or exuberance. All the walls of the house are covered in paintings, his and others'. There's a terrace on the first floor where we sit for a while under the stars, listening to the sound of waves, the swish of branches overhead. After a while we go up a level to his studio where he shows me his art. The paintings tend to be abstract renderings of the political and mystical. The political ones depict the despair of the intellectual humanist. One of his series is in black and white and shows sections of the human body in various postures of power; it is a commentary on the oppression of the weak. Another series shows the human head and torso defaced and rendered grotesque with abrupt and haphazard-looking brushstrokes. Man turned beast.

Adjacent to the studio is his library. I met someone in Toronto who had visited Nadir's house in Moshi when they were both in their teens. And what she remembered were the books, Nadir's pride in them. He had shown her his books as he now does to me. The pride of place here is taken by his first editions. From him I learn that there is actually an archaic law in place that forbids importing or owning indecent pictures, sometimes as innocuous as simple nudes, and therefore he's had struggles to release art books from Customs. In one instance his office assistant had to seek help from a relative in the security services.

People like him, educated abroad and living on the edges of society, find camaraderie with a few like-minded souls and a few expatriates. The latter are his patrons, those who seem to understand his art and encourage him. There is no other patronage of the arts in town. No one would understand his madness. And yet the same would be true if he were to move overseas, I reflect to myself, having observed Chinese, Pakistani, and Punjabi artists floundering in neglect in Toronto. When all's said and done, despite foreign influences, he belongs here, where he has a context.

Later we sit on the terrace and have dinner as a gentle breeze blows in.

I first met Walter Bgoya at a dinner party in Issa Shivji's house.

Shivji is an institution in the country. If you say you know Shivji, they—almost everyone, it seems—look at you with respect. He is consistent, he speaks his mind, he is honest. I lay a claim to him because we went to the same high school, he three grades higher than I.

I remember him as a founder of a student representative body in our school, called the Pupils' Own Council (POC); it was a radical idea, allowed perhaps because the principal was an Irishman who loved our school where, he told us once, the attitude to learning was so much better than in British schools. POC created great excitement, and I recall Shivji on the stage with others giving a spiel. He was also involved in a movement called Moral Rearmament (MRA)—which was at the time making a push in Asia and Africa. This was an embarrassing episode, I believe, in Shivji's life. He would have been sixteen or seventeen. Those were the days of our idealism, and these involvements reflected that idealism. One day some MRA representatives from England or America came to our school and made a big impression, selling a lot of books, which we could barely afford. But MRA was not heard of much again. Perhaps it was banned by the government, which also banned POC for supporting a student protest at the university. Shivji was a brilliant student and went on to study law. From all that I have heard, often with envy, the University of Dar es Salaam was a place throbbing with radical new ideas and optimism. It was where Uganda's future president Museveni, and Tanzania's, Mkapa, studied. Mahmood Mamdani of Uganda was here, as were Walter Rodney of Guyana and the Kenyan Swahili poet Abdilatif Abdalla (who became a jailmate in Kenya of the author Ngũgĩ). Professors of a liberal bent converged from all over the world, including Canada. Later Shivji became a professor here, writing books and opinions, keeping in mind always the interests of the common people.

When I first returned to Tanzania, after a long absence and having just finished my first book, I went to meet Shivji—a person I had come to admire from a distance for his consistency, against what I saw as my own inconstancy and betrayal. I had never spoken to him before. We became friendly, though not quite friends, for he is a private person. He lived in Upanga in the same area and in the same kind of flat I had lived in during high school, and he has continued to stay there when anyone else with his influence would long ago have moved on to Oyster Bay.

It was at a dinner party at his modest home that I met Walter. At the end of the evening Walter drove me and another guest back. All I recall of that other passenger is that she was an Asian and had returned from the United States for a visit; when we dropped her off on India Street—the Bohra area—she quickly produced a black veil, put it on, and quite nonchalantly went on her way. The Bohra mulla in India had recently decreed stricter orthodox observances for his followers. Then Walter dropped me off nearby at the Flamingo on the perpetually potholed Jamat Street; it's always surprised him whenever I stay there, but it's at the heart of the Dar I grew up in.

During my next visit to Dar, I was a guest of the International School, which put me up in Oyster Bay. I had been asked to meet the pupils of every grade in the school. This was the first time I had stayed in that beautiful, breezy area by the ocean, and the sense I had then was of how times had changed. Oyster Bay was still lovely, though a bit more crowded; egalitarian. One evening when I returned to my hotel, a note was waiting for me, from Walter, chiding me for not having informed him that I was in town. We met several times during that visit; once we ate at an Indian vegetarian restaurant; a few days later he took me to his home in Gaam, like Shivji's a modest place, where I met his wife, Frida, and his young son, Mkuki, who made a drawing of me—which he showed me years later when he had returned from the U.S., a professional designer.

Walter had just left TPH, Tanzania Publishing House, and was now a dedicated independent publisher of Swahili books in a sliver-thin market. When I left Dar after high school, there were several bookstores in town, some of them new—the book business was booming. Now there was one belonging to a church and another, a meanly stocked, dusty one run by TPH. Life could not have been easy, and one could not help but admire Walter's dedication. His office was in Kariakoo, behind Msimbazi Street—whose hustle and bustle becomes ever more forbidding with the years. It was where my grandmother, an uncle, and an aunt had their shops once, when my family moved to Dar from Nairobi. From Msimbazi, at the intersection of my aunt's provision store, I walked three blocks on an unpaved street through a residential neighbourhood, passing bungalow-style traditional homes with sloping iron roofs, inquiring here and there for Bwana Bgoya, until I arrived at the house that was his office. There was an outer room, with a secretary, and an inner room where he sat surrounded by books—all that he would need, but it was not downtown where a professional business should be. The very site of a publishing firm in that humble neighbourhood spoke of resolve and rebellion. He told me how hard it was to sell books in the local market, spoke of everything he had tried, including book vans. There was an international collective based in London on which he relied to distribute abroad.

Since then he seems to have done well, though there have been snide remarks—the barest hints—I have heard about him and his old pal, former president Ben Mkapa. Perhaps the president put in a word or two in his favour. Perhaps it's the economic boom, however selective it is. But surely he deserves some reward for the essential but very thankless service he has performed for the country. There is no other publisher like him in East Africa. His new office is in a smart new business complex on the airport road, and occupies a good portion of the ground floor, the several rooms separated by glass walls. He has also bought the old TPH bookstore—which was one in name only—on Samora Avenue and converted it into a unique outlet for African titles. But Walter is not a businessman, not a good investment. A venture into a restaurant—an excellent one—is bound to fail because it is in an area where expats don't go out to dine. He needs to move it, but where to find investors? His wealthy friends, Harko is one, know that Walter Bgoya is not a businessman. Still, even as he plans to move—office rent is too high—he thinks of new ventures. He organizes an annual book fair. And every month his son holds an open mike with book readings and jazz at the office premises.

Once when I was in Dar, Walter was seriously ill, being treated in South Africa. Our common friend Fawzi gave me the news, and together we phoned him to wish him luck. We were not sure he would survive.

I had never heard of Fawzi before she rang me up one day while on a visit to Toronto and introduced herself; we met briefly then, and later again when I visited Dar. She was head of a women's organization and the large front section of the office was buzzing with activity, with young, bemused-looking foreign interns hanging around. Fawzi, a flamboyant presence who dresses colourfully, often looks angry, and she is quick to speak her mind, but she is a warm personality and perhaps emotionally vulnerable. She is one of the

Zanzibari exiles, her family having lost everything in the revolution, but now is able to maintain a home on the island. She is also a victim of Zanzibar's barbaric forced-marriage episode of the 1960s. While walking home from school one day in Zanzibar, she says, she caught the eye of an official of the revolutionary government in his car. One day he knocked on the door and told her father he wished to marry her. Fawzi had taken the long route home from school that lunchtime and was not back. Her father, with the inspiration of the desperate, quickly told the man she was already engaged to be married very soon. A groom was sought overnight by the anxious, frightened family, and she was convinced to marry him. The alternatives were unthinkable. She was sixteen, he in his twenties, from a known family. The marriage never worked. It never could have, she says. All her ambitions and dreams for the future were laid aside by that single episode. She later married a charismatic professor at the University of Dar es Salaam, and her memories of being a member of a support group of campus wives in the 1970s, a "chapati-maker" to the intellectuals who discussed all the great topics of the day, still rankles her. But she's made herself known as an activist and feminist, and was on the board of the Zanzibar International Film Festival. She is still connected to her own family, and can hardly go out with the guys for a drink at night—it's not done. She has brought up a son, sent him to university in the United States. Now she has a grandchild.

When I meet her most recently, at al-Qayyum, the new kabab and bhajia place, she looks beleaguered. Her sister's granddaughter was one of three girls who drowned in an accident outside Toronto, and the grieving sister is visiting. And the building in Upanga where both Fawzi and her son own apartments was recently slated for demolition, to put up one of those high-rises that are supposed to turn Dar into New York. The development company is of course partly owned by a high-placed government official. She's managed to have an injunction passed, and waits.

She has stories, many stories of Zanzibar and herself that she's hoarding and wants to write up.

I call up Shivji and ask him if he has time to meet. Of course, he says, let's meet at Barbecue Hut tonight. And so I go to the place, in Upanga, famous for its barbecued chicken, chips, mishkaki, and a kind of naan. I am early and therefore find a table outside on the patio.

The restaurant is in the middle of a row of townhouses in the Khoja Ismaili community's extensive cooperative housing development. In the 1950s, the Ismailis had resolved collectively that every family should be able to own its own flat. When the cooperative development came up, the roads were mud trails and much of the area was wooded; frogs were heard all night, and snakes abounded; nevertheless many families from bustling Kariakoo moved their residences to Upanga. To visit family here, in the country so to speak, made for a good Sunday outing but it was a long trek through the streets of Gaam. I wonder now what zoning regulations were flouted to put up this restaurant in the midst of a completely residential neighbourhood. From where I sit I see a tall new building rising up on the site of a former block of flats, the scaffolded structure looming grotesquely in the dark, a godzilla waiting to devour everything below.

The street outside is broken and potholed, over which large SUVs arrive, bouncing on their springs. They park, families emerge and enter joyously through the restaurant's wide entrance; this is a crowded, popular place. The owner, Sadru, comes to meet them. A big man with cropped hair, he's a good host, greeting new arrivals, kissing babies, Asian and African. He tells me the fish is excellent, he bought it himself soon after it was caught. I tell him I'm waiting for Shivji, and his esteem goes up several notches. He's been to Canada, he says, but saw no reason to stay there. He has a daughter in Boston. When people started leaving in a panic in the early 1970s, he picked up a few properties at a few thousand dollars each. Now—he doesn't tell me this, though it is implied—each is worth a few hundred thousand dollars.

Shivji arrives. Simple and professorial, wearing shorts and faded shirt and sandals—in the former Tanzanian, not to say Gujarati, way. You don't show off. Following retirement, he was recalled by the university to take up the Julius Nyerere Research Chair in Pan-African Studies. Since Nyerere is to Tanzania what Gandhi is to India, Jinnah to Pakistan, and Mandela to South Africa (of which he was the greatest champion when it needed champions), Shivji's status is extremely elevated. Now and then he gives an opinion in a newspaper, in Swahili. People listen.

We talk about this and that, including our families. I remind him about my recent visit to Dodoma, where I spoke at the university at the invitation of his daughter, a faculty member. He glows with pride. He tells me his department is organizing an event to honour Walter Rodney, the Guyanese historian and intellectual who taught in Dar in the 1970s—will I be around then? He gives me the date. He reiterates what many people on the left say, that the economic condition of the country is worse than what official statistics reveal. Food prices have gone up, people can't afford to feed themselves. Even the KT Shop, he says, is becoming unaffordable. He walks a mile and a half to the chai place early every Sunday morning, and he's observed that the number of patrons has considerably declined. Twenty percent increase over most items in one go.

I would like an in-depth chat with him, but this is not the time. We get up when we finish, and go out and have kahawa from a street vendor across the road, and since I hanker for a tea, he says, Why don't you come home for tea. Shamelessly I accept.

Over tea, which he makes, his wife also having joined us, we arrive at that irresistible and obsessive subject, the state of the Khoja community, in which we both grew up, and to my great surprise he recites a line from a Gujarati bhajan, "Raakh na ramakada . . ." These toys made of ashes, which my lord Rama made . . . It's part of our Indian heritage, isn't it, he says.

At some point he mentions two episodes from his life.

He grew up in a small village, in extremely modest circumstances. One day, his father being away, their landlord, a community man, came over and threatened to throw them out. His mother pleaded and cried for the man to show some mercy. Finally she took off her siri—the nose stud—the last bit of jewellery she possessed, and said, Here, keep this, until my husband arrives. It was a wounding, unforgettable experience for the eldest boy, who witnessed his mother's humiliation.

Another incident involving rent occurred when the family had moved to Dar. The property was owned by a lawyer. Lawyers, Shivji says, were like gods, arrogant men whom you approached with trepidation. They were from wealthy families, which had afforded to send them to England to study. Shivji's father went to the landlord to plead for an extension, taking his son with him. He received the haughty reply, Why do you people breed if you can't afford to feed your kids?

I think it must have been then, Shivji says, when I was ten, that I resolved that I would be a lawyer.

He became one, and also a champion of the poor. And I realize that I have been privileged to have caught this very private person in a special moment, some chemistry having worked as the three of us sat with tea in his house at around ten at night, when he felt like revealing these experiences.

Of all these old leftists, I find myself personally closest to Walter; I can banter and joke with him, speak freely and let him contradict me if he wants to. When he smiles, he seems intimate. I've been meaning to sit down with him for a long chat, and finally a few days before my departure from Dar I text him: "How about meeting this afternoon for a tête-à-tête? Kili or New Africa." Kili is the lounge of the Kilimanjaro Hotel; it's cool, quiet, posh, and anonymous and you are not badgered by the waiters. You can stay as long as you want. Kilimanjaro has had several name changes, but this was its original name. Here sometimes I come to rest and make notes, after a day's running about in the sun. New Africa Hotel is a modern high-rise built upon an old, much beloved colonial watering-hole. The two are close to each other and face the harbour. "New Africa," comes Walter's reply. And so at six I go there and wait for him in the bar.

It's a good place to sit and wait without being hassled; the TVs show constant cricket and football. But it's Friday and the bar is crowded: young Indians (from India) on business; local business types; musicians making a deal. When Walter arrives we decide it's far too noisy and get up to go elsewhere, and it's to the Sheraton that we repair. Here we sit on the veranda facing the pool, and we talk.

It's hard to speak to Walter on personal matters. I want to ask him how he managed to move from his modest Kariakoo office to the modern premises on Nyerere Road; what kind of success allowed him to open a restaurant or buy a bookstore, drive an SUV. I can't, quite, but somehow we get on the subject of the failure of the left. He knows I've been meeting the others, Harko and Shivji in particular.

He says the problem with the left is that they went out of touch with the basics, became too theoretical and idealistic. I am not interested in the abstractions of the consitutional debate—he says, exaggerating surely—but I am concerned with how to change the attitude of a policeman who thinks nothing of bashing a suspect's head in. The basics, respect for life. Here we are—he gives an example—at a live mike organized by Mkuki, people come on the stage auditioning jazz, reciting poetry, and these guys (the old intellectuals) are still discussing politics, the constitution. There's live art in front of them! Fantastic jazz, poetry! They're deaf to it.

He had to bring up his children while struggling as a publisher, with no foundation money to support him, no guaranteed academic salary, or wealthy relatives. He must have had some foreign support, but I don't mention that. He couldn't afford the thousands of dollars required for the good—private—schools, whereas others had the means to send their kids off to exclusive schools in Dar or abroad. He had two daughters who were enticed into going to the U.S., where they became stranded and couldn't complete school. He didn't hear from them for a whole year. It was only after the American amnesty for aliens that they could go on to finish their education. He gets passionate, his eyes spit fire, and I feel privileged and moved to be given this confidence. The veranda is surrounded by lush greenery, the air is warm and humid; the tables are full but not loud, the guests are mainly tourists. I wonder if he picked this spot because it makes us anonymous. He carries the wounds of having lived through socialism's lean years and the costly war with Uganda, and the satisfaction of having survived pursuing a dream. I feel, vainly perhaps, that I've earned, I need this confidence. In him I see that other life, the one I left. The road not taken.

—

But how different the country has become, since socialism was kicked aside, when the generation of idealists has aged, when collective concerns have been replaced by individualistic ones. We are at Ali's house, also in Oyster Bay, some six of us. I met Ali at a reading at Novel Idea, the bookstore that's a sign of the new times, following which he's organized this luncheon on a Sunday. Nadir shows up and Walter, and Abdu, a media person, and his wife, Jane, a medical doctor, and Mehboob, a publicity and financial consultant. We sit in the living room in a circle; wine flows freely, the conversation is loud and passionate, about the status of the country and its future. The leadership is held up in utter contempt—what do you say of a government that cannot pay the medical interns their allowances, threatens them when they protest, and immediately gives its own members a handsome raise in their own allowances? Is there hope for the country? Abdu asks. He is pessimistic. He's made a documentary on a serious cultural issue but to have it shown on the national station he's required to bribe someone. He will not do it. Walter, the father-figure in this crowd, scolds him. It is better to show the film, even if you have to bribe—what use is a film in storage? What contribution do you make by your obstinacy? Abdu has children studying abroad and he wonders if they will return. What opportunities can the country offer them? He accuses the older generation of idolizing Nyerere, whom he blames for the nation's current complacency and hostility to entrepreneurship; and surprisingly it is the Asians among us who defend Nyerere's old order, however flawed his policy of socialism. What Nyerere bequeathed to the country was a sense of nationhood, the people's sense of themselves as Tanzanians, that the neighbouring countries envy. The irony of course is that with the broad brush of racist generalizations of the period, most Asians were portrayed as greedy Shylocks and exploiters, with long straws to suck the blood of the poor, and it was Nyerere's nationalizations of private property that largely contributed to Asian flight. Still, among the Asians, in Tanzania and abroad, Nyerere has left a deep impression, he is still respected, even loved, for his honesty and humility. He was a man of the people.

Time flies, it gets dark. The snacks Ali had provided for a plain lunch are long gone. Walter gives me a ride back, and I tell him I'm hungry, rather hoping that we might get a quick something on the road. Come home, he tells me, we'll eat there. He calls Frida to tell her to order barbecue chicken, and we drive to his home in the dim, old section of Nyerere Road—where he's lived as far back as I've known him—park the car and walk through a dark alley, climb precariously up the dark stairs to the second-floor apartment. It's late, Frida has stayed up, and it takes a long time for the chicken to arrive; meanwhile Walter's feeling sick from the wine he's had, and he lies down on the sofa as I watch the news on an Iranian channel, and soon he falls asleep. When the chicken arrives, I eat by myself, as Frida sits beside me, chatting, and I then leave.

22.

Omba-omba: The Culture of Begging

IN 1961 AS THE "WINDS OF CHANGE" ushered in the country's independence, a euphoric slogan was heard around the country: *Uhuru na kazi*, meaning "freedom and work." The idea was common sense. We had our own flag and anthem, we had our beloved president; no longer were we an insignificant part of the British Empire, a pink smudge on the map, overseen by the colonial government and His Excellency the Governor, in a hierarchy where the white man, the bwana, was superior. But freedom came with responsibility; there was a price to self-respect and dignity: hard work. We would have to work for ourselves to make progress. In the years that followed, growing up in the postindependence heyday, we schoolboys and schoolgirls of the nation were exhorted by another slogan: be self-reliant. *Jitegemee*—"Help yourself." And yet another one: Nyerere's words, "It can be done, play your part." There were many self-help projects in the country. It was implicit in the mood of those Cold War years that it was shameful to be reliant on other nations more powerful and consequently to be subject to their demands. The British and the Europeans were, after all, the former "colonial masters." What sort of independence was it if we had to go to them, begging bowls in hand, in order to feed ourselves? If they still told us what to do? In 1965 West Germany stopped its military aid to Tanzania in protest against an East German consulate in the country; the government said, So be it, and refused to accept all West German aid. The conflict was resolved in a few months, but the East German consulate remained, standing large and solid, on Upanga Road. Tanzania did need military aid from West Germany, especially after the scare of the army mutiny of the previous year. But this was a matter of principle. We ran our own country.

What has happened since then? A new term came into circulation, *donor*; it denotes a benevolent, foreign entity that looks after you; and the head of state's job description apparently includes touring the world seeking more aid from "the donor community." The donors make demands on economic policies, and surely they have their political and strategic motives behind their beneficence. A few years ago, I heard a news report that at an international conference, the Tanzanian president had told the audience that his country was so poor it could not afford mosquito nets for its people. Immediately a benefactor came forward, a Hollywood actor, with an offer to donate the nets. For those of my generation who have not forgotten the calls for self-reliance and dignity, who volunteered to build houses during our vacations, and recall the pride we felt at Nyerere's rebuff of a pushy foreign power, this is humiliating. Surely there are enough wealthy people in the country, those who own office towers and insurance companies, who own mines and export fish, who could make the donation? According to a news report in the *Citizen*, wealthly Tanzanians own a few billions stashed away in offshore accounts. How can a government that purchases costly military equipment, and pays its members lavish travel allowances, say it cannot afford mosquito nets? One wonders, how does the leader of a nation feel, making that statement at an international conference? Have we lost all dignity?

Here I must answer a rejoinder. I left the country after high school, therefore I missed the hardships that others endured in the years that followed. What right do I have to show this outrage? It is easy for me, in the comfort of my situation in North America, to condemn the nation's reliance on foreign aid. To which I answer that leaving a place does not sever one's ties to it, one's feeling of concern and belonging. We are tied to our schools, our universities, our families even when we've left them—then why not to the place of our childhood, of our memories? Surely a returnee has some claim to the land which formed him—which is not in some godforsaken corner of the globe but in the centre of his imagination. And surely distance lends objectivity, allows one to see a place as the world sees it.

I often find myself protesting that media images to the contrary, Africa is not simply wars, HIV, and hunger; people don't simply drop dead on the streets out of sickness and hunger. (Just as I had to explain to my host family in New Jersey, way back when I was a student, that lions didn't come roaming into our sitting rooms.) I speak of East Africa, of course. Despite hardships there is *life* there; people sing and laugh and play music; they go to school, they get married. In many towns, the markets are abundantly full; life is teeming, so much so that Toronto, upon my return, often feels rather moribund. Sitting on my couch at home I sometimes find myself, a modern-day Don Quixote, sparring with the television, railing against reporters who fly from one starving place to another, presumably in helicopters—with all good intentions, how can one even question that?—and, with the brand-name pained expressions and sober voices that we know so well, point at the distended belly of a toddler, the fly-covered nose of a child, the shrivelled buttocks of an old man. Why don't you go somewhere happy, just for a change, I protest; report on a wedding, a taarab concert, a school games day; show a well-endowed man or woman (but not a fat politician). People do celebrate, not only in Texas but also in Temeke.

Once, on a visit to Durban, South Africa, I was asked to speak to a high school class. The teachers and principal advised me to explain to the kids my occupation. I began to do that, but I found it difficult to sound convincing. Why wasn't I a doctor, a pharmacist, a politician? And so I changed tack and told them the importance of telling stories: we should tell our stories so we can be a part of the world community; if we don't remember our histories, if we don't tell our stories, then the world tells our stories—and do you know how the world sees Africa? Wars, HIV, and hunger. Is this how you see yourselves? The class—some of the girls at least—looked aghast. Really, sir, is that how they see us? When I finished, a girl came up to me and said, "Sir, one day you will hear from me. I will become famous." Bravo. Tell it to them.

African countries need aid, yes, just as many parts of the world do, including the poverty-stricken, desperate parts of the wealthiest nations. (More than half of Canada's aboriginal population lives below the national poverty line.) But equally—I would maintain, more than that—Africa needs to be included in the world community as an equal. Not very long ago I would stare in despair at the world weather maps on TV, which showed Africa rather as the empty geographical space of previous centuries. It seemed that now Africa had no weather, just as then it had no recognizable life.

And so, admitting my comfort in Canada, which has been generous to me and given me a home from which to observe and write, and even rail at television news, I plead my ties and empathy to and my love for the place where I was born—where I walked to school and returned home drenched with sweat, went to community festivals and the excellent library, and to cricket and football matches.

Over the years serious questions have been raised doubting the benefits of foreign aid. Reams of paper have been produced of studies and statistics—foreign aid, an industry in itself, has also spawned an academic industry. Studies show, for example, that aid does not create investment. There is, in fact, a correlation (though not necessarily causal) between *decreasing* per capita growth in Africa and massive *increases* in foreign aid. In her book *Dead Aid*, Zambian-born Dambisa Moyo has produced a scathing critique, seeing aid as more the problem than the solution to Africa's woes. She pulls no punches. "Aid is not working," she says flatly. "It is these billions [of aid money] that have hampered, stifled and retarded Africa's development." The reasons are obvious, examples speak for themselves right across the continent. Corruption, repression, dependency, haphazard planning, civil wars, all of these have been abetted by foreign aid. Concludes Dambisa Moyo, "aid is not benign—it's malignant."

In the view of its patrons, Africa lies like some comatose patient, taking in infusions of aid until one day it will revive and start running. This view is mechanistic, and also patronizing. It creates a global divide between white and black, rich and poor, giver and receiver, bwana and masikini. It is worse than colonialism in the simple sense that no realistic end seems to be in sight. Africa keeps begging, aid keeps arriving, always from the West. "The most infuriating thing about the Planners," says William Easterly in his book *The White Man's Burden*, "is how patronizing they are . . . any time you hear a Western politician or activist say 'we,' they mean 'we whites' . . ." "Bono said, 'it's up to us.' Sachs writes of 'our generation's challenge.' Gordon Brown . . . saw himself telling Africans: 'We will help you build the capacity you need to trade.'"

And what will the Africans do? "We are building villages in Mozambique," says a man from the World Development Network to me in Toronto, sounding excited, and then this globetrotter puts in an aside: "Have the Africans learned to do anything themselves?" Which is a sentiment echoed by Paul Theroux in his travels: "Where are the Africans in all this? . . . in forty years of charity the only people dishing out the food and doling out the money are foreigners."

The other end of the foreign-aid equation is what one observes on the ground, what aid has done to the dignity of a people since the time of independence, how pride and self-respect have yielded to an attitude of beggary. Foreign assistance—in a word, baksheesh—has created so much dependence all over the country that it's akin to a dope fix.

In Tukuyu, the old town in the southwest that I visited, a branch road from the highway is rough and broken. The area is wealthy farm country; there is an abundance of food. On either side of this bone-breaking road are fine properties; tea is grown, and banana, and avocado and beans. And yet it's proved impossible to get that road fixed. The residents await baksheesh to complete the repair. An elderly school trustee in the area says there are no textbooks in schools, and she cannot get to the schools because the roads are so bad. Taking a walk in the same neighbourhood, one is approached by a boy, who begs for money to pay school fees; the gesture seems casual, he thought he'd just ask and try his luck today. Walking past a school, taking me for a white man, kids come running to me, hands outstretched. It's a habit. The white man gives.

And so this returnee cannot help asking, What happened—to the pride, the head held high, eyes on the future that belonged to us, to Africa? Is this the promise of independence? Is there an end in sight to this addiction?

According to a Norwegian report, in 1993 there were 224 registered NGOs—non-governmental organizations that take care of the civil order in society—in Tanzania; this number had risen to 8,499 in 2000. The number today is presumably greater by several factors. (It seems, perhaps pointedly, not to be counted anymore.) It is now a basic tenet; it is blithely accepted that the social welfare of the people is the responsibility of organizations in the private sector, the foreign-funded NGOs. As Issa Shivji succinctly states in the edited volume *Development in Practice*,

> most of our NGOs are top-down organisations led by elites. What is more, most of them are urban [that is, Dar es Salaam] based. In the case of Tanzania, NGOs did not start as a response to the felt need of the majority of working people. It is true that many of us within the NGO community are well intentioned and would want to contribute to some cause, however we may define it. It is also true that many NGOs do address some of the real concerns of the working people. Yet we must recognise that we did not develop as, nor have we as yet managed to become, organic to the mass of the people. The relationship between NGOs and the masses therefore remains, at best, that of benefactors and beneficiaries. . . . Our accountability is therefore limited, and limited to a small group. In fact, we end up perhaps being more accountable to our donors than to our own members, much less to our people. . . . *[W]e are funded by, and rely almost exclusively on, foreign funding. This is the greatest single limitation. . . .*

> *Very few of us can really resist the pressures that external funding imposes on us.* [Italics mine]

The government never took on, or it soon abdicated, its responsibility for the social and cultural welfare, and the health, of its people; now thousands of expatriates and their local agents provide essential—and sometimes useless—services. In this new scramble for Africa, young men and women arrive from abroad as the new benefactors, managers, and teachers, the bwanas and bibis, to hold the hands of the locals, often knowing little or nothing about the culture of the place they have come to. Meanwhile, locally educated men and women who cannot find good jobs await foreign projects to help them earn a decent living, send their own kids to good urban schools. You see them at the coffee shop of Dar's Mövenpick (now Serena), the supplicant and the benefactor seated at a small table, the donee and the donor, one—to use crudely racial depictions—black, the other white. Often the "white" are embarrassingly young. All these workers, local and foreign, make up the urban elite, driving SUVs, visiting western-style restaurants, sending children to expensive schools, and generally living a western lifestyle, the vast majority of them in Dar es Salaam, which is currently—and this is hardly surprising—one of the most expensive cities in the world. Running an NGO is like owning a business, I am told, it's like having a shop of one's own; opportunists and cynics will run several NGOs at once, in any field that's "trending." Business people try a hand at it, for commissions and kickbacks; university lecturers become "consultants." Not surprisingly, their students take extra classes to learn how to start their own NGOs.

At the other end, in the developed world, this foreign-aid system provides opportunities for western youth to travel abroad and seek foreign experience for their resumés; and it's an opportunity for retired people to do something in their sunset years to give worth and purpose to their lives. Africa gives and is exploited as it receives.

It can only be laudable for individuals and organizations to provide services where there are no alternatives. Relief organizations help the diseased and the disabled, orphans and victims; church, mosque, and temple bodies run decent schools. The human instinct for pity and kindness, for charity, can hardly be denied or dismissed. Even in the advanced economies there are charities running soup kitchens, sheltering the homeless and the abused, assisting immigrants, providing safe needles to addicts, promoting culture. What is unsettling in a place like Tanzania is the scale of dependence and expectation; it's as if the majority of the population, from the university graduate to the subsistence farmer, exists with its hand perpetually outstretched, in expectation of assistance, a job, a handout. When the social sector is run by foreigners, and the urban cost of living is pushed up to accommodate their lifestyles, which are vastly beyond those of the great majority; when a total dependence is created on the "donor"—what does this do to the self-image and the dignity of a dependent population that not long ago celebrated its *independence* from Europe? When in order to raise funds, the donor resorts to the slick strategies of the consumer market in its home country to promote its "product," portraying a nation at its weakest—pathetic faces, distended bellies, running noses stuck with flies, bony buttocks again—how does the world see Africa? How do Africans living abroad face their world?

—

An entire nation wearing castoffs, clothes designed and manufactured elsewhere, worn before by others, only enhances the local perception and feeling of privilege versus underprivilege, giver and receiver, there and here. It is true that with the castoffs, the so-called mitumba, the people at least dress well; what disturbs is the scale, and the price paid is self-respect. Theroux, who came out with such a negative and disturbing view of Africa in *Dark Star Safari,* observed, "The foreign clothes were like proofs of this shadow existence . . . and I imagined the wearers to be the doppelgängers of the folks in that other world."

Social services, roads, schools, vocational training are all due to foreign benefactors. Every schoolchild in the West wants to throw a quarter at Africa. Africa, in that very pathetic sense, is sexy. A family goes to Tanzania and donates a bunch of pencils. A Toronto broker donates a writing prize, a Vancouver doctor donates a school prize. A Los Angeles businessman installs a solar plant. In Zanzibar a foreign NGO wants to teach culture to the locals; another, how to cope with emergencies. A girl in England gets some money from a project and provides free lunch at a school in Malawi. Of course she is received well. I can imagine myself a schoolboy in Dar and well-wrapped beautiful packages arriving by air to give us a free lunch. We'd have been delighted, our eager hands stretching out to receive these lovely goodies. But what does all this constant foreign charity tell a child about its own society? And while one can hardly deny or denigrate the motives, the good purpose in the giving—at the end of the day Africa seems to be there to make people in the western world feel better, more moral.

The Kony episode of March 2012 was a signal lesson in the media manipulation of Africa's problems and at the same time all the complexities involved in what seems to be the simple idea of giving.

The Kony YouTube video, describing the mass atrocities of Joseph Kony and the Lord's Resistance Army (LRA) in Central Africa, was made by an American NGO called Invisible Children; it went immediately viral, taking the world—at least that portion connected by the social media—by storm. The LRA stands accused of brutal killings, sexual slavery, and kidnapping children. Celebrities such as Oprah Winfrey, Mia Farrow, and Rihanna began Tweeting their support after the video came out, and within a few days it had attracted tens of millions of views on YouTube and garnered hundreds of thousands of dollars in donation. This was the kind of world event that makes people feel good. But which people, in this instance, and why?

There were immediate objections to the video—its manipulative inaccuracy and timing; its open call to yet another American intervention; its simple-mindedness—it was "pitched to a five-year-old's sense of right and wrong," according to a *New York Times* article. When I read a report on selected African criticisms of "Kony 2012," I couldn't help saying, At last—though not without an unnerving sense of irony. Suddenly—to interpret these African responses—their part of the world was in the news; millions in the West talked and read about it, pitied it, and blogged and Tweeted about saving it. But where, in this narrative, was Africa itself? Where were the *Africans* themselves in it? Africa had become a public-relations opportunity; a plug for the social media and the wonders of technology; an opportunity for those with a few dollars to spare to feel good about themselves. A blackface comic, except that the comedy was tragic.

Rosebell Kagumire, a Ugandan blogger, observed, ". . . this is another video where I see an outsider trying to be a hero rescuing African children. We have seen these stories a lot in Ethiopia, celebrities coming in Somalia. . . ." The video only furthers "that narrative about Africans: totally unable to help themselves and needing outside help all the time." Another blogger, T.M.S. Ruge, wrote, "Africa is our problem, we hereby respectfully request you let us handle our own matters. . . . If you really want to help, keep the guilt and charity in your backyard. Bring instead, respect, and the humility to let us determine our destiny." And novelist Teju Cole Tweeted provocatively about "the banality of sentimentality" and the "White Saviour Industrial Complex." Others saw a "White man's burden" message repropagated. Showings of the film in Uganda met with anger and even a riot.

More Africans should rise to voice such sentiments. Depictions such as Kony 2012 are humiliating and offensive. It is outsiders who write these narratives of hunger, disease, and war, in the process making careers for themselves. Reporters have dedicated themselves to hopping from one trouble spot to another wearing earnest faces and seeing nothing in between. And yet, having said this, who would deny that the realities they depict actually exist? How to reconcile "Africa is our problem" with the sad truth that much of Africa depends on foreign aid like a patient permanently hooked to life sustenance? In Dar es Salaam it's difficult to come across anyone who lives comfortably and does not depend for their living on some foreign connection.

Some years ago I was invited to a meeting of publishers held in Tanzania, at an expensive new resort in one of the smaller national parks. The meeting was called to brainstorm the problems faced by the African publishers, and I had been invited as a writer. Among the problems discussed were the small book markets, distribution, the payment of royalties, and lack of funds. I must admit to my naïveté at the time. It surprised me to discover that this worthy meeting had been organized by a foreign donor, whose representatives were also present. To add to my discomfort, in one private moment at the coffee urn, a senior foreign representative, a publisher in his home country, said to me what he honestly believed, that African novelists couldn't write. I could have named a dozen good, and some great, African novelists from different parts of the continent, but I named a few. Perhaps he did not consider Gordimer or Coetzee as African, because they are white; or Tayeb Salih, a Sudanese; perhaps he thought Achebe and Soyinka were mere hacks. Obviously the man had given me his confidence having taken me for a foreigner. On the final day of the meeting, a Tanzanian government minister arrived to give blessings. I asked him then why the government would not assist publishing and cultural enterprises the way many western governments, such as

Canada, regularly did. I was not being entirely naive at this point, I also wanted to provoke. My question was met with such a silence in the room (besides a grin from the minister) that I realized then how alien and misplaced I was at that meeting. Some African publishers stared at me as at a madman. I have always wondered if they understood me at all.

23.

The New (Asian) African: Politics and Creativity

ONE AFTERNOON AT A TEA following a seminar on Gandhi, in Shimla, India, to my utter astonishment I was approached by a woman who spoke to me in Swahili. Veena Sharma—small, soft-spoken, and sari-clad—was not from Africa but she had spent some years in Dar es Salaam in the 1970s, reporting for All India Radio. She seemed to know all the important people in Dar, people whom I, a student from modest Kariakoo and Upanga, had only read about. Her interest in Africa remained. Four weeks later, at the tea lounge of the India International Centre in Delhi, Veena introduced me to a woman called Urmila Jhaveri.

Coincidences happen; this one seemed miraculous. As I stood chatting with Mrs. Jhaveri in a Gujarati as formal as I could muster, I couldn't help but wonder at the improbability of this meeting. We both came from Dar es Salaam, she was a fellow mhindi from Africa—that was enough to be excited about. It was also one more demonstration of the fact that East African Asian identity is real, and becomes evident especially outside of that milieu. But there was more to our meeting, and this my new acquaintance could never have guessed.

The name Jhaveri takes me to one of my earliest memories: I was eight, my family had moved to Dar from Nairobi, and my mother had opened a shop in a new building on Uhuru Street, on the second floor of which we now lived. Independence was around the corner, and the first-ever general election in the country was about to take place for representatives to the Legislative Council. White-and-black posters with photos of the candidates had been pasted on the buildings of Gaam and Kariakoo, exhorting, "Vote for Jhaveri!" or "Vote for Daya!" Young Asian men came around to the shops to canvas, saying, "Ma, are you going to vote?" Daya was the doctor who treated my grandmother, and he had my mother's vote. He was from our own community, moreover, and that was the extent of our politics. K.L. Jhaveri, a criminal lawyer, however, had the backing of Nyerere—leader of the African TANU party—and won the seat. Years later he wrote a book about his political life, *Marching with Nyerere: Africanisation of Asians*. The subtitle is significant. It is a bold assertion, it is unequivocal, it speaks to the time.

K.L. was from Dar, Urmila from Pemba. That afternoon in the tea lounge in Delhi she sounded wistful about Dar, where she had spent her adult years, and missed its familiarity, having left only the previous year because K.L. needed constant medical attention. Their daughter was settled in Delhi.

When I visited them at their suburban home a few days later, K.L. was seated on a sofa, an extremely frail-looking man, literally skin and bones, shorn of all flesh. He was lively, however, and complained about the Indian production of his book. In Delhi he was keeping himself busy writing—though you wondered how in his fragile state he managed even to finger the keys. Urmila and I had bhajias and tea. She said she was writing her own memoir. It would be a valuable contribution to East African history, though I wondered if it would be allowed to see the light of day.

As the call for African freedom rose in the 1950s, and in the years thereafter for real freedom—from "neocolonialism"—the Asians faced a choice of loyalties. The shopkeepers and small-business people, in the manner of their class everywhere, were nervous about change. Most of them merely eked out a living; they had been protected by the colonial administration, and the only nation they knew was their small and exclusive community. Our longtime barber, Madhu Bhai—who passed by our shop every month to cut my brothers' and my hair outside on the patio in full view of the public—was one of those who succumbed to his fears and left for Gujarat, much to my sorrow.

Among the professionals and the educated, however, there was an elite that responded positively to the call for freedom. The Jhaveris reflected the optimism of that class—educated abroad, still in their thirties, and savvy about the world. Well aware of India's own struggles and excited about African independence, they moved in the enlightened and secular circles of the Asian Association (founded in 1950). The questions they posed themselves, often expressed in their bulletin, *The Tanganyikan,* concerned the future of Tanganyika—which they saw as democratic and nonracial—and the role of the Asians in it. In a report to the Association, for example, K.L. Jhaveri opposed the proposal of the government-supported Capricorn Society, which would restrict the role of the Africans using economic and other criteria and called for a federation with Kenya and Rhodesia. And in an eloquent article, Amir Jamal, the future minister for finance, said, "The Asians of Tanganyika . . . have a great opportunity of making a significant contribution to build up a strong and stable society. What is needed is a complete change in their outlook towards the realities."

Sophia Mustafa, of Qadiyani (Ahmadi) background and wife of a judge, ran for the Legislative Council in the Moshi area. Soon after that election, she wrote a book titled *The Tanganyika Way*, and it quite catches the excitement, the freshness, and perhaps the naive idealism of the period. Wearing a sari and not very fluent in Swahili (she was born in India), she enthusiastically embraced the idea of citizenship above race, and exhorted fellow Asians to think beyond communal and racial identities. In a speech she gave to the Asian Association, she said,

> I . . . appeal to you all here to forget your various sects or communities as such, and all consider yourselves as Asians. And, when you have succeeded in dissolving your mutual differences and antagonisms, you will go further and sink your race as a distinctive factor and consider yourselves as Tanganyikans.

A dramatic and bold statement. Sophia Mustafa came not only from a racial minority in Tanganyika, but also from a small and oppressed minority among Muslims; the Partition of India was recent memory. It is not surprising then that she spoke for dissolving differences among Asians. She envisioned a future in which Asians did not only run shops or work as white-collar professionals but also farmed and worked with their hands. (The Gujarati trading class did not traditionally dirty their hands.) In a moving passage she describes the moment when the constitutional conference of March 1961 concluded in Dar es Salaam, and a garlanded Julius Nyerere emerged from the hall to be driven slowly in a motorcade, holding up a placard that said, "Independence 1961." The governor of Tanganyika turned to her and said, "Was this not the day we were all waiting for, Mrs. Mustafa?"

Her book ends with a collective rallying call for the new Tanganyika. But the politics of the time were tumultuous. In a short time would come the revolution of Zanzibar, the attempted coup in Tanganyika, the union with Zanzibar, and a policy of socialism that lasted two decades. She herself left politics, and like Urmila Jhaveri much later, she had to leave the country for the sake of the health of her ailing husband. I met her in Toronto in the 2000s, and she died soon afterwards, shortly after her husband. She had written two novels, one of them set in Kenya, where she had spent some time.

The most powerful, admired, and enigmatic Asian in politics, however, was Amir Jamal. Educated in India, where in 1942 he happened to attend a Congress meeting in which Gandhi gave notice to the British to "Quit India," Jamal kept his distance from communal affiliations. From 1961 to 1980 he held various ministerial positions in government, including that of minister of finance. The website of the Brandt21 Forum (of the Centre for Global Negotiations) writes,

> Jamal's utter integrity, dedication and selfless service, along with his political ability, were recognized throughout Tanzania, and Jamal was repeatedly elected with ever-increasing majorities from predominantly African constituencies.

He died in 1995 in a Vancouver hospital after a year of illness. According to Sophia Mustafa, Nyerere made a call to Vancouver begging that the body of his friend be returned to Tanzania to receive full honours. The plea was rebuffed by those concerned. If this story is true, it encapsulates completely the straitjacket that the Asian had to escape in order to join mainstream society.

Because of the violence of the freedom struggle in Kenya and, since early colonial days, the presence of white settlers, whose ideas about the country's future leaned towards the models of South Africa and Rhodesia, Kenyan politics was always more colourful and louder than that of Tanzania. Kenyan Asian demography was also quite different from that of Tanzania, a fact often not realized or simply ignored; it comprised not only the Gujarati shopkeeper class but also the descendants of the Punjabi indentured workers who had come to build the railway in the early twentieth century, and a sizable professional elite—doctors, lawyers, teachers—who arrived much later. The presence of the white settlers meant that business was more profitable. They spent more freely.

And yet Kenya had—perhaps because of better education and better economic status—produced some remarkable Asian activism, since as far back as the 1920s, in the form of legal and publishing services for African activists (including Jomo Kenyatta), opposition to apartheid, and promoting labour relations. In her book *Challenge to Colonialism*, Zarina Patel writes passionately of the contributions to modern Kenya by the businessman A.M. Jeevanjee (AMJ), who was also her grandfather, and other Asians:

> Led by AMJ and Manilal Desai, [the Asians] put a halt to the settlers' bid for self-government. . . . They enabled Harry Thuku to meet with Marcus Garvey, Mbiyu Koinange to travel overseas. . . . They established newspapers

> in Kenya and gave access to their presses to the African nationalist movement. . . . [They] were instrumental in founding the trade union movement, which was a leader in the struggle for independence. In fact, the first public demand for Kenya's independence was made by Makhan Singh, an Asian. . . . [It was] Ambu and Lila Patel who spearheaded the Free Jomo Kenyatta movement.

After independence, however, the potent brew of Kenyan politics, with its corruption, tribalism, and violent vendettas, made it impossible for the Asian minority to raise its voice. They were too small in number, they were a soft touch—traders and white-collar workers mostly—and they were uncertain and nervous. In the clamour for new opportunities, amidst all the tribal and personal rivalries, the Asians were too easily shoved aside. Makhan Singh, who had spent ten years in colonial detention, was ignored by the new leaders. Pio Gama Pinto, the journalist who spent four years in detention for his support of the Mau Mau and whose activism continued, was assassinated. In a climate of increasing corruption and state violence, it was far too easy to intimidate the Asians, blame them all for exploitation and racism—to call them the Jews of Africa who bred uncontrollably and dangerously. On their part the Asians remained insular: it was in their character. They could join in the nation-building—donating blood, helping to build a school or distribute food, et cetera—but at the end of the day they reported to family and community. Their predicament was put succinctly and with some bitterness by a Sikh gentleman, who was quoted in the papers: "The problem with us Asians is that we are not white enough to be white nor black enough to be black." The white man who had been top dog during colonialism now came as a benefactor and representative of Europe. He was cool. The Asian "Jew" moved into the background.

In December 1995, in *The New York Times* there appeared an obituary of a Ugandan Asian. London's *Independent* carried his obituary the following month. This in itself is remarkable. Uganda, except for war or disease, is hardly of global interest, and the Asian from there even less so. But the deceased, aged fifty-seven, was Rajat Neogy, someone very special. He was founder and editor of the hugely influential literary magazine *Transition* that came out of Makerere University in Kampala in the 1960s. Neogy was born in Kampala in 1938 and had studied in London. There's not much known about him that's published, but he had come blazing onto the African literary scene. *Transition*'s pages gathered a remarkable array of literary and political luminaries—James Baldwin, Wole Soyinka, Chinua Achebe, Kofi Awoonor, a young Paul Theroux, Christopher Okigbo, Ezekiel Mphahlele, Okot p'Bitek, Tom Mboya, and Kenneth Kaunda. Benjamin Mkapa, the future president of Tanzania, was associate editor. Ali Mazrui followed him. Said Henry Louis Gates Jr. of Harvard about Neogy after his death, "This man created an African-based journal of letters that everybody in the intellectual world, it seemed, was excited about. He fought fascism in blackface, and that was rare and courageous." Ngũgĩ would credit the publication of a story in *Transition* as a turning point in his life.

The post-independence 1960s was a particularly thrilling and creatively fertile period for Africa; so much seemed possible and within reach. Reflecting the intellectual fervor and political idealism of these years, Makerere University had became a literary hub. A new literature was in the making, and the young people were busy defining their role in it. In 1962 the first African Writers Conference took place at Makerere, a milestone that is still remembered. Soyinka, Achebe, Ngũgĩ, Nkosi, Taban were present, Soyinka later saying of it, "We went to join a convocation of writers and intellectuals from every corner of the continent. . . . We were on safari on African soil: the signs along the way all showed the same slogan: Destination Kampala! Africa's postcolonial renaissance." There would have been few other places in the world where there was such an excitement about new literature, new ideas, and new politics. The inspiration arrived at this conference for a new publishing imprint of literary titles called the African Writers Series, which was soon launched by Heinemann in the U.K., with Achebe as the series editor. The excitement reached as far as my high school in Dar, where literary competitions were held, new drama was produced, and a parade of literary luminaries passed through, including Chinua Achebe. When many years later my first novel was published in this series, it was for me a moment of arrival. The headmaster who brought Achebe to our school, Peter K. Palangyo, himself turned out to be a novelist.

Besides Neogy, the editor of *Transition*, several Asian writers were a part of this emerging East African literary consciousness centred in Kampala: Bahadur Tejani (b. 1942 Uganda), Peter Nazareth (b. 1940 Uganda), Amin Kassam (b. 1948 Kenya), and Yusuf O. Kassam (b. 1943 Tanzania). All were near-contemporaries of Ngũgĩ wa Thiong'o (b. 1938 Kenya), who was already claiming attention as J.T. Ngũgĩ. Here was an opportunity for forming an Asian African identity through literature.

It was typical of those times that Wole Soyinka in his anthology *Poems of Black Africa* (1975) includes the poetry of Amin Kassam, Yusuf O. Kassam, and Bahadur Tejani. "Black" in the title denotes southern Africa, embracing while not denying ethnic or racial particularities. It is a generous anthology, as is evident from Soyinka's introduction. But—one imagines, from this distance in time—for these young Asian writers the exuberance and power of the African literary consciousness around them must have been intimidating. Theirs was not an easy place to be. There was first the whole historical baggage of India to confront; education demands an honest appreciation of identity and history, and India surely had to be confronted—it could not be dismissed simply as poor and out there. But more than that was the all-consuming presence and pull of community and family—by which, in fact, India manifested its presence in most of us, through religion and language, customs, foods, and traditions. (Nazareth was a Goan; Amin Kassam, Yusuf O. Kassam, and Bahadur Tejani, Khoja Ismailis.) And finally there was the consciousness, all the time, especially in Kenya, of being the Other, an insecurity enhanced by frequent discussions of the "Asian question," and frequent racist provocations by African demagogues.

To write meant to write with your whole being, and that was hard to do, with family looking on, the community watching nervously, and presumably the father wondering what the future was in all that scribbling, why not marry and settle down in the age-old fashion? And so, whereas the poetry of Okot p'Bitek, for example, is firmly grounded on African soil and fully confident of its intent, and Taban Lo Liyong writes an essay with provocative gusto about the barenness of East African writing, while the black African poets struggle with their gods and tangle with their native languages and speech rhythms, their village life and urban squalor, all the three Asian poets mentioned above, and several others who wrote occasionally, seemed largely to prefer the safety of the universal, the minimal, the casual observation—and even the obscure and abstract, shying away from their gods and languages, their traditions and personal lives. To ground their creative output in Africa, it would have to be grounded in Asian Africa, their own lives and experiences as Asians from their respective communities, which could not have been easy—on one hand to produce a genuine aesthetic and make yourself understood and accepted; on the other, not to offend the home gallery. The result was a nervous uncertainty to the writing, a wavering aesthetic.

In some of his poetry, however, Tejani directly confronts his dilemma of being different, an Indian in Africa, revealing a personal anguish that is a consistent thread. Tejani in particular is deeply attracted to the physicality of the African, compared to the bloodless reserve and interiority of the Asian. In one poem, "Lines for a Hindi Poet," he uses a scene witnessed in a New Delhi park—two dogs freely mating—to call for a loosening of Asian attitudes to love and sex. The result is an incantation:

> Lord! Lord!
> Let the brown blood
> rediscover the animal
> in itself,
> and have free limbs
> and laughing eyes of
> love-play.

In "On Top of Africa," Tejani again laments the difference,

> I shall remember
> the dogged voice of conscience
> self-pity warring with [the] will
> of the brown body

to keep up
with the black flesh
forging ahead
on the way
to Kilimanjaro

Fiction gave greater scope for in-depth and honest portrayals of Asian life. In his novel *Day After Tomorrow* (1971), Bahadur Tejani pursues his theme of Asian inadequacy. His protagonist Shamsher, who grew up in the countryside, is in love with Africa—its simplicity and honesty, its majesty and grace; he dislikes the Indians around him. He observes, "The estrangement with their environment and with the people around him made him feel that all Indians were the remnants of a decaying civilization." (One detects echoes of V.S. Naipaul.) Elsewhere, at the Kampala football stadium, he observes:

> The African people, full of physical vigour and joy of life, flocked in large crowds to watch their players perform. The whole place rang with ululations and joyous shouts so that the very walls of the stadium trembled with it. As if lusting to participate in the struggle.

And of an African woman he sees there he writes:

> He was captivated by the graceful movement of the Muganda female. Her elegant dress that exaggerated her back-swing. The sharp delicate features and the glow of the fresh skin reminded him of the sun dying in a clash of hot sympathy for the earth.

The novel is sketchy and schematic, simple and romantic, forgiveable in a young man's first effort; there is no complexity of characters or even ideas; it examines Asian life very perfunctorily (compare Ngũgĩ's treatments of Kikuyu life, which are so grounded in the earth of Kenya). The Asian woman is hardly observed. In a sari, one might argue, she would look as elegant as Tejani's Muganda female, with a "back-swing" as well. Is a taboo at work here or simply disinterest? The novel however has some beautiful descriptions of Asians in a rural setting, and the awesome, looming greatness of the African continent. And it does explore the idea of what a new Asian African might be. In his Epilogue, in which the author pessimistically addresses the reader directly, he rejects the idea of the separation of races, very much as Sophia Mustafa had suggested:

> We in East Africa, numbed by our pluralities, have decided to erect the one firm ideal of multi-racialism: that is, to keep quiet. To display a deliberate sense of graceful relaxation which is meant to show the non-existence of tension.

For Tejani, then, as for Sophia Mustafa, a mere racial coexistence was unacceptable. There had to be a single identity.

A new East African literary consciousness had thus emerged. The Asian writers were part of it and spoke confidently of a collective "we" and a collective future. "What is our East African culture?" Neogy asked, for example, in his editorial for the first issue of *Transition*.

And then suddenly everything changed. Africa, it seemed, had stepped out of its early, idealistic phase. Neogy was put into detention in 1968 for criticizing the Uganda government, after which he left Uganda. He died in San Franciso. Idi Amin appeared and expelled the Asians of Uganda ("the engineers of corruption"). Tejani ended up teaching in New York, where he would write fantasy and comic fiction and poetry. Amin Kassam and Yusuf O. Kassam disappeared from the literary scene, and Peter Nazareth, after two novels, became a literary critic in Iowa.

That creative spark, inspired by the promise of a new dawn, a new Africa, with all its excitement and uncertainty, was gone.

Was that creative spark, that hope, doomed from the beginning? A cultural magazine is a broker, a provider of sorts—was Neogy and his *Transition* a mere broker, a deliverer of goods—that typical, stereotypical role of the Asian in Africa?

Peter Nazareth's novel *In a Brown Mantle,* written just before Idi Amin had his dream, presents an extremely pessimistic portrayal of the Asian's fate in Uganda. (The country is actually given a fictitious name, and the Asian home and family are hardly portrayed.) In the novel, Deo D'Souza is an idealistic young Goan who leaves his civil service job to work for the political party that brings the country its independence. He is assertive about his African-ness. But he is never fully accepted—"When will you return home?" is a taunt he often hears. Fed up with the racism, and the cynicism, political corruption, and betrayal that had set in, he leaves the country, saying, "Goodbye Mother Africa—your bastard son loved you."

A tough, moving testament. But one has to pause here: *loved* you? No longer *loves* you? What then does it mean to belong? There were Asians who never left Uganda even after Idi Amin's dictat—and were never heard of again. I met an Asian woman in Vancouver who told me, after visiting her Ugandan homeland more than twenty years after Idi Amin, "I did not mind seeing that Africans had taken over my father's business. At least that way they could come up." That's belonging, from the gut.

For three decades Peter Nazareth championed African literature. Dozens of writers passed through his department in Iowa City. But he never visited his native Uganda. I have given this phenomenon much thought, and have convinced myself finally that the turning-away from Africa by many Asians was not from bitterness, entirely, but also from pain and grief.

Those Africans—in East Africa and elsewhere—who cheered Amin's decision could not have imagined that their boxer hero would end up killing thousands of Africans within a few years, turning the Nile red, and would cause a war that would cripple the area economically for many years; and that that mild ethnic cleansing in Uganda was but a foreshadowing of the genocide of Rwanda. Indeed, the goading racist stereotypes, so manifest in the pages of the *Uganda Argus* at the time, were reminiscent of the antisemitism of Europe of three decades before. (On their way to India, many Asians left Kampala for Mombasa in sealed trains.)

In a 2012 article in the electronic African magazine *Pambazuka*, Ngũgĩ paid a tribute to the Asians of East Africa, pointing out their contributions. In particular he mentions his days at Makerere:

> The lead role of an African woman in my drama, *The Black Hermit*, the first major play ever in English by an East African black native, was an Indian. No make up, just a headscarf and a kanga shawl on her long dress but Suzie Wooman played the African mother to perfection, her act generating a standing ovation lasting into minutes. I dedicated my first novel, *Weep Not Child*, to my Indian classmate, Jasbir Kalsi. . . . Ghulsa [Gulzar?] Nensi led a multi-ethnic team that made the costumes for the play while Bahadur Tejani led the team that raised money for the production.

He adds:

> It was not simply at the personal realm. Commerce, arts, crafts, medical and legal professions in Kenya have the marks of the Indian genius all over them. Politics too, and it should never be forgotten that Mahatma Gandhi started and honed his political and organizing skills in South Africa. . . .

If only he—or someone—had said this thirty years earlier. In an issue of *Transition* in 1967, Wole Soyinka had issued a scathing warning to African writers: ". . . would a stranger to the literary creations of African writers find a discrepancy between subject matter and environment?" There was a "lack of vital relevance" in the writing, he charged. "Reality, the ever present fertile reality was ignored by the writer and resigned to the new visionary—the politicians."

24.

Nairobi, Lost and Regained?

As I recall it, on the road from Dar, Nairobi would always first appear in a distant haze, a mere suggestion—and the heart thrilled. After a journey of a full day or more, having left the coast for the grassland, and stopped at the junctions Morogoro, Korogwe, Mombo, Moshi, and Arusha, past the border post at Namanga, having sighted giraffes and zebra in abundance, the bus would take a final turn and there it would suddenly be, the city rising from the plains. Perhaps the mystique was due to the long expectation—each arrival was, after all, a return to native soil. Nairobi was my family's original original home. We left it when I was four and a half, soon after my father died. We went from temperate suburbia to sweltering Kariakoo, from wearing shoes and sandals even at home to mostly barefoot on the pavements. For many years Dar remained our exile. My brother treasured his Nairobi school blazer and tie, my sisters their green cardigans. As we trudged over rough road and over mud, and waded through pools of rainwater to get to school, our former schoolbus was vivid on our minds. We had owned a car in Nairobi, the licence plate number never to be forgotten, tee-eight-oh-one-six. In Dar our neighbours often placed us as Nairobi people, and even now sometimes I have to explain that I am originally from Nairobi. We never had a family presence in Dar.

My earliest memory of Nairobi is of my father opening the front door of our Desai Road home at night and with his pistol shooting at the dark emptiness outside, while my mother fretted behind him. It was the Mau Mau period, when many Asians and Europeans were expected to keep guns for safety. We had left class and cool weather behind but also the dark fearsome nights of Nairobi. That perhaps contributed to my mother's decision to leave the city. One day her two older sisters arrived from Dar, they all sat down on a mat on the floor, had tea and had a good ritual cry over my good father's untimely demise, and convinced my mother to pack and leave to join her mother and nine brothers and sisters. She was never sure she made the right decision.

Nairobi began its existence in 1899 as a railway supply depot in the masai plains.

As the "scramble for Africa" began, following the Berlin conference of 1884-85, which portioned off Africa among European powers, the British claimed the territory today known as Kenya, which became known as British East Africa. To develop the interior, construction of a railway began, to go from Mombasa to Uganda; completed in 1903, it was called the Uganda Railway. From a bare waystation on the Masai plains, Nairobi became a metropolis and the capital of the colony, its cultural and economic life dominated by the Europeans and the Asians. The two races (and the Africans) lived separately, of course, in a kind of semi-apartheid, but Nairobi had the caché of being the most westernized and modern city in East Africa.

I returned to Nairobi for the first time with my mother and older brother when I was ten, brought along partly as a reward for doing well in school, and also—I now realize—because on the way back my brother would be left behind in Mombasa, and she had to have someone to travel back to Dar with her. In Nairobi she had family business to attend to, and things to buy for her own shop (much as women now head off to Guangzhou in China for the same purpose). From Nairobi she brought selections of cloth and toys to sell, and new ideas and fashions—we believe she introduced the "sunsuit" to Kariakoo. For that visit, I had formed great expectations of Nairobi, sometimes called "Little London." By all the nostalgic accounts in the home, it lived up to that nickname, a fantastic place, clean and beautiful, with handsome houses and parks with fountains and band stands. There were buildings into which cars drove up, and drive-ins where you could watch movies from your car, and splendid new cinema houses; there were shops selling goods undreamed of in Dar. There was our old home in Desai Road, and the khano where I was registered at birth and whose askari—the security guard—a short, brown, wrinkled man in a khaki uniform, we remembered fondly. Lest we forget this paradise, Kenya Broadcasting Corporation's "Hindustani Service" was a daily reminder.

During that visit, we stayed in Ngara, an Indian suburb behind the museum and the city centre, where one of my aunts ran Windsor Hotel. It catered to Europeans, and consisted of several bungalows spread out on a lot, the main one with long corridors, terrazo floors, a large dining hall, and a bar with slot machines. Like most of residential Nairobi, this area evoked in you silence and awe. Every morning my little cousin would be driven to a nearby kindergarten, my uncle singing to her a ditty in English about the *abc*s. I recall breakfast on a table with white cloth, the silver tea service, the smell of toast and butter, and sitting down to eat a crisply fried egg with a fork and knife. After a useless struggle, the egg goes flying, the waiter looks on in silence before stooping to pick it up. His look tells all. We had truly come down in our lot. During this visit I met an old woman, my grandmother's sister, who had brought my father up. The family owned a high-class safari-outfitting company, where—I guess—the famous "white hunters" would have shopped for gear.

Subsequently I visited Nairobi every few years. One of my sisters came to survey secretarial colleges here and ended up getting married. And when socialism put the crunch on Tanzania's Asians, my mother—even though she was in no position to be affected—succumbed to panic and moved with my two brothers back to Nairobi. I was at the time studying in Boston, and the abandonment of my Dar home that I had now come to love caused me considerable grief. It was to Nairobi that I would go to visit my family, now living on 5th Parklands Avenue. The flat came with a dog called Foxy, whose diet consisted of throwaway stale chapatis from the neighbourhood. The prayer house was across the road, and at four in the morning when people went to meditate there, the dogs from the neighbourhood would gather on its cricket ground and howl together as though in their own prayer. Compared with Dar, Nairobi was a dog city, reflecting partly the influence of white settlers, and partly the fact that its quiet, dark suburbs were prone to robberies. But you would not see a dog being walked in these neighbourhoods, they all remained behind the fences. What dogs those were who gathered outside the prayer house would always remain a mystery; but at a little past 5 a.m., when people began to emerge from their meditations, the dogs would trot off in their own different directions. Foxy was one of them.

Now as we arrive by bus from Arusha, Nairobi doesn't appear all of a sudden, the enigma in the distant mist or haze, a fantasy beckoning from the grassland; it's simply there, suddenly, following a spate of

Masai villages, a couple of cement factories, and—with increasing traffic—shops and guest houses that all merge into a great urban sprawl. Evening has fallen and the highway is lit up. And as we proceed, a strange panic seizes me: isn't there any familiar landmark left, has it changed so dramatically in the six years since I was last here? Is Nairobi lost to me now? But then comes the clock tower on Uhuru Highway, the Parliament building and the old downtown to the right—there is Kenyatta Avenue, we turn into Koinange Street near Karimjee Gardens and there's the chicken place across, at which corner we drop off some passengers, and this is Nairobi. That old thrill returns.

Nairobi used to be an Indian and "European" town, its city centre defined by the backbone of Government Road with its suiting stores, safari outfitters, sports shops, chemists, book shops, and the Kenya and Twentieth Century cinemas. For Asians, the heart of Nairobi city centre was the Khoja Ismaili khano at the head of Government Road, a greystone two-storey structure with a clock tower. Indian Bazaar came off here in one direction, with a string of clothing stores followed by spice and grain merchants. Farther up, Government Road met the rather posh Delamere Avenue, where a policeman in white uniform and helmet stood on a pedestal smartly directing traffic. To one side of him was the New Stanley Hotel, the watering hall for the whites.

Opposite the New Stanley, occupying a corner, was a child's version of heaven: Woolworths, in a burst of light and colour, displaying in its windows and on its shelves and counters heaps of exciting stuff bidding for the heart, especially if you were from humble Dar. Toys and games, cricket bats and balls, chocolates and candies, story books and comic books, imported from England, of course; and pencils and pens, paint boxes and compass boxes, school satchels and school bags. Mostly unaffordable, but you could not return to Dar without coming away with some mementos from here—tall pencils with a plastic toy or a crook and a frill at the top were an affordable favourite.

From the Khoja khano, on the other side of Indian Bazaar ran away the informal and hectic River Road, where many Indians lived and ran shops for Africans, and where one was also likely to be pick-pocketed. Behind River Road were the Odeon Cinema, which showed Hindi films, and Indian restaurants. And then came the valley of the Nairobi River, beyond which were the Indian suburbs of Ngara, Pangani, Parklands, reachable by the single Limuru Road which went all the way down into the Rift Valley and Nakuru, Naivasha, and then back up to Kisumu at Lake Victoria (and Kampala, if you were so inclined), following the railway.

The old khano looks faded now, and insignificant, dwarfed by the tower across from it (on the site of which an Indian corner store would display condoms in its window). The wide front entrance had streams of Ismailis going in and out everyday, but now the door is closed for security reasons and you enter through an invisible side entrance in an alley. Just inside the main entrance was a large reading room with an oval table. Desperate Tanzanian Asian boys hung around the khano in the 1970s, having escaped the trials of socialism by means licit and otherwise; they would come here to the khano lobby to rest and exchange notes, always bewailing the low value of their currency—100 Tanzanian to 60 Kenyan. (Now it's 1,600 to 60.)

If Dar es Salaam snacks on kababs and bhajias, Nairobi does so mostly on cakes and pies. But Nairobi, like Dar, has changed. Government Road is now Moi Avenue, Indian Bazaar is Biashara (Business) Street. The streets are more crowded, the population of the city having multiplied more than tenfold. And following the "Indian Exodus" of 1968, when all those who were not citizens had to leave for Britain, the stores are mostly owned by Africans. Upscale shopping has moved to the malls, one of which, Westgate Mall, was the site of a recent horrific terrorist attack. Many of the old, squat colonial buildings of grey stone are gone, replaced by towers. But Macmillan Library stands intact within its compound, right behind Indian Bazaar, though it looks forlorn; the mosque next to it, however, has expanded and imposes on the area. There is a "Somali Mall" where once Indian shops stood; and there are more women in hijab, some of them running the shops, than was once conceivable.

And yet, despite the changes, Nairobi has maintained a level of integrity. The streets in the city centre are identifiable (and walkable), the suburbs with their bungalows and apartments are mostly intact, and the more grotesque and vandalizing forms of development have been avoided.

Still, Nairobians uniformly complain—as people do in Dar—about the traffic, the corrupt cops, the haphazard construction. But there is a difference. Traffic is dense in Nairobi, but it moves, doesn't come to an absolute standstill awaiting divine intervention; the drivers are smart and sophisticated, they manouver through traffic; Dar—portions of it—are crippled at rush hour. In Nairobi, flyways and walkways have appeared, new roads created, old roads widened to ease traffic. There is green space and the houses have gardens. Am I simply revealing that thrill and that bias of the native returning? Yes, but even in the past, arriving from beloved Dar, the comparison was inevitable, starting with the weather, and one was always awed.

In Nairobi, service is crisp, efficient. We want to open a bank account; a young assistant manager at the DT comes with me to help me get a photo taken. At the studio-cum-shop, it takes exactly four minutes. While I wait, I notice two photos of the "boss" taken with presidents Clinton and Obama; could they be real? Not likely, but I don't ask. Next door the name board of a beauty salon, hanging over the sidewalk, displays four identical images of Mrs. Obama. The Obamas are big in Kenya. In Dar, you might find photos of Obama displayed, but also "Osama" written on the backs of buses. That evening I send a scanned photo page of my passport to the bank manager. He duly acknowledges receipt early the next morning. Now really. Forget Dar, even Delhi isn't as efficient.

Why this difference in the two cities? Weather is one factor, of course. The January heat in Dar is such that the pursuit of a single chore wears you out. But it's also the people, the culture. Dar is Swahili, a culture of ustarabu and kusubiri—patience and style; a willingness to see humour; an identity tied to language. The irony is that with such a strong identity, there is not a sense of public space. In Nairobi a few years ago I was told that the people of a neighbourhood were collecting money to buy cars for the police—who claimed they did not have them; and others were petitioning against the opening of a bar in their neighbourhood, in violation of zoning laws. Jeevanjee Gardens, once slated for development, was saved due to the efforts of concerned citizens.

The problem with Nairobi is personal safety. It always was violent, and it's become progressively more so. Exaggerations aside—I have been advised not to walk through crowded city streets in broad daylight—it's impossible in Nairobi to meet a person who has not experienced violence, or does not know someone who has. In Dar, where dinner parties are held in Oyster Bay roof terraces and outdoor barbecue places open specifically at night, in Nairobi's Muthaiga the wealthy hold elaborate luncheons with imported wines, fortified behind gates and guarded by dogs. Tanzanians will agree, yes, Nairobi is wonderful, the cultural life is superb, the weather is ideal, service is efficient—it's way more advanced. Would you want to live there? No.

Better the laid-back slowness, the informality, the waiter who does not know Cabernet from konyagi. We'll get there eventually, in our own way.

The University of Nairobi, formerly Royal College, is located in what once was an exclusive white enclave, some hundred yards from Norfolk Hotel and not far from the city centre. The Norfolk with its elegant veranda bar (the Lord Delamere Terrace) thrives on its colonial look and reputation, the ugly memories of racism now mostly forgotten. Tourist brochures give lists of famous people who stayed here in the past—Theodore Roosevelt, Karen Blixen, the cast of *Mogambo*, Ernest Hemingway, and presumably his one-time wife, Martha Gellhorn (whose close friends the Blocks owned the hotel for a period). The bar was the watering hole for the "white mischief" settler crowd, and Lord Delamere, it's said, once rode into the dining hall on his horse. But what's history or quaint colonial folklore for the tourist may not be worth remembering for the Kenyan African. "Coolies" would bring in the white patrons on hand-pulled rickshaws, and a bumpy halt would get the African a lash on his back right outside where the taxis now stand and the security guard frisks you.

In the heyday of the 1960s, when the East African community was real and a political federation still viable, Tanzanian students were sent to the University of Nairobi to study engineering, all expenses paid. (The affiliated University of Dar es Salaam was where Kenyans came to study law and learn left-wing politics.) It was a thrilling three years in the metropolis, a time away from community and family eyes, a time to flirt with the opposite sex. Nairobi was where you dressed smartly. It was cool enough to do so, and you didn't sweat much. The boys immediately upon arrival proceeded to the friendly Indian stores on Government Road to be fitted with blue blazers with an insignia sewn on the breast pocket, identifying them as proud Nairobi undergraduates. This dress code was not official, however—some inspired shopkeeper had simply invented it to make profit. I spent three quite carefree months in the engineering faculty, and recall walks to the post office to check mail in the evenings, dining in the women's hall with Asian girls—and frequent visits to the dean to have my major changed. I had requested to study electrical engineering, my government had enrolled me for civil engineering, where it insisted that I stay. If the Tanzanian bureaucracy had relented, life would have taken a different course. As it was, a warm letter arrived from an American university with a promise of financial assistance, and I left, but with a vow to return that was never quite fulfilled.

Now it is decades later and I am back, walking on the still sedate-looking Harry Thuku Road, the 1960s-style engineering buildings on one side of me. Where I had once studied mechanical drawing and electrical circuits, I notice, there is now also a space science department. The squat police station lies ahead, at the corner on University Way, which has acquired two more lanes and a pedestrian overpass. Across on the other side, is the old city centre. This time I am here as a guest of the literature department to give a keynote address, and I speak about the years in East Africa following independence, and in particular about the young Asian politicians, intellectuals, and writers who sought to define themselves as Africans. The subject has a resonance today, especially in Nairobi; how much, I will soon find out. The older faculty members wistfully remember those years, when Ngũgĩ wa Thiongo was around, and the younger professors sound a little envious. I have come as an African, and I speak as an African, and I am in my native city. Nevertheless, I did not expect the welcome I receive. Nairobi in the past, despite its attractions, always seemed . . . formal, somewhat hostile, a city where the bitter whiff remained of the acrimony of racism and colonial rule. But much has changed. A new generation has arrived. During this visit I have noticed confidence and ease, and I am received warmly, as a man from Nairobi who lives abroad. Two days before, I had sat down to give a workshop to a group of young Asians and Africans, and felt perfectly at ease. And when my hosts took me to a somewhat deprived primary school in one of the Nairobi slums, at the inaugration of its library, my escort told the all-African youngsters, Don't pay attention to his skin colour, he is an African like you. It was a moving moment. Perhaps my own ease comes from the fact that I am also from Canada and Tanzania. And I have had the luxury of distance, reflection, and years in which to come to terms with myself, with the realization that I am always from a minority—though, somewhat quixotically, I never think of myself as such—wherever I go, and therefore I do not have to prove anything.

But now I am made to realize that there is indeed some resentment left over in Nairobi, only it has moved elsewhere.

After my lecture, a member of the audience, Neera Kapila—who was a kind host during a previous visit—comes forward and presents me with a book she has authored. It deals with Asian contributions in the formation of modern Kenya, and as she makes the presentation she tells me that it is a corrective to the fact that "we" have not been represented adequately in the national narrative. A pregnant moment. It highlights a grievance and an ache, feelings and sentiments I understand and yet that are quite beyond me now.

In the white settler world of Kenya, described in many books, most famously by Elspeth Huxley, Beryl Bainbridge, and Isak Dinesen, and romanticized by Hollywood and British television, the Asians hardly existed if at all. Following independence, they have been either caricatured as venal and alien, or simply ignored. There have been a number of books about Kenyan Asians, but they are hardly known outside a niche audience. (Ironically, the Nairobi booksellers, who are Asian, happily peddle the "white mischief" tales, which seem to sell briskly.) This cultural argument, this feeling of neglect is—to a large degree—typically Kenyan: Tanzania and Uganda are not the stuff of adventure and romance; and Tanzanian Asians (except the Zanzibaris) never cared much for history, they are simply there.

Of course, unfairness, injustice, and discrimination should be highlighted; this is how a society corrects itself. Self-correction happens to be a constant feature in the evolution of North American identity—for example, in the representations of minorities (of Asian, African, and other origins) in film and television and in the textbooks over the decades. A dangerous new trend in Kenyan (and occasionally Tanzanian) thinking is the openly racist argument that would distinguish the "indigenous" African from the others. Therefore, Neera Kapila's book has a place as a corrective and a prompt to the national conscience, as does the Asian newsmagazine *Awaaz*, as does the Asian Heritage Exhibit now looking for a permanent home.

But the otherness can also become a debilitating marker, a permanent self-identity, as it has become in India, where one cannot simply be an Indian, and minorities and the majority are defined by the constitution. In Nairobi now this sense of an Asian "we" unsettles me. It should not be there fifty years after independence.

The question arises, But where have the Kenya Asian historians and romanciers been in any case? I have met many of them over the years; but they all seem to have been sucked into the bane that is the pariochialism of their own narrow Indian community, a black hole that draws in the bright-eyed idealists and turns them into caste and sectarian functionaries.

Where are the Asians? This question is asked at Kenyatta University when I speak there. There is not a single brown face but mine in the packed hall. I put this question to Sarita, a brilliant young Kenyan who studied at Cambridge and London and returned. She is of the new generation. For her holidays she goes up Mount Kenya with her young family. But in answer to my question, she replies that local facilities at the universities are so inadequate that she herself would prefer to send her kids to Oxford or Cambridge if she could. As would many others, undoubtedly, of whatever race—but would these Kenyan Asians of a fourth generation return? Or will the Asians only continue to deplete and further marginalize themselves?

We leave for Arusha and Dar early next morning, departing by minibus from the Karimjee Gardens. With us are a few Israelis on their way to climb Kilimanjaro; a woman in hijab on her way to Mwanza; a Chinese girl with only a few words of English and Swahili. The university is a short walk away, so is the khano. The air is cool and bracing—so unmistakeably Nairobi in the morning. Can a place leave such an indelible mark that you can breathe it every time? I imagine, perhaps. I realize I have been reclaimed, partly, as I always seem to be.

25.

Closing the Circle

It's a bright Sunday morning in Dar, and I'm sitting in the front row of a gathering inside a quietly festive Diamond Jubilee Hall, in Upanga, ten minutes' walk away from my former home, wondering how I allowed myself to slip into my predicament. Actually I'm panicking. A few days before, I was approached by some people to speak words of wisdom to a graduating class of young students; I could be as brief as I wanted; I might speak of careers in science and the arts. They, everyone, would be delighted and honoured. There are ways of approach that appeal to your vulnerability, and I knew I could not refuse without sounding brash and arrogant. These people were from my tribe, so to speak: I came out of them, we had lived and prayed together, we went to the same schools. The ties were emotional. The fact that intellectually I had gone my own way was irrelevant.

Now here I am, and to my utter bewilderment I find out that the graduating kids are from an early-childhood learning program. I've been tricked, it appears. In the hall, buzzing with excitement, there are a few dozen four-year-olds, their proud mothers and fathers with them, smiling nervously, along with leaders of the community. What do I say to these little ones? What do I know to say to them?

Words of wisdom? Careers? Science and arts? Earlier this morning I prepared some lines to say to teenagers; now as the proceedings begin, and the leaders get up on the stage to speak, followed by a teacher, my predicament only deepens.

The graduating class arrives one by one on the stage, each child dressed in a well-wrought costume that signifies a message, followed by a beaming young mother, her comforting hand touching the child's shoulder. This is no ordinary graduation. The majority of the kids are Asian, but there are some who are African and mixed-race, and all belong to the community—how times have changed. As the teacher calls out a name, a child comes forward from the wings, with the mother standing behind, and recites in a unique manner, sometimes prompted by the mother, the name of a career to match the costume he or she is wearing: I am an astonaut; I am a scientist; I am a poet.

It's not for me to tell them anything, it's they who are telling me, they of the new Tanzania, the future, with their own dreams to follow. And am I the same person, who sits here now wrenched, having been where I've been to and done what I have done, who at their exact age played in the mud of Uhuru and Sikukuu streets?

They'll go where they want to, and become many things, and perhaps some of them will even return. Which is what, I think, I said to them.

Select Glossary

Asian
"South Asian"; since people originally arrived in East Africa before the subcontinent was partitioned, and most early Asians arrived from Gujarat and Kutch, I have also used the more evocative term *Indian* in this book, when it applies.

ahsante
thank you

bajaji
the Indian-made autorickshaw (made by the Bajaj company)

bana
Stanley's pronunciation of "bwana"

Bhadala
a traditional seafaring community of Kutch and Gujarat

Baluchi
people originally from Baluchistan (now in Pakistan)

biriyani
a spicy, flavoured rice-and-meat dish

duriani
the tropical fruit durian, with a characteristic smell

gaam
town; downtown

jambo
hello

karibu
welcome

Khoja
traditionally a community from Gujarat and Kutch; also, based on religious practice, referred to as "Ismaili," which term however occludes ethnicity or place of origin. Another branch of the Khojas are the Ithnasheries, who split away in the nineteenth and twentieth centuries to join the mainstream Shia faith.

maalim
a Muslim practitioner of traditional medicine, sometimes an exorcist

mandazi
a fried bread

Mhindi
an Asian or Indian (from "Hind")

mtumwa
a servant or slave

Muganda
a member of the Baganda people of Uganda

Mungu
God

Mwarabu
an Arab

Mwenyezi
Almighty

nani?
who?

omba
from "kuomba," to beg

starehe
(in context, although probably not used this way anymore) relax; don't trouble yourself

thuppo!
a form of hide-and-seek

wadi
neighbourhood

Bibliography

2. Gaam, Dar es Salaam: The India Town

Markes, Sarah. *Street Level: A Collection of Drawings and Creative Writing Inspired by Dar es Salaam*. Dar es Salaam: Mkuki na Nyota, 2011.

Sulemanji, Muzu. *Contemporary Dar es Salaam*. Dar es Salaam: Mkuki na Nyota, 2010.

Sykes, Laura, and Uma Waide. *Dar es Salaam: A Dozen Drives Around the City*. Dar es Salaam: Mkuki na Nyota, 1997.

4. The Road to Tanga
5. Tanga, Decline in the Sun

Crichton-Harris, Ann. *Seventeen Letters to Tatham*. Toronto: Kennegy West, 2001.

Dundas, Charles. *African Crossroads*. London: Macmillan, 1955.

Farwell, Byron. *The Great War in Africa, 1914–1918*. New York: Norton, 1986.

Hill, Mervyn F. *Permanent Way: The Story of the Kenya and Uganda Railway, Being the Official History of the Development of the Transportation System in Kenya and Uganda. Vol. 1.* Nairobi: East African Railways and Harbours, 1957.

Hordern, Charles. *History of the Great War: Military Operations East Africa. Vol. 1.* London: The Imperial War Museum, 1941.

Von Lettow-Vorbeck, Paul. *My Reminiscences of East Africa.* Uckfield, Sussex: Naval & Military Press Ltd., 2009.

Young, Francis Brett. *Marching on Tanga*. Uckfield, Sussex: Naval & Military Press Ltd., n.d.

6. India and Africa: Of Entrepreneurs Old and New

Barbosa, Duarte. *A Description of the Coasts of East Africa and Malabar: In the Beginning of the Sixteenth Century.* Translated by Henry E.J. Stanley. London: The Hakluyt Society, 1866. Google Books.

Burton, Richard. *Zanzibar: City, Island, and Coast.* 2 vols. London: Tinsley Brothers, 1872. Google Books.

Desai, Gaurav. *Commerce with the Universe: Africa, Asia, and the Afrasian Imagination.* New York: Columbia University Press, 2013.

Goswami, Chhaya. *The Call of the Sea: Kachchhi Traders in Muscat and Zanzibar, c.1800-1880*. New Delhi: Orient Blackswan, 2011.

Mangat, J.S. *A History of the Asians in East Africa c. 1886 to 1945*. Oxford: Oxford University Press, 1969.

Patel, Zarina. *Challenge to Colonialism: The Struggle of Alibhai Mulla Jeevanjee for Equal Rights in Kenya.* Mombasa, 1997.

Seidenberg, Dana April. *Mercantile Adventurers: The World of East African Asians 1750–1985*. New Delhi: New Age Publishers, 1996.
Visram, M.G. *On a Plantation in Kenya*. Mombasa: M.G. Visram, 1987.
Visram, M.G. *Alidina Visram the Trail Blazer*. Mombasa: M.G. Visram, 1990.

7. Kilwa, the Old City
8. Quiloa, the Island

Barbosa, Duarte. *A Description of the Coasts of East Africa and Malabar: In the Beginning of the Sixteenth Century.* Translated by Henry E.J. Stanley. London: The Hakluyt Society, 1866. Google Books.
Battuta, Ibn. *Travels in Asia and Africa.* Translated and selected by H.A.R. Gibb. 1929. Reprinted. New Delhi: Low Price, 2004.
Camões, Luís Vaz de. *The Lusiads.* Translated by Landeg White. London: Oxford University Press. 1997. Reprinted 2008.
Cliff, Nigel. *Holy War: How Vasco da Gama's Epic Voyages Turned the Tide in a Centuries-Old Clash of Civilizations.* New York: HarperCollins Publishers, 2011.
Correa, Gaspar. *The Three Voyages of Vasco da Gama and His Viceroyalty, c. 1583.* Translated by Henry E.J. Stanley. London: The Hakluyt Society. 1869. Google Books.
Dunn, Rosse E. *The Adventures of Ibn Battuta.* Berkeley and Los Angeles: University of California Press, 1986.
Elton, J. Frederic. *Travels and Researches Among the Lakes and Mountains of Eastern & Central Africa.* From the journals of the late J. Frederic Elton. Edited and completed by H.B. Cotterill. London: John Murray, 1879. Google Books.
Hamdun, Said, and Noel King. *Ibn Battuta in Black Africa.* 1975. Reprinted. Princeton, NJ: Markus Wiener, 1998. [Translations of Battuta differ slightly from Sutton and are more detailed.]
Mackintosh-Smith, Tim. *The Travels of Ibn Battutah.* London: Folio Society, 2012.
Miehe, Gudrun, Katrin Bromber, Said Khamis, and Ralf Grosserhode. *Kala Shairi: German East Africa in Swahili Poems.* Koln: Rudiger Koppe Verlag, 2002.
Milton, John. *Paradise Lost.* 1667. Ed. Christopher Ricks. New York: New American Library, 1968.
Sheriff, Abdul. *Dhow Cultures of the Indian Ocean.* London: Hurst Publishers, 2010.
Sutton, John. *A Thousand Years of East Africa.* Nairobi: British Institute in Eastern Africa, 1990.
Waugh, Evelyn. *A Tourist in Africa.* 1960. Reprinted, Boston: Little Brown, 1986.

9. The Mystics Down the Road: Discovering the Sufis

Becker, Felicitas. *Becoming Muslim in Mainland Tanzania, 1890–2000.* Oxford: Oxford University Press, 2008.

Martin, B.G. *Muslim Brotherhoods in 19th-Century Africa.* Cambridge: Cambridge University Press, 1976.
Nimtz, August H. *Islam and Politics in East Africa.* Minneapolis: University of Minnesota Press, 1980.
Schimmel, Annemarie. *Mystical Dimensions of Islam.* Chapel Hill: University of North Carolina Press, 1975.

10. Burton and Speke, and the East African Expedition of 1857

Burton, Richard. *The Lake Regions of Central Africa.* 1860. Google Books. Published with an introduction by Ian Curteis as *The Source of the Nile.* London: Folio Society, 1993.
____. *Zanzibar.* 1872. Google Books.
____. "Zanzibar; and Two Months in East Africa—Part II." *Blackwood's Edinburgh Magazine.* Vol 83, March 1858. http://www.bodley.ox.ac.uk.
Grant, James Augustus. *A Walk Across Africa.* 1864. Google Books.
Goswami, Chhaya. *The Call of the Sea: Kachchhi Traders in Muscat and Zanzibar, c.1800-1880.* New Delhi: Orient Blackswan, 2011.
Harrison, William. *Mountains of the Moon.* Formerly published as *Burton and Speke.* New York: Ballantine, 1982.
Henderson, Louise. "John Murray and the Publication of David Livingstone's Missionary Travels." http://www.livingstoneonline.ucl.ac.uk/companion.php?id=HIST2
Jeal, Tim. *Explorers of the Nile.* New Haven: Yale, 2011.
Krapf, Johann. *Travels, Researches and Missionary Labours.* 1860. Google Books.
Livingstone, David. *Missionary Travels.* 1872. Google Books.
Morehead, Alan. *The White Nile.* 1960. Reprinted. London: The Reprint Society, 1962.
Speke, John Hanning. *Journal of the Discovery of the Source of the Nile.* 1863. Google Books.
Stanley, Henry Morton. *How I Found Livingstone.* 1872. Google Books.
Tajddin, Mumtaz. "Tharia Topan, Sir." http://www.ismaili.net/Source/mumtaz/Heroes1/hero099.html

11. The Old Westbound Caravan Route

Finke, Jens. "Traditional Music & Cultures of Kenya. Meru-History." http://www.bluegecko.org/kenya/tribes/meru/history.htm
Hill, Mervyn F. *Permanent Way: The Story of the Kenya and Uganda Railway, Being the Official History of the Development of the Transportation System in Kenya and Uganda. Vol. 1.* Nairobi: East African Railways and Harbours, 1957.
Stanley, Henry Morton. *How I Found Livingstone.* 1872. Google Books.
Wikipedia. "Books Published Per Country Per Year." http://en.wikipedia.org/wiki/Books_published_per_country_per_year

12. Bongoland: Something Is Happening

Mwapachu, Juma. "The Education Climate—Turbulence or Tsunami?" *The Citizen.* May 19, 2013.

13. Kigoma and Ujiji: The Long Road

Brode, Heinrich. *Tippu Tip: The Story of His Career in Zanzibar & Central Africa.* 1904. Reprinted. Zanzibar: The Gallery Publications, 2000.

Encyclopaedia Britannica. 1911. http://en.wikisource.org/wiki/1911_Encyclopædia_Britannica/Ujiji

Page, Melvin E. "The Manyema Hordes of Tippu Tip: A Case Study in Social Stratification and the Slave Trade in Eastern Congo." *The International Journal of African Historical Studies,* Vol. 7, No. 1 (1974), pp. 69–84. http://www.jstor.org/stable/216554

Stanley, Henry Morton. *How I Found Livingstone.* 1872. Google Books.

Wikipedia. http://en.wikipedia.org/wiki/Ujiji

14. The South Coast: A Journey Shortened

The Citizen. "Premier Calls for Calm as He Visits Riot-Hit Areas in Mtwara." May 23, 2013.

15. The Southern Highlands: Tukuyu—Neue Langenberg
16. The Southern Highlands: Mbeya

McCormack, Patricia. "Lady Chesham Beats Drums for Africa." *Palm Beach Daily News,* January 29, 1962.

Theroux, Paul. *Dark Night Safari.* New York: Houghton Mifflin, 2003.

Time. "Zambia: The Hell Run." February 25, 1966.

Waugh, Evelyn. *A Tourist in Africa.* 1960. Reprinted. Boston: Little Brown, 1986.

Wikipedia. http://en.wikipedia.org/wiki/Chief_Mkwawa

World Council of Churches. "Moravian Churches." http://www.oikoumene.org/en

17. Book, Medicine, and Spirit

BBC. "Living in Fear: Tanzania's Albinos." http://news.bbc.co.uk/2/hi/africa/7518049.stm

Ismail, Hasani bin. *Swifa ya Nguvumali.* Translated by Peter Lienhardt. London: Oxford University Press. 1968.

New York Times. "Crowds Come Over Roads and by Helicopters for Tanzanian's Cure-All Potion." March 28, 2011.

RNW Africa Desk. "Tanzanian Medicine Man with a Nation on His Doorstep."

Radio Netherlands Worldwide Africa. March 28, 2011. http://www.rnw.nl/africa/article/tanzanian-medicine-man-a-nation-his-doorstep
Swantz, Lloyd W. *The Medicine Man Among the Zaramo of Dar Es Salaam*. Uppsala, Sweden: Nordic Africa Institute, 1990.
Tanganyika Standard. "White witch-doctor dies in crash." August 30, 1957.

18, 19, 20: Zanzibar

Attwood, William. *The Twilight Struggle*. New York: Harper Collins, 1989.
Bennett, Norman. *A History of the Arab State of Zanzibar*. London: Methuen, 1978.
Burgess, Thomas G. *Race, Revolution, and the Struggle for Human Rights in Zanzibar*. Athens, Ohio: Ohio University Press, 2009.
Burton, Richard. "Zanzibar." *Blackwood's Edinburgh Magazine*. Vol. 83, Feb. 1858.
____. *Camõens: His Life and His Lusiads*. 1881. Google Books.
____. *Zanzibar: City, Island, and Coast*. 2 vols. 1872. Google Books.
Camõens. *The Lusiads*. Translated by Landeg White. London: Oxford, 1997. Reprinted. 2008.
Correa, Gaspar. *The Three Voyages of Vasco da Gama and His Viceroyalty*. c. 1583. Translated from the Portuguese manuscripts by Henry E.J. Stanley. London: The Hakluyt Society. 1869. Google Books.
Fazal, Abdulrazzak. "Recollections of Zanzibar in the 1950s and Early 1960s." http://zanzibar-stories.blogspot.ca/2010_07_01_archive.html
Goswami, Chhaya. *The Call of the Sea: Kachchhi Traders in Muscat and Zanzibar, c.1800-1880*. New Delhi: Orient Blackswan, 2011.
Hamad, Seif Sharif. *An Enduring Trust*. In Burgess, Thomas G. *Race, Revolution, and the Struggle for Human Rights in Zanzibar*. Athens, Ohio: Ohio University Press, 2009.
Hunter, Helen-Louise. *Zanzibar: The Hundred Days Revolution*. Santa Barbara, California: Praeger, 2010.
Ingrams, W.H. "The People of Makunduchi, Zanzibar." *Man*, Vol. 25 (Sep., 1925), pp. 138–142. http://www.jstor.org/stable/2839717
Issa, Ali Sultan. *Walk on Two Legs*. In Burgess, Thomas G. *Race, Revolution, and the Struggle for Human Rights in Zanzibar*. Athens, Ohio: Ohio University Press, 2009.
Juma, Abdurahman. *Unguja Ukuu on Zanzibar: An Archaeological Study of Early Urbanism*. Uppsala: Afrikansk och jämförande arkeologi. 2004.
Kamm, Henry. "Zanzibar: An Improbable Island Emerging From a Violent Past." *The New York Times*. December 6, 1975.
Kapuściński, Ryszard. *The Shadow of the Sun*. New York: Vintage, 2001.
Kilimwiko, Lawrence. "The era of forced marriages and mass murder." *The Citizen*. October 13, 2011. http://www.tanzanianews24.com/the-era-of-forced-marriages-and-mass-murder/

Lyimo, Karl. "Rewriting history ignored by the victors." *The Citizen.* January 21, 2012. http://allafrica.com/stories/201201231623.html
Mustapha's Place. "Unguja Ukuu – a Gem of Zanzibar." http://www.mustaphasplace.com/blog/unguja-ukuu-gem-zanzibar
New York Times. "Kenya on Alert." March 1, 1964.
Okello, John. *Revolution in Zanzibar.* Nairobi: East African Publishing House, 1967.
Petterson, Don. *Revolution in Zanzibar.* Boulder, Colorado: Westview Press, 2002.
Ruete, Emily (Princess Salamah bint Said). *Memoirs of an Arabian Princess from Zanzibar.* 1886. Mineola, NY: Dover, 2009.
Sheriff, Abdul. Editor. *The History & Conservation of Zanzibar Stone Town.* Zanzibar: Department of Archives, Museums and Antiquities, 1995.
____. *Slaves, Spices, & Ivory in Zanzibar.* Dar es Salaam: Tanzania Publishing House, 1987.
____. *Dhow Cultures of the Indian Ocean.* London: Hurst, 2010.
Singhji, Virbhadra. *The Rajputs of Saurashtra.* New Delhi: Popular Prakashan. 1994.
Stanley, Henry Morton. *How I Found Livingstone.* 1872. Google Books.
Time. "The Cuckoo Coup." May 1, 1964.
Wikipedia. http://en.wikipedia.org/wiki/Zanzibar_revolution

21. The Old Warriors: Dar es Salaam Again

Mohammed, Omar. "Five Questions with Painter and Architect Nadir Tharani." http://www.vijana.fm/2011/03/24/five-questions-with-nadir-tharani/
Tharani, Nadir. http://www.nadirtharani.com/

22. Omba-omba: The Culture of Begging

Allafrican.com. "Tanzania: Mkapa can finally afford to help the poor." http://allafrica.com/stories/200502080883.html
Citizen. "More Details Emerge on Offshore Billions." February 18, 2014.
Easterly, William. *The White Man's Burden.* New York: Penguin, 2006.
Moyo, Dambisa. *Dead Aid.* Toronto: Douglas & McIntyre, 2009.
NBC News. "Celebs, Big Donors help fight Africa's war on Malaria." http://www.nbcnews.com/id/39656433#.URKXEqXonTc
New York Times. "African Critics of Kony Campaign See a 'White Man's Burden' for the Facebook Generation." March 9, 2012.
____. "Tanzania calls dispute with West Germany over." June 29, 1965.
Shivji, Issa G. *Development in Practice*, Vol. 14, Number 5, August 2004, p. 689. http://www.un-ngls.org/orf/cso
Theroux, Paul. *Dark Night Safari.* New York: Houghton Mifflin, 2003.
Vassanji, M. G. "The Trouble with *KONY 2012.*" *Maclean's*, March 15, 2012.
Wikipedia. http://en.wikipedia.org/wiki/Kony_2012#Negative

23. The New (Asian) African: Politics and Creativity

Brandt 21 Forum. "Amir H. Jamal: Biography." http://www.brandt21forum.info/Bio_Jamal.htm
Eckstein, Lars. Ed. *English Literatures Across the Globe: A Companion.* Stuttgart: UTB, 2007.
Gurr, Andrew, and Angus Calder. *Writers in East Africa*: Papers from Colloquium. Nairobi: EALB, 1974.
Jhaveri, K.L. *Marching with Nyerere: Africanisation of Asians.* New Delhi: B R Publishing, 1999.
Kemoli, Arthur. *Pulsations: An East African Anthology of Poetry.* Nairobi: EALB, n.d.
Mustafa, Sophia. *The Tanganyika Way.* 1961. Reprinted. Toronto: TSAR, 2009.
____. *In the Shadow of Kirinyaga.* Toronto: TSAR, 2010.
Nazareth, J.M. *Brown Man, Black Country. A Peep into Kenya's Freedom Struggle.* New Delhi: Tidings, 1981.
Nazareth Peter. *In a Brown Mantle.* Nairobi: EALB, 1972.
____. *The General Is Up.* Reprinted. Toronto: TSAR. 1991.
New York Times. "Rajat Neogy, 57, Founder of Journal on Africa." December 11, 1995.
Patel, Zarina. *Challenge to Colonialism: The Struggle of Alibhai Mulla Jeevanjee for Equal Rights in Kenya.* Mombasa, 1997.
____. *Unquiet: The Life & Times of Makhan Singh.* Nairobi: Zand Graphics, 2006.
Soyinka, Wole. *Poems of Black Africa.* New York: Hill and Wang, 1975.
____. "The Writer in an African State." *Transition* 31, June-July 1967.
Tejani, Bahadur. *Day After Tomorrow.* Nairobi: EALB, 1971.
wa Thiong'o, Ngũgĩ. "Asia in My Life." *Pambazuka* 585, 17 May 2012.
Zettersten, Arne. Ed. *East African Literature: An Anthology.* New York: Longman, 1983.

24. Nairobi, Lost and Regained?

Kapila, Neera. *Race, Rail & Society.* Nairobi: Kenway, 2009.
Patel, Zarina. *Challenge to Colonialism: The Struggle of Alibhai Mulla Jeevanjee for Equal Rights in Kenya.* Mombasa, 1997.

Photo Captions

Sources and Credits

The epigraph at the front of this book is from *Cahier d'un retour au pays natal* by Aimé Césaire, translated by Emile Snyder (Paris: Éditions Présence Africaine, 1971, pp. 60-61).

The poem excerpt on p. 11 is from "The City," by C.P. Cavafy, translated by Lawrence Durrell, in *Justine* (New York: Pocket Books, 1961. p. 227).

The map of Kilwa on p. 100 is by map-makers Georg Braun & Franz Hogenberg. http://www.raremaps.com/gallery/detail/17056/Aden_Arabiae_Foelicis_Emporium_Celeberrimi_Nominis_quo_ex_India_Aethiopia/Braun-Hogenberg.html

Other material quoted in this book has been taken from the sources cited below. Full publication details may be found in the Bibliography.

pp. 35-36. Charles Hordern. *Military Operations East Africa. Vol. 1.* 251; Francis Brett Young. *Marching on Tanga.* 1, 264

p. 48. Byron Farwell. *The Great War in Africa.* 173

p. 49. Byron Farwell. 175

p. 60. Richard Burton. *Zanzibar: City, Island, and Coast Vol 2.* 11

pp. 80-82. J. Frederic Elton. *Travels and Researches.* 71, 86, 102

p.81. Johann Krapf. *Travels, Researches and Missionary Labours.* 424

p. 88. Evelyn Waugh. *A Tourist in Africa.* 71

pp. 91-92. Gudrun Miehe, et al. *Kala Shairi.* 287, 294

p. 97. John Sutton. *A Thousand Years of East Africa.*

p. 99. John Sutton. 81

p. 102. Gaspar Correa. *The Three Voyages of Vasco da Gama.* 84

p. 103. Luís Vaz de Camões. *The Lusiads.* 22; Gaspar Correa. 292

p. 116. Richard Burton. *Lake Regions.* 21

p. 117. Louise Henderson. "John Murray."

p. 119. Richard Burton. "Zanzibar; and . . ." In *Blackwoods.* 289

p. 121. Richard Burton. *Lake Regions.* 100

pp. 122-23. Richard Burton. *The Source of the Nile.* ix, xi, 9, 11

p. 125. John Hanning Speke. *Journal of the Discovery of the Source of the Nile.* xvii, xiii, xxvii, xxii

p. 127. Richard Burton. *Lake Regions.* 35

pp. 127-128. Henry Morton Stanley. *How I Found Livingstone.* 8-9, 37, 50

p. 129. Richard Burton. *Zanzibar Vol 2.* 179

p. 130. Henry Morton Stanley. 28

p. 131. Richard Burton. *Lake Regions.* 22, 424

p. 132. James Augustus Grant. *A Walk Across Africa.* 48

p. 136. Henry Morton Stanley. 28

pp. 190-91. Henry Morton Stanley. 409

p. 218-219. *Time.* February 25, 1966

p. 236-237. Evelyn Waugh. 105

p. 238. Paul Theroux. *Dark Star Safari.* 286

pp. 260-261. Henry Morton Stanley. 2-3

pp. 265-266. Richard Burton. *Zanzibar Vol. 1.* 104-109

pp. 274-275. Don Petterson. *Revolution in Zanzibar.* 3-4; *Time.* January 24, 1964

p. 279. John Okello. *Revolution in Zanzibar.* 73,86

pp. 280-281. John Okello. 120, 126, 187

p. 282. Don Pettersen. 173, 175

p. 284. *The New York Times.* February 29, 1964

p. 285. John Okello. 197; *Time.* May 1, 1964

p. 289. Abdulrazak Fazal. "Recollections of Zanzibar."

pp. 289-290. Thomas G Burgess. *Race, Revolution, and the Struggle for Human Rights in Zanzibar.*

p. 290-291. Richard Burton. *Zanzibar Vol.1.* 83

p. 294-296. Emily Ruete. *Memoirs of an Arabian Princess.* 40, 103, 105, 253

p. 330. Dambisa Moyo. *Dead Aid.* 9,29,47

pp. 330-331. Charles Easterley. *The White Man's Burden.* 26

p. 331. Paul Theroux. 272

p. 332. Issa Shivji. In *Development in Practice.* 689

p. 335. Paul Theroux. 273

pp. 336-37. *The New York Times.* March 9, 2012

pp. 342-343. Amir Jamal. In. K.L. Jhaveri. *Marching With Nyerere.*

p. 343. Sophia Mustafa. *The Tanganyika Way.* 83

p. 344. Brandt 21 Forum.

pp. 345-346. Zarina Patel. *Challenge to Colonialism.* 220-221

p. 347. Henry Louis Gates Jr. In *The New York Times.* December 11, 1995

p. 348. Lars Eckstein. *English Literatures Across the Globe.*

pp. 350-352. Bahdur Tejani. *Pulsations* 120; *Day After Tomorrow.* 35, 141

p. 353. Peter Nazareth. *In a Brown Mantle.* 75, 114, 150

pp. 354-355. Ngugi wa Thiong'o. In *Pambazuka News 585.* May 17, 2012

p. 355. Wole Soyinka. In *Transition 31.* June-July, 1967

Acknowledgements

I MUST THANK ALL THOSE WHO over the years during my travels have provided much help, friendship, hospitality, companionship, and those moments of inspiration that have infused not only this book but also others. They are:

(Tanzania)
Fatma Alloo, Mkuki Bgoya, Walter Bgoya, Harko Bhagat, Mehboob Champsi, Ramesh Chauhan, Shabir Jaffer, Feroz Jafferji, Colonel Ameen Kashmiri, Nawroz Lakhani, Yasmin Lakhani, Ali Mawji, Karim Mitha, Sadru Mitha, Omar Mohammed, Beatrix Mugishagwe, Mpeli Nsekela, Charles Nsekela, Azim Premji, Issa Shivji, Natasha Shivji, Parin Shivji, Abdul Sherriff, Abdu Simba, Muzu Sulemanji, Mohamed Sumar, "Taju," Nadir Tharani. Also, TPH Bookstore and Novel Idea.

(Kenya)
David Angell, High Commissioner of Canada, Muthoni Garland, Alex Kandie, Neera Kapila, Begum Karim, Pyarali Karim, Aleya Kassam, Dawn Makena, JKS Makokha, Zarina Patel, Zahid Rajen, Jayant Ruparel, Sultan Somji, Radha Upadhyay.

(Canada)
Iqbal Dewji, Zahir Dhalla, Hassan Jaffer, Moe Jiwan, Karim Ladak.

(Elsewhere)
K.L. Jhaveri, Urmila Jhaveri, Abdulaziz Lodhi, Veena Sharma, Farouk Topan.

For their encouragement and making this book possible in various ways, Bruce Westwood, Lien de Nis, Kristin Cochran, Lynn Henry, Tracy Bohan, and Jacqueline Ko. And, of course, for this and much more, Nurjehan.